The de ... ut Tanner couldn't leave. Carly was walking out toward him.

Damn! He had hoped to be long gone before she saw him. Now he'd be forced either to tell her the truth or to make up a reasonable explanation of why he was there.

Before he could manage either, Carly halted abruptly. Tanner squinted his eyes; tears were running down her face. He moved quickly toward her, but not fast enough to save the two cups from sliding out of her fingers and onto the floor. It hit him hard to see her this way. It dawned on him she must be feeling she had been through hell. He reached for her and she nearly fell into his arms, clinging to him with all her strength.

God, he thought, feeling her soft body against his, *she's shaking all over*. She must have been scared to death. He felt guilty for what she had been through, yet extremely relieved that she was all right.

He pulled her even tighter against his chest and pressed his lips to the top of her head, just holding her.

No Easy Way Out

Rebecca Blanchard

TUDOR PUBLISHING

NEW YORK AND LOS ANGELES

No Easy Way Out
Front Matter
Sharol-Area 75   11-12-87

Published by
Tudor Publishing

ISBN: 0-944276-01-6

Printed in the United States of America

First Tudor printing—1988

To dedicate this book to one person is impossible. I love my husband, Curtis, whose support and help has kept me going, but if my mother, Elnora Ortiz, hadn't dragged me to my first writer's meeting, I never would have become a writer. And I owe my deepest gratitude to Keith Cockrell, whose interest and criticism was invaluable.

So . . . Curtis, Mother, Keith . . . This book's for you.

No Easy Way Out

CHAPTER ONE

The small beige and tan yacht sliced through the choppy gray depths of the Intracoastal Canal, parting the water and peeling it back in white-capped waves. Slickened by the late evening rain, the twenty-foot mast stood naked of its off-white sails, emphasizing the barren edges of Bolivar Peninsula. Opposite was a tiny sliver of an islet inhabited by a small herd of goats. Its land held just enough foliage to sustain them, no more.

Carly Jameson stood at the wheel of the sleek vessel squinting her eyes, finally able to see, through the misty spray, that she had reached the less populated end of the peninsula and was nearing the mouth of the canal that led into Galveston Bay.

So what do I do now? She eased off the throttle and allowed the boat to drift for a moment, hoping to hear the clanging bell of at least one buoy. All she heard was the rumble of thunder.

She cursed, wishing she could delay because of

the weather, or because it was rapidly getting dark, or even because she didn't have the faintest idea how she was going to complete the last leg of her journey. She knew only that she had to secure her berthing spot within the next hour or lose it. Her father's name still had clout, and although usually she was reluctant to use it for what might seem a rich spoiled girl's whims, this time Carly had felt no compunction at all in using it in order to bump another vacationer out of his reserved yacht space. The waterfront was where she had to be, and what better lodging than a yacht? Still, the marina's manager had given her only until nine o'clock to arrive.

She braced herself against the roll and dip of the boat. The thought of returning home to the disappointment or guilt she was certain would be on her brother's face was the catalyst she needed to strengthen her nerve. Ellis was just too ill to take control of things, and Therese had to be found, soon. Carly knew that the responsibility of bringing her wayward sister home rested entirely on her shoulders. And find Therese she would. There was no way Carly was going to believe that her sister had simply vanished into thin air.

Pressing down on the throttle, Carly sent the boat cutting through the water. With the wind and rain whipping her reddish brown ponytail across her chapped face, she prayed that things would finally start working in her favor. They just had to.

It was hard going, but she managed to cross the bay and slip through the ship channel with thirty minutes to spare. She notified the harbor master that she was near and radioed the yacht basin's manager to confirm her reserved berth. Everything was set. As the basin came into view, Carly cut the motor. This was the tricky part, she knew. She'd never docked the yacht before. In fact, she couldn't recall ever having paid attention when her brother had either. Ellis had taught her much about steering and maneuvering the craft, but that had always been in open water—in clear, sunny weather. Well, docking couldn't be that hard; all she had to do was let the boat coast in between the two piers, toss the lines, and let the men on shore secure them. She could do that.

The bow of the yacht was straight on target and she was almost in place when a ground swell caught it and sent it crashing into the pier. A loud thud was followed by a horrible scraping noise. If she hadn't been hanging on so tightly to the wheel she would have fallen.

"Oh my God! What have I done?"

"Hurry! Grab the line and dally it!" she heard someone yell. "Lady, bump the motor! No! Never mind! Don't do a thing!" the same man shouted.

I won't, she cried silently. *Just get me secured!*

A few moments later a man in a yellow slicker jumped aboard. "Are you all right, ma'am?" Carly nodded vigorously. "Do you mind if I finish this for

11

you?"

With pleasure Carly stepped out of his way.

Hank Armand managed the heavy wooden door and a tray of food with the ease of a man with two arms, although he was minus one. Moving into the small room, he placed the tray on a teak coffee table and sternly eyed the blond-haired man lounging on the rust divan. Tanner Barnes was staring back with an equally intense expression on his own lean features.

"I take it by the sound of all that racket a few moments ago that she has arrived," Tanner said, pulling the ends of his robe over his bare calves.

"Yeah. Seems she had a little trouble docking." Hank covered his grin with a discreet cough.

"And?"

"She's reported in at the marina office and seems to have settled down for the night." Hank thrust his hand into the front pocket of his white duck slacks.

"That's not exactly what I meant, Hank." Tanner's impatience was evident in the way he pushed his lean body up and swung his legs to the floor.

Hank knew what Tanner wanted but hesitated before giving him the information. He pulled his hand from his pocket and ran it through his thick black hair, wondering what Romeo would think if he told him she made him feel . . . cautious. Hell,

Tanner would laugh him out of the cabin.

"She's beautiful, Tanner," he answered quietly but truthfully. "Even drenched and windblown."

Tanner's brow slashed upward. "Good. Sometimes a photograph can be deceiving."

Hank didn't respond but knew by the look in Tanner's blue eyes that Tanner felt he had everything under control. And Hank wasn't about to tell his friend that from what he had seen Tanner had his work cut out for him.

"Have you radioed Omi?" Tanner asked, tilting his head back. Hank nodded. "Stupid question, huh?" An answer wasn't necessary. "Well, what did he say?"

"He said that he was depending on you and your debonair charm. That time was the main factor."

"No kidding," Tanner replied sarcastically. "Well, it can't be too soon for me either. I'm sick and tired of the rat race." Lifting his head he smiled devilishly. "But what a way to end fifteen years of service. If Carly Jameson is even half as promising as her picture indicates, I'll leave the bureau with a helluva bon voyage!"

Hank smiled too, but the humor never reached his black eyes.

Carly was working up a sweat. "Damn!" she nearly shouted as one handlebar of the bicycle caught on the door for the third time in her attempt to get it out of the cabin. With her patience long gone, it took every bit of self-control she had to keep from shaking the vehicle until every nut and bolt fell off. She'd had enough trouble the night before docking the yacht; she certainly didn't need the hassle this bicycle was causing. Opening her hand, she released her grip on the bicycle and let it drop to the floor, then dusted her hands free of imaginary dirt. In this frame of mind she knew it was best simply to leave it alone until she calmed down. She stepped out into the early morning sunshine and took several deep breaths of the tangy sea air. At least the rain had stopped sometime during the night; that comforting thought was soon replaced by her dread of the heat she knew would soon be beating down.

She paced around the deck, trying to decide how—if she ever got that stupid bicycle out of the cabin—she was going to get it off the yacht and onto the dock. She peered over the railing and saw that it was just a small drop to the wooden pier and that all she had to do was toss the bike a few feet over the side to hit the landing. *And*, if she managed that without losing it to the watery depths, she thought somewhat doubtfully, the first thing she had to do was check with the marina office. Perhaps they had a safe, reasonably priced store-room where she could park it.

Carly pushed away from the metal railing and turned to face the remaining chore. She wished she didn't need the bicycle so badly. The thought of pedaling all over an island that was infested with tourists was not her idea of fun, but limited funds had cut out any notion of finding alternate means of transportation. Her heart felt heavier than usual as she stood gazing through the cabin doorway at the twisted handlebars and wheels. A year ago she had never dreamed of being in such dire financial straits. Now she even hesitated before buying a soft drink from a vending machine.

"I have to find Therese!" The minute the words were out of her mouth she cringed. *Oh, God, Therese,* she silently cried. *There are so many reasons I need to find you.*

Carly felt self-pity creeping up on her, but for the moment she was powerless to stop it. So much had happened in the past eight months. So many times she had needed her sister for support, for comfort. At times a deep resentment against Therese's gallivanting ways settled over her, and at other times a gnawing fear that something disastrous had happened ate away at her. Therese had never felt the slightest guilt at just picking up and taking off for God only knew where, and more often than not she was late in letting her family know where she was. But she had never been silently absent for such a long time.

Now time had become a critical factor, and even the hired detectives had come up empty-handed. Therese's whereabouts were unknown, and that left Carly searching on her own, starting with the last place her sister had been known to be—Galveston Island.

Carly bent over and gripped the black plastic covering on the bicycle handlebar, and already it was hot to the touch. At least her clothing was appropriate for the humid heat. Her loose-fitting white shorts and pale blue midriff top were made of lightweight material, cool feeling and cool to look at. She straddled the front wheel of the bicycle and lifted it up with the intention of walking backward, slowly and carefully leading the vehicle out onto the deck. First one handlebar came through the small opening, then the next. She was just about to ease the rest of the bike out when a yell from the neighboring yacht startled her.

"Ahoy, there," came a man's silence-breaking call.

The bicycle fell and Carly nearly with it. Righting herself, she jerked around and looked up to see a man in his late thirties peering down at her.

"Having difficulties?" he asked, and Carly, giving him a what-do-you-think look and planting her hands on her hips, prepared to get rid of him with as little conversation as necessary. Undeterred, he placed his hand on his yacht's railing and leaped over the side, landing gracefully on her deck.

Why not let him help you? a little voice asked her, and for a moment Carly wanted to shrug and agree, but then she felt her hackles rising at the nerve of the man taking it upon himself to come uninvited onto her yacht. The bicycle had become a personal challenge to her, as ridiculous as that thought might seem, and she didn't want anyone touching it now that she had mastered it this far.

"Actually no," she said, and when he looked puzzled she gestured toward the cabin door. "I'm not having difficulties now."

"Of course you're not," he replied, "now that I'm here." He gave her a wide smile, revealing straight, even teeth. Carly could have sworn they even glimmered in the sunlight. Her hands knotted into fists as she realized what a very handsome man she was staring at. His blond hair, streaked with silver from the sun, curled against the collar of his brightly patterned Hawaiian shirt. The planes of his darkly tanned face were sharp, with deeply etched grooves slashing each side of his mouth. But it was his eyes, such a striking royal blue even in the bright morning light, that captured her attention. She imagined they changed shade with his moods, which right now seemed a little too friendly for her liking.

"Look—" she began.

"Tanner," he answered.

"I'm really in a hurry, so if you wouldn't mind . . ."

"Don't mind a bit."

Carly sighed; he wasn't going to be easy to get rid of. "I'm sure you don't, but I wanted to do it myself."

"Why?"

Why? What would he think if she told him it was because she had come a long way with the type of responsibility she had never had before, being the youngest of three children. Although the bicycle seemed like a small thing, it was extremely important to her that she do everything, *everything* by herself.

"It's become a matter of my besting that heap of metal." God, that sounded stupid.

"I've watched you wrestling with that thing for the last half hour, and you'll be lucky if you're not covered with bruises. What difference does it make who gets it on shore as long as it gets there?"

He had a point. Carly shaded her eyes with the palm of her hand and saw how rapidly the sun was climbing. If she was going to make it to the other end of the island before the day became scorching, she had to get on her way.

"I guess it doesn't make any difference; it's just that when something doesn't go right, I tend to work myself into a state over it and then I want to finish what I've started just for personal satisfaction. It can be a bad fault." She smiled wanly. "Especially when it kind of makes me look like a fool."

"Not a fool. And believe it or not, I understand what you're saying, although in this case I think you should concede defeat and let me help you." His eyes had lightened just a shade, and as he waited for her okay, he slid his hands into the pockets of his khaki shorts and tilted his head just slightly to the left, smiling a crooked half grin.

Her heart fluttered. She couldn't believe how instantly attracted she was to this man. "I agree. And I'd really appreciate it if you'd wrestle this heap of junk to the pier for me."

"Your wish is my command."

Carly stood to the side and watched as Tanner easily maneuvered the bicycle to the deck. He kicked the stand down, then lifted the bicycle over the rail and placed it on the wooden pier. Although he seemed to have done everything right, the bicycle tilted over and crashed. Tanner flinched, a look of disbelief coming over his features.

"My fault," Carly said, trying not to laugh. "The bike's old, and I'm afraid I overoiled the kickstand, because it's been doing that ever since I worked on it."

"I take it your battle with that thing has been going on for some time?"

" 'Fraid so." She sighed. "Look, I'm really grateful, and I don't mean to sound rude, but I have a lot of things to do this morning. And if I don't leave now it's going to be too hot . . ."

"A vacation shouldn't be hurried," Tanner said, his smile doing funny things to her equilibrium. "Why not come over and have a cup of coffee with me first, before you go do all those *things* you

19

have to do?"

She stepped back. "I'm sorry. I can't." She went to the cabin door. "Thanks . . ."

"Hey, wait a minute. You never told me your name."

"Carly." She left him standing there. In the cool interior of the small cabin she took a deep breath; then, with a small shake of her head, she checked her tote bag for the address book she needed, made sure she had enough money handy, and slipped her sunglasses on top of her head. She flipped through the book, found the address she needed and then unfolded a map of the city to find the best route to take. From previous visits she knew better than to ride down Seawall Boulevard; it would be packed with people, bicycles, and wind gliders. She recalled the street, lined with palm trees that ran through the heart of the city and searched for it on the map. Broadway, that was it, but it went only a little over halfway to her destination. *Oh, well, I'll ride as far as it takes me and then pass over to Seawall,* she decided. She crammed everything into the large canvas bag, slipped it over her shoulder, and started on her way.

When she stepped onto the deck she felt a slight pang of disappointment that Tanner had gone. She glanced up at his yacht but saw only a dark-haired, one-armed man, who tilted his head in greeting. Carly casually waved her hand, then left her yacht and climbed onto the bicycle.

20

Tanner sat in much the same position he had the night before, with his feet resting on the teak table. There wasn't much else to do, he decided, until someone reported something. He crossed his legs at the ankles and his arms over his chest, then admitted to himself that he was genuinely bored.

His thoughts drifted to Carly Jameson and he smiled. Hank had been right; she was beautiful. But Tanner had expected a more worldly person, someone like Therese. Carly was nothing at all like her sister, not in appearance, not in personality. In fact, it was her very vulnerability that bothered him. Could he pull this off without hurting her? he wondered, then immediately felt irritated with himself. Hell, she's nothing more than an assignment. The easiest one he'd ever have. Wasn't that what Omi had said?

God, could he suddenly be having an attack of conscience after all these years? Tanner reaffirmed his belief that it was past time for him to get out of the program. He loved his country, it was the best in the world, but working in the unit wasn't the answer for him any longer. He wondered what exactly it was he was searching for, what it would take to make him happy. How did one find new kinds of excitement when one had been everywhere and done everything?

He sighed. He couldn't answer his own questions.

Carly, with sweat literally running down her face, rang the doorbell for the eighth time. *Dammit, answer the door!* she wanted to shout. When she had called earlier, Lisa Curtis had said she would be at home waiting, that she had things to tell Carly. Therese had roomed with Lisa for six months or more, and Carly knew Lisa was the only one who could help her at this point. She was probably the only one Carly knew who had any inkling of Therese's whereabouts. So why wasn't she here? Carly thought as she angrily pounded on the wooden door.

"Hey, lady, she ain't home," a young Mexican gardener yelled from where he was working beneath the concrete stairs of the apartment complex.

Carly's chin fell to her chest. "Do you know Lisa?" Carly asked hopefully, rubbing her aching knuckles.

"Don't *know her*, know her, but I'd like to. Real fox, ya know what I mean?"

Carly descended the stairs and stood on the sidewalk peering at the young man. "Did you know her roommate, Therese Jameson?"

"Was she the blond that lived here about a year ago?" he asked, rubbing a grubby hand against his cheek.

"Yes, she lived here until about eight months ago."

"Nother fox," he said. "But I ain't seen her in

a long time. Don't even 'member why she left."

Carly felt her spirits rise and fall at the same time. "Do you happen to know where Lisa went?"

"Naw, she just climbed into her little sports car and left about thirty or forty minutes ago. Looked in a hurry too. She's usually decked out, but she was a wreck when she left. Ya know, I don't think she's ever up this early in the morning."

And she wouldn't have been this morning if I hadn't called! Dammit, I should have just ridden out here on the chance that she'd be home. Now it'll be hell catching up with her! Carly thought angrily, wishing now that she had believed the detective agency when they'd told her how hesitant Lisa Curtis had been in helping them. But Carly had thought they were giving her the runaround in order to get more money out of her. Well, they had proved her wrong, and now she was stuck with going to the club where Lisa worked each night and trying to catch her there.

Carly cleared her throat. "Would you be interested in making a little money?"

"That depends. Whatcha got in mind?"

She flushed and was glad her overheated face hid the sign of her embarrassment. She had been going to ask him to call her when Lisa returned but then remembered that she didn't have a phone. "Oh, never mind." She spun on her heel and left a bewildered-looking gardener staring after her.

Carly lifted the bicycle from its reclining

position on the grass and climbed onto it, wincing when her sore bottom came into contact with the seat. Feeling defeated, she pedaled across the street and up the slight hill to the seawall. At least this far out on the island there were no tourists clamoring all over the place as they did on the central section of the beach.

The manager of the marina was a nice man, Carly thought as she parked the bicycle in a storage room in back of the office building. He'd even loaned her the key to the door, since there was nothing in the room but a few battered tea crates and some empty boxes. He should have refused her after the way she had pressured him into giving her a berthing spot—not to mention her near wrecking of said spot—but he seemed a very easygoing man, a person who didn't hold a grudge.

As Carly pulled the key from the lock, she was undecided about which she should do first—call Ellis or take a cool shower and then call him. Her skin felt tight from the dried perspiration coating her body, and her parched lips tasted salty. Her stinging back indicated she'd had enough sun for one day. She decided to call her brother and get that over with. The thought of climbing aboard the yacht and then leaving it again was distinctly unappealing; it would be too much of an effort for her trembling legs. She just hoped it wouldn't take her body long to become accustomed to pedaling the bicycle.

Carly had spotted a pay phone near the dock and made her way toward it. She dug through her purse but to no avail. She had plenty of credit cards, but not the one she needed for the telephone. Damn! She refused to call collect. She'd already taken off without Ellis's knowledge or consent—because when she had told him of her plan he'd been against it—and when he finally heard from her it was going to be bad enough. If he knew how unprepared she was, he'd really taunt her, which was the last thing she needed.

Selecting a handful of coins from her purse, she inserted one and informed the operator that she wanted to place a call to Beaumont, Texas, and to please allow the phone to ring an extra long time—which it did.

"Hello." A feminine voice came across the wire.

"Hold, please?" the nasal tone of the operator instructed. "Insert two dollars and twenty-five cents, please, for the first three minutes." Carly heard a faint ringing noise each time a quarter slid into the slot.

"Tina, it's me, Carly. Is Ellis able to come to the phone?"

"Where are you! We've been worried sick." Tina's tone was less than cordial.

"I'm in Galveston. Will you please get my brother?"

"I can't believe you've actually gone through with this. Do you realize what stress you've caused him? What this could do to his morale?"

Carly wasn't sure if Tina was asking or demanding. "Yes, I'm quite aware of what he's going through!" Carly decided Tina was demanding. "But it can't be helped. Now, will you bring my brother to the phone or not?"

She heard a sigh. "Just a minute. He's in the dining room."

For several minutes there was silence, then a break in the connection as the operator intruded. "If you wish to speak longer, deposit another two dollars, please." Carly inserted the money and heard a rushed "thank you" for using that particular phone company—as if she had a choice, she thought sourly.

She willed Ellis to hurry. At this rate she'd barely get to say hello before they were disconnected. She didn't have enough change for another three minutes' conversation.

"Carly?" The familiar baritone warmed her. "Carly? Where the hell are you?"

"In Galveston." She rushed on before he could interrupt. "Listen, Ellis—"

"No, you listen," he interrupted tersely, "because I've got a few things to say to you, little sister." The last didn't sound like an endearment.

"Ellis, shut up!" For a stunned moment neither said a word. Carly couldn't believe she'd actually said that to her brother. She shook her head as if to clear it, then stiffened her spine and continued. "I had to come. You know I did. I'm supposed to meet Lisa Curtis this evening—" God forgive me for lying, Carly said to herself—"and she's promised to tell me anything she can about Therese."

"For God's sake, Carly, do you really believe you're going to get anything out of her? If the best men in the state failed, what makes you think you'll succeed?"

"Once I've explained why we have to find Therese, I'm sure she'll be willing to give us all the help she can," Carly answered, crossing her fingers. "I'm sure Therese told her of the ugly falling-out she and Dad had and that she never wanted to see him again, but . . ." Carly's voice cracked. "But she doesn't have to worry about that now, does she?"

Ellis sighed, much as Tina had, but Carly detected the pain it held. "No," he answered somberly. "Carly, be careful. You're all I've got right now. . . . And call me as soon as you've heard what Ms. Curtis has to say."

"I will. Ellis, please, try not to worry. I'll be fine."

"I can't help but worry, babe."

"I know. I love you."

"Love you too."

The line was severed by his hanging up, and for

a moment Carly stood still, holding the gray receiver. She was worried. Perhaps she was piling too much on Ellis too soon. He'd been gravely injured, and his recovery greatly depended on his frame of mind. Still, Carly thought defensively, Tina King had been hired to take care of him. She was young, attractive, and a great therapist. If anyone could inspire Ellis to try harder, it was she. Her tongue was sharp, and her no-nonsense attitude left little opportunity for Ellis's anger to overrule her. Yes, Carly thought, Tina would be in control of the situation, leaving Ellis little time to dwell on his baby sister's out-of-character behavior.

Carly placed the receiver back in its silver cradle and made her way to the yacht, her only goal to have a cool shower wash away her fatigue.

Tanner was lounging on the deck of his much larger yacht. Sweat beaded on his forehead and the sun beat down on his bare chest. Dark glasses reflected a harsh glare off the water and hid his alert indigo eyes.

The squeak of deck shoes signaled Hank's arrival, and he sat up.

"She's finally contacted him," Hank said casually.

"And . . .?" Tanner brushed the beads of perspiration from his forehead and pushed back his hair in one move.

"It was what we expected. She made the move

against his wishes. He's irritated with her, but she's set on trying to find out what she can."

"Well," Tanner said quietly, "let's just watch her for awhile. Lisa should have satisfied her curiosity for the time being."

Hank shook his head negatively. "Lisa apparently wasn't at home for Carly. Carly's going to try and corner her at the Diamond Lounge."

Tanner sat up straight. "Damn! I don't want her going to that dive. What the hell is Lisa up to?"

Hank sat across from Tanner. "She must have her reasons."

"Or something has come up." Deep in thought, he gazed off into the distance. "Contact Lisa and see what's going on. It looks as if I may have to start working sooner than I thought."

"What's wrong with that?" Hank asked.

"Nothing," Tanner snapped, then looked away when Hank's dark eyes looked full at him.

"Then there shouldn't be any problem," Hank said, pushing himself out of the chair and leaving.

And there won't be, Tanner thought. He had reevaluated Carly's file after he'd talked to her that morning and had come to the conclusion that she wasn't a very gutsy person at heart. In fact, she had been coddled and protected all her life—until the accident. It must have been hard on her, he thought, being thrust into the business world so suddenly on the heels of her father's death and her brother's brush with death, especially in a business that was floundering. But she had done all right. It wasn't her fault that the economy had taken a dive or that her father had written an airtight will, stating that all three children had to hold a daily position within his company for one year—beginning on the anniversary of his death—or all would forfeit their inheritance. Nor was she to blame for wanting to find Therese. It was just that he couldn't allow her to do so, at least not yet.

Carly was really a victim. Old Jameson had been a selfish bastard. He'd wanted Therese under his thumb so badly he'd made sure of it one way or the other, even if it had taken his death to do so. But in trying to tie Therese down, he'd ended up hurting his youngest and most favorite child. Tanner wondered if Carly had even thought of that. Surely she had.

After having studied her file, Tanner made a few adjustments in his strategy. Having been in the business of reading people and their motives for so long, he knew that Carly was uncertain about her undertaking, and he planned to use that in his favor. He would gain her confidence and allow her to lean on him, enabling him to be a part of her dilemma openly. He had an assignment to carry out, and Carly was that assignment. He had to ensure that she didn't learn of Therese's location. It was just that simple.

He spotted Carly slowly walking toward the dock and stood up, immediately detecting the weariness in her pace. It would be easy for him to take advantage of her, he thought, studying her as a man would a woman, not an assignment. He'd always admired Therese's figure, but he had to admit that baby sister's put hers to shame. Carly wasn't very big—medium height and average weight, but it was the way it was all distributed. Her waist was tiny, and he knew his large palms could easily span it. He flexed his fingers; then, realizing what he was doing, clenched them into fists. His eyes moved down to admire her long, lean legs, then up to the hem of her white shorts and over the gentle curves of her hips. Her bare stomach was flat. The cropped-off edge of her blouse reached just below the fullness of her breasts. Tanner took a deep breath and stepped toward the bow, anticipating her arrival.

As Carly neared, her features came clearly into focus. Her long chestnut curls were now twisted up and pinned to the back of her head. They bounced with her every step, just like another part of her anatomy. Her cheeks were red, overheated; her expression sad. She stopped suddenly and glanced up. Tanner stared down into her shaded green eyes and smiled.

"Hi ya, sailor," she said huskily. "Buy a girl a drink?"

He made himself ignore the tightening in his groin and answered, "They're on the house."

CHAPTER TWO

"**H**ow about an ice-cold margarita?" Tanner asked from his lofty position. "I make the best in the state."

Carly shook her head. "I'd prefer a cold soft drink if you have one."

Tanner grimaced in mock distate at her preference, then winked. "Come on up, Carly."

He moved to wait for her at the top of the accommodation ladder. Actually, he decided as he watched Carly pull herself up, this assignment wasn't going to be as bad as he'd first imagined. All he really had to do was keep Carly from messing up Therese's investigation and give Therese time to complete her mission. Lord knew she deserved that much. Therese had been successful in infiltrating the smuggling ring where none of the others had even come close, including himself. Years of work were about to pay off. He knew Carly thought her family's welfare rested on bringing Therese home.

And, it did, he had to admit, but there were still several months to go before the old man's will had to be fulfilled, and Therese would be home in plenty of time to see that it was. Was there really a need to make Carly dependent on him? Hell, yes, he thought, temporarily anyway. He had to keep her out of that dive—at least until Lisa was found. The Diamond Lounge was bad news, especially for someone as green as Carly Jameson.

Tanner pinched the ridge of his nose. What had happened to Lisa? Her orders had been simple and to the point. Had she carried them out, Carly would have been feeling much easier about Therese—and he, much easier about Carly.

Carly climbed carefully up the ladder, almost wishing she hadn't made the spontaneous request. The backs of her calves felt weak, and it took a tremendous effort just to lift each foot to the next rung. As her head rose above the side of the craft she came face-to-face with Tanner, who was braced on his hands leaning toward her. His smile was devilish, the dark lenses of his glasses unsettling. For a split second she felt hesitant about moving any closer. The urge to descend the ladder and leave was strong, but when Tanner placed his palm over her hand she unwittingly climbed up another step.

"What's the matter?" Tanner asked, his voice a little rough.

"Nothing," she answered weakly. "I'm just

pooped and not really certain I can make it over the side." She felt a smile breaking across her face. "What's worse is that I don't think I can crawl back down either. Would you mind if I just sorta' hang here for a while?"

"That tired, huh?" He smiled sympathetically.

"Just about."

"Well," he drawled, slipping his hands beneath her arms, "I can't leave you here. What would the neighbors think?"

Effortlessly, or so it seemed to Carly, he hoisted her over the side and stood her on the deck. She closed her eyes, trying to gain her equilibrium, but the spinning in her head got worse.

"Hey, are you all right?" The concern in his voice seemed magnified as it penetrated the roaring in her ears.

Carly couldn't answer. She seemed unable to do anything except blink against the white spots flashing behind her lids. Slowly the sound died down and she was able to focus on Tanner's face.

"I guess I got too much sun today. Listen, I'm sorry, but I'm going to decline the drink. I think I'd better lie down for awhile."

"Why not come in and rest in my cabin?"

"No, I . . ."

"Carly, we both know you can't make it back down the ladder. Come on, rest awhile, and when you feel better we can share that drink."

The muscles flexing in his arms made Carly

realize that she was holding onto him and he to her. When his fingers lightly squeezed her bare waist she stepped back too quickly, and swayed.

"Here, sit down," Tanner said and helped her to the chair he had earlier vacated. "Wait just a second." He left her and stepped across the deck, disappearing into the yacht's cabin. She faintly heard him speak to someone before he returned to help her to her feet. With great gentleness, Tanner placed his arm around Carly and led her into the cool, darkened cabin. Unaccustomed to the darkness, she blindly followed him as he steered her through a hatch into another room.

Tanner sat her on the edge of a bunk and swung her feet up. Carly couldn't believe how docile she was being as he pressed her back against a pillow. He was a virtual stranger, but she didn't feel threatened.

"Thanks, Hank," she heard Tanner say; she was curious about who was in the room, but she had already closed her eyes and was too tired to open them.

"Carly, this should make you feel better." Tanner spoke quietly, but despite the warning Carly flinched at the touch of the cool, damp cloth he placed over her forehead.

"I think she'll be okay after she rests, Tanner," a deeper voice said as Carly drifted into a swift, deep slumber.

"For a second there I thought she was going to pass out on me," Tanner said, removing the dark glasses from where he had shoved them on top of his head. He placed them next to the bowl of water Hank had set on the nightstand.

"Too much sun'll do that," Hank replied. "And she's had more than her share. Look how red she is."

Tanner silently agreed as he stared at Carly's bare midriff and long legs. She was going to be as sore as hell by the time she awoke. He was more concerned, however, at the lack of color in her face. She was ghostly white and a greenish ring had formed around her mouth.

"She'll sleep for a while, Tanner. Let her rest while we find out what's going on with our friend."

Tanner lifted a brow and nodded, but remained where he stood. Hank left the room alone.

Leaning over Carly, Tanner plucked the washcloth off her forehead. It was already extremely warm. He shook out the folds and dipped it into the cool water, then squeezed it. He eased his weight onto the edge of the bed and placed the cloth back on her brow. Smiling faintly as she stirred, he wondered if the tiny moan she'd emitted was from relief or displeasure. Cautiously, he brushed the tip of his middle finger across her cheek, pushing a lock of hair away from her face; then he, too, left the room, closing the hatch securely behind him.

Tanner walked through the cabin. The crackle

of static led him to Hank's whereabouts.

"What've you come up with?" he asked, stepping into the room.

"Nothing, yet. I may have to go ashore and make a call." Hank frowned as he spun around in his chair. "I don't like this a damned bit. Lisa should have been at her apartment."

Tanner agreed.

"If Omi had changed her orders he'd have informed us." Hank pointed at a table covered with the latest in high-tech radio equipment. "I've sent word for him to contact us. Do you want to wait for him, or do you want to try phoning Lisa?"

Tanner grimaced, not really wanting to talk to his superior. "I'll stay here. Carly might wake up and be alarmed if she sees your ugly mug."

"Like hell. She'd prefer my pretty face to yours any day."

"Wise up, Armand. Once a woman looks at this heavenly profile you fade into the woodwork."

"That's not what Consuelo said the last time I was with her," Hank stated smugly.

"When were you with Consuelo?"

"All the times you weren't." Hank laughed, leaving a stunned Tanner looking after him.

Tanner slid into Hank's chair and had to smile. Of course he knew Consuelo slept with whomever was game, but he'd been vain enough to think that at least when he was in Mexico she'd reserved herself solely for him. He laughed out loud. Hank had certainly deflated his swollen head this time. But why should he care? No woman was worth jeopardizing a friendship, especially his with Hank.

He flexed his shoulders and grimaced as his bare back stuck to the chair. He needed a shower. He looked at his own chest and saw that even though he was darkly tanned, his skin held a pink cast from the miserable heat he had endured while waiting for Carly's return. She was more than well cooked herself and was going to be in a lot of pain. Maybe that would keep her immobile for a few days. Somehow he doubted it.

A shower sure sounded good. If he turned up the frequency on the radio and left the door open, he'd be able to hear any incoming calls over the rush of the water. If he hurried, he'd be in and out before Omi even had time to waddle to the station's base or before the whine of the radio could wake Carly.

Tanner swung the door to the head open. Without hesitation he stripped off his shorts, turned on the water, and stepped beneath the cold spray.

"Come in, Santa Anna, this is the Alamo. Dammit, Santa Anna, come in!"

Tanner left the shower, grabbing the first thing his hand touched to wrap around himself as he wondered just how long Omi had been calling. A short towel, which didn't quite reach around him, was the best he was able to do. He held it on his hip by the corners, cursing as it threatened to slip.

"Crockett back, Alamo. I read you loud and clear."

"Where in hell have you been?"

"In the shower," Tanner answered.

"Where's Anna?" came the heavily accented voice.

"Anna's on shore leave. Won't I do?" he joked, knowing it wouldn't be well received by his superior. The towel slipped lower and he grabbed it; then, blinking drops of water out of his eyes, he jerked it off and briskly rubbed his face and hair. If Carly came in, he thought, grinning, the sight of his nudity would send her running.

"Ann left word for me, remember?"

"Right. What's going on with Curtis?" Tanner was already tired of talking to Omi. Since he had announced his intention to leave, the little man had treated him like a traitor.

"What do you mean . . ." Static blocked the rest of Omi's words. Tanner cursed, hating to ask Omi to repeat himself, so he didn't.

"There was no one at home when our friend went by the apartment," Tanner stated, hoping Omi knew what he was talking about without his having to make it any clearer. Sometimes Tanner was amazed that a man in Omi's position could sometimes be so dense yet other times be so damned clever. *I just hope I'm out of this line of work before I begin to understand his reasoning,* Tanner thought.

"No one home?"

Why couldn't Hank have been here? Tanner didn't know how it was that Hank could always communicate with Omi; when he used the same, plain-speaking terms, Omi always got them screwed up. Tanner was just about to begin an explanation when Omi broke through again.

"Crockett! What are you doing, standing with your finger up your . . ."

"I read you, Alamo," Tanner said, cutting off the last of Omi's acerbic remark.

"I don't know what's going on down there, but Curtis was supposed to have been at the apartment all this morning. Have you tried to make contact this afternoon?"

"Anna's on it now," he replied.

"Where's the girl?"

"Here. Sleeping. She's under the weather," Tanner explained.

"Good. I'll see what I can find out. Have Anna contact me as soon as he returns."

Gladly, Tanner thought but said dryly, "Roger Wilco." He could almost see the short, stocky officer scratching his head while he mentally went over the information he'd been given.

"Button your lip, Crockett . . ." At Omi's words, Tanner flipped the radio off and went in search of his clothing.

"Why are you wearing my clothes?" Hank

asked Tanner.

"I didn't want to risk waking Sleeping Beauty, so I borrowed some of yours."

Hank stepped further into the radio room, eyeing Tanner sternly. "I take it you've spoken to Omi."

"And I take it you didn't reach Lisa."

Neither said anything for a moment. Tanner stood up and thrust his hands deeply into the pockets of his jeans. "Something stinks!"

"What did Omi have to say?"

"He doesn't know any more than we do. There weren't any changes in Lisa's orders. Whatever's happening, she's doing this on her own, and I hope like hell she knows what it is." Tanner's frustration showed in his stiff stance.

"Tanner, she wouldn't do anything without cause."

"I know. What did you come up with?"

"An unanswered telephone."

"Damn!" Tanner was ready to punch something. "Radio headquarters and see if they want us to find Lisa tonight. I'm going on deck."

Tanner was gazing at the water when Hank joined him several minutes later. He pulled a pack of cigarettes out of his pocket and extended it to Tanner.

"We're to keep Carly on board until they find out what's happening with Lisa. Cornwall will be doing all the legwork."

Tanner took a cigarette and ran it between his finger and thumb before placing it to his lips. Hank flicked a lighter and touched it to the tip, repeating the process for himself. Both exhaled a stream of smoke.

"Cornwall, huh? When did he arrive?"

"Late last night. He's booked at the Galvez."

Tanner nodded. "Seems like our simple assignment is becoming complicated."

"They're usually the worst ones," Hank agreed.

"*Now* you tell me." Tanner scanned the waterfront, his brows knitting.

"How are you going to keep Carly aboard?"

"I think I have a simple solution. We'll just do a little deep-sea fishing tonight."

"You hate to fish," Hank replied, massaging the stump of his arm.

"I only hate fishing when there're no fish biting. I think I'll take a stroll around the basin and pick up some bait. Maybe I'll find out what's running—if anything."

"What if she wakes up?"

Tanner grinned. "You'll think of something."

Carly tossed feverishly on the bed, moaning softly in her sleep. She suddenly sat upright. Sweat poured off her, and for a moment she felt completely disoriented. Her eyes darted around the cabin as her heart beat rapidly against her chest.

She wasn't certain if it was from her dream or the fright of not knowing where she was. Taking in the elegance of the interior, she drew a deep breath of relief as she remembered where and how she'd ended up in Tanner's . . . What's his last name? she thought, realizing she didn't know it. She lay back down on the pillow, throwing her arm over her eyes.

Her head ached horribly and her skin was stinging all over. It was dark outside and probably too late to find Lisa. Damn! When were the cards going to start falling in her favor?

She carefully turned her head on the pillow. Why do dreams have to be so real? she thought, remembering vividly why she had awakened. For some reason she'd been dreaming of a red dirt road —similar to those in East Texas—when she'd seen Therese and started running toward her, laughing and crying in relief. As if in slow motion, Therese had turned, her face grimacing sadly as she looked at her sister. She'd held up her hand to ward Carly off and then started running away, going too fast for Carly to catch her. Suddenly Carly found herself on the bicycle, pedaling with all her strength but going nowhere. The dirt had become mud, and Carly had startled herself awake fighting the sensation of being sucked into its red depths.

The dream had been real enough, Carly thought, but she had no idea what it meant—if anything. She rubbed her eyes, then pushed herself up, swinging her legs over the edge of the bed. She groaned at the soreness in her legs, then drew her breath in sharply as her burning skin protested the sudden movement.

"Great," she muttered, wishing she'd had more sense than to forget to use a sunscreen.

Someone had turned on a small lamp and left a bowl of water resting on the table. Tanner, she thought, spotting his sunglasses. She dipped her fingers into the water and splashed the drops on her face. The small clock sitting on the nightstand read ten o'clock. How long had she slept—seven hours? Impossible. She had to get out of there, get back to her yacht.

Carly stood up and felt the room sway. At first she thought she was still suffering the after affects from the afternoon, but she soon realized it wasn't her, it was the yacht that was rocking. The ground swells must have gotten bigger, she thought, wondering if they were in for some bad weather. She glanced out the porthole, but it was too dark to see anything. Turning, she caught her reflection in a small mirror mounted on the bulkhead and frowned at her haggard look. Her hair was a mass of tangles; the rubber band holding it would probably have to be cut out. She smoothed it as best she could, splashed more water on her face, and left the room.

Tanner's yacht was much larger than hers, and so she wasn't surprised to see such elegance. The

sitting room held dark wood furniture. The uphol-
stery, a rich, rust leather, felt softer than it looked as
Carly trailed her fingers along the back of a chair.
There didn't seem to be anyone around, and Carly,
although hesitant about snooping through his living
quarters, didn't want to leave without at least
thanking Tanner and letting him know that she was
going. She walked forward and opened a heavy
metal hatch, sticking her head through to see if
anyone was there. It was the galley, spotlessly clean
and totally unoccupied.

Carly sighed. Perhaps she should just call out
to Tanner instead. Surely he would hear her and
come. But what if he had left her here alone and
gone out for the evening? She imagined he led a
very active social life; he was too friendly and too
good-looking to want to spend his time alone. Carly
felt a twinge of envy. It would probably be
extremely nice to be the center of a man's attention,
she thought, but she hadn't the time to worry about
such matters now. Maybe after Therese was found
and things settled down at home she would meet
someone she could really care for.

"Tanner," she called before she realized it.
"Tanner?" Her voice rose a fraction. "Ohhh!"

A tall, one-armed man had entered without her
hearing him.

"I didn't mean to startle you," he said quietly,
his voice a deep, mellow bass. He reached out a
hand. "My name's Hank. I saw you earlier, but I'm

afraid you were a little out of it and we weren't properly introduced."

With her heart beating rapidly, Carly barely touched his fingers in greeting. Then she recognized him as the man she had seen on the deck earlier that morning and relaxed. "I'm Carly, and I'm sorry about this afternoon. It's really rather embarrassing. That was the closest I've ever come to passing out."

"Are you feeling any better?"

"Some. But my head's aching, and I'm sure I'll be peeling in a few days." She grimaced comically.

"I think you're right." Hank smiled, and Carly thought his black eyes were almost as beautiful as Tanner's deep blue ones. Both men were eye-catchers, but Hank seemed a more serious-minded man than his friend. "How about a couple of aspirins?"

"Please, if you have some handy."

He walked to a cabinet and removed a bottle of white tablets. He handed it to her and then set a glass in the sink and turned on the faucet. Carly wondered what had happened to his arm.

"Is Tanner still here?" she asked hopefully.

Hank nodded. "Topside." He handed her the water and watched as she downed the medication.

Carly didn't want to seem pushy, but she was ready to leave; already she was feeling weak again. "Would you mind taking me up there?"

"Not at all," Hank said, taking her by the arm.

She isn't going to like this, Hank thought, and he was glad that Tanner would be the lucky one who got to deal with Ms. Jameson's temper if she became angry, for he, Hank, planned to quietly slip away. He was not one to enjoy an emotional display, especially if it were being performed by a female, and he had the feeling that this one, if she ever cut loose, would be hell to handle. He'd seen her with the bicycle.

Carly's sunburned skin was extremely sensitive to the night's chilly breeze, and her teeth began to chatter, but not for long. When she saw nothing but water for miles around, her jaw clenched.

"Where are we?" she asked, feeling a surge of anxiety.

Hank was saved from explaining as Tanner appeared.

"Good, you're up. How are you feeling?" Tanner asked cheerfully.

Hank decided to depart then. "If you'll excuse me," he said, "I think I'll turn in for the night. It was a pleasure meeting you, Carly."

She ignored his retreating form and answered Tanner's question. "Fine," she said sharply. "Why didn't you wake me up and let me know you planned on doing some late-night fishing?" Carly saw the fighting chair anchored to the deck and the thick rod mounted on the chair.

"It was sort of a spur-of-the-moment thing," he said. "I went ashore earlier and learned that the

48

ling were hitting. You were sleeping so well that I didn't want to wake you, but I didn't want to miss the chance to reel one of those monsters in, so I decided to head out. I'm sorry. I didn't think you'd mind." Tanner modified his voice to sound truly apologetic.

Carly felt contrite. He had gone out of his way to her help her today. It wasn't his fault that she had slept so long. She must have looked like hell when he first saw her, for she still felt haggard, but she had planned to find Lisa Curtis, and now she was going to lose another day. Carly sighed. She wasn't really angry at Tanner, just at the circumstances she found herself in.

"No, I'm sorry. I overreacted at finding myself out in the middle of the gulf. I should be thanking you for taking such good care of me, and I do. Thank you, that is."

He smiled. "No problem. It isn't every day I have a beautiful woman swooning in my arms," he said, tongue in cheek.

Carly smiled. "Swooning?"

"Uh-huh. Right into my arms," he said, his voice lowering an octave.

The smile abruptly left Carly's face. His eyes no longer held the glint of humor. In the darkness of the night, they matched the deepened color of the sea. He stepped directly in front of her, not touching her, but she could feel the heat from his body on her bare stomach. She tilted her head back, looking up into his face, and knew he was going to kiss her if she didn't do something to prevent it. She placed her hand on his shoulder and stepped back. Her earlier thoughts of him were right—he was used to being entertained, only she couldn't allow him to start something she had no intention of finishing. Besides that, she'd met him just brief hours before.

His smile reappeared as he accepted her silent rebuff. He straightened and looked off across the water. "I hope you're not in a hurry to get back. It's rare that I get time to do this sort of thing."

She grinned, and it felt good. Since it was too late to continue her search for Lisa Curtis that night, she gave in.

"If you don't mind having me aboard, I'll be fine below deck. As tired as I am it doesn't matter where I sleep, just as long as I do." She rubbed her arms against the brisk chill of the wind.

"If you're sure?" he asked, turning his gaze back on her.

"Positive. Would you mind if I took a shower though?"

"Help yourself," he said; then, noticing her chattering, he added, "Come on. I'll get you all set up."

Carly followed him below deck and back to the cabin where she had slept. As she watched him pull a gray warm-up suit out of a drawer she decided that anyone who knew her would never believe she had spent the night on a stranger's yacht.

He turned. "This will swallow you, but at least you'll be warm. Come on." He gripped her hand lightly and led her back the same way she'd taken earlier.

She suddenly felt a little nervous and pulled her hand out of his. "If you'll just point me in the right direction, you can get on with your fishing."

"It'll wait," he said, stopping because she had.

"No, no. I don't want to interfere with your plans," she replied.

He raked his hand through his windblown hair. "Am I making you nervous?"

"No. . . . But what if you hook a fish while you're gone?" she said too quickly.

"That's doubtful. A ling has to be antagonized into striking and since I'm not trolling, only a brain-damaged fish would be likely to bite." Carly smiled. "Have you ever seen a retarded ling?"

She laughed openly. "No. In fact, I've never even seen a ling."

"Then I'm not in any serious trouble."

"Unless another type of fish is hungry."

"I'll worry about that when the bow of the yacht is jerked under water. Come on," he said. "At least let me make sure you have a towel. What kind of a host would I be if I let you drip dry?"

"One who could be thoroughly enjoying himself on deck."

He placed his hand beneath the dangling curls

51

on the nape of her neck and lightly massaged her neck. "My mama raised me better than that. This way, my dear." He pulled her forward and through the door.

As Carly showered, Tanner gathered a few extra things he thought she would need and was waiting for her when she finished. He knocked on the door.

"Carly, here's some lotion for your sunburn."

She cracked the door, and he handed her the plastic bottle and a comb. It was a few minutes before she came out. Tanner frowned.

"I know I look a mess," she stated, referring to her wet hair, as well as the way the warm-up suit swallowed her, "but I can't get this rubber band out. Do you have any scissors?"

"Somewhere. Hold on."

He pulled open several drawers before he found them. "Turn around."

Carly stood as still as she possibly could with his warm breath coursing down the back of her damp neck. He was so close, her back touched his chest when he stooped to clip the band.

"I don't want to cut your hair, but that thing is on there tight."

"If you can just lift one of the circles and snip it, I should be able to get it out," she responded.

"I'm trying to, but it's all tangled."

Carly couldn't control a small sigh. "Here, let me lift my hair, and you see if you can find an easier place underneath."

"I don't think I've ever seen so much hair on a human head," he said, bending to peer beneath the wet, tangled mass. "But it's beautiful." He planted a moist kiss on her nape.

Carly stiffened. "It's also a pain," she said quickly, "especially at times like this."

"Ah, there!" he said, and Carly heard the snap of the rubber band. She gingerly pulled the end of the band, frowning as it clung painfully to a few tangled strands. She tried to step away from him, but he stopped her, and with his help they worked the band out. Her hair tumbled down in a mass of wet curls.

She stepped away and mumbled a thanks, refraining from rubbing her neck where he had kissed her. She felt a little breathless, and raked her fingers through the tangles as a distraction. She turned to face him, intending to ask him where she was to bed down, but when she looked at him her tongue seemed to stick to the roof of her mouth. In the light, his every feature was perfectly defined. His lean face was serious and his eyes were slightly squinted as if he saw something in her as extraordinarily appealing as she seemed to in him. It had been a long time since she'd felt her stomach quiver from a man's look, but Tanner's gaze was having that effect on her. He was obviously a man who knew what he wanted . . . she didn't know what to do, so she did nothing.

Then he was next to her, lowering his head and kissing her before she could blink. His warm breath fanned her cheek, evoking a response, and she found herself lifting her arms and encircling his neck to bring him even closer. He was tall and broad shouldered, and she felt completely swallowed in his embrace. He moved his mouth slowly over hers, his vast experience evident in the way he made her react. Carly felt her excitement wane as a fear grew that she was in over her head.

Tanner felt her pliable body tense and knew that to push her now would be a mistake. She was nothing like he'd originally thought she would be. It would take a little more time before she willingly accepted him as a man. He broke the kiss and lifted his head, allowing Carly to step out of his arms.

"Uh, where would you like me to sleep?" Real smart question, Carly, she thought, berating herself and hating the heated sensation tingling her cheeks.

He must have taken pity and chosen to ignore her blunder, Carly decided when he remained silent. He blinked, then smiled. "Have you ever fished for ling?"

It wasn't the response she had anticipated. "No."

"Would you like to?"

"Well, I don't know. I'm not really wild about catching something that's slimy and scaly and . . ."

"I assure you, if you catch one you won't have to touch it," he said, grinning.

"I don't know," she said again, frowning at the thought. "I just hate to bait a hook and all, and I know how men hate to have to interupt what they're doing to . . ."

"It doesn't bother me a bit to touch a squid."

"Squid."

He nodded. "To begin with. If that doesn't appeal to the ling, I'll change to mullet."

"I don't think . . ." she began, wrinkling her nose.

"You don't have to fish. You could just keep me company."

He looked disappointed, and Carly felt contrite. "It's not that." She hesitated, thinking fast. Her eyes lit up. "You see, I talk too much and always frighten the fish away. My brother just hated me to tag along with him when I was little . . ."

His laugh completely blew her explanation.

"Carly, the fish can't hear you."

She smiled weakly. "Oh, all right." She had given in, but she was going to hate every minute of it.

CHAPTER THREE

Carly almost wished she had left her hair in the tangled ponytail, for it kept blowing in her face. The fighting chair was comfortable, but instead of just keeping Tanner company, she was now seated with a heavy saltwater rod mounted to her chair. Tanner had convinced her that she didn't have to fish, just sit there in case the second line he'd put out was more successful than the first. Well, she thought, if this wasn't fishing, then she was a squid! But she had to admit it was quite enjoyable, resting in the moonlight and having a quiet conversation with such a handsome, pleasant man.

It seemed like ages since she'd had any time to relax. Her life had been in a turmoil for so long. . . . She squelched the memory of Ellis's accident and her father's death. She wouldn't allow the peaceful atmosphere to become cluttered with the painful reminder of how she'd ended up with

Tanner in the first place. She wanted to enjoy it without the headaches and heartaches.

Turning her head to the side, she watched Tanner slowly twist the reel around as he had done continuously since getting her settled. He'd placed her chair starboard, while he remained seated at the bow. She smiled inwardly, realizing how easy he was to talk to. Maybe it was his age, she thought. He was older than any man she had ever dated, and even better looking than Lane, the only man she had ever slept with. But Tanner didn't seem the least bit concerned with his handsomeness. She found that endearing, for Lane had been a snob from the word go. Too bad it had taken her so long to recognize it.

Tanner looked up and saw her watching him. "Why not give it a try?" he asked, pointing toward the reel.

"I'd better not," she said with a sigh. "If you should happen to snag Jaws I'll need my hands free to shoot the harpoon." They both laughed.

"Carly, how long are you going to be staying in Galveston?" he asked quietly after a few moments.

She shrugged. "I'm not sure. No longer than I have to but as long as necessary."

He looked puzzled and Carly smiled. "I'm here to . . . handle some business, and until I'm satisfied with the outcome I'll stay."

"Pretty heavy stuff, huh?"

"Yes. Probably the most important thing I'll

ever handle."

He swiveled his chair around and leaned forward. "Maybe you'll settle it fast"—he smiled at her look of surprise—"and be able to spend a few days with me."

Carly didn't respond. Lying back, she scanned the moon-glistened water. *Just my luck,* she thought, *I meet a man I like, really like, and I can't afford to get to know him better.* She frowned, pushing a lock of hair out of her face. How unjust the entire matter was, she thought. Time ran as freely as water, and hers was quickly running out. Finding Therese was the most important thing in the world right now, much more important than her wishing to stay in Galveston to try and make something special happen with a man like Tanner.

The problems in Beaumont were never ending, but she'd left them anyway. Her family's business, which she had done her best to straighten out, was now in the hands of her father's best friend and long-time employee, Jackie Edward, instead of Ellis's, as it should have been. Carly knew that Jackie would do the best he could with the floundering Steelworks. Still, she had hated to leave it at such a crucial point. She felt sick every time she thought about the three hundred people they'd been forced to lay off, but there wasn't anything else they could have done. At the time, she'd cursed her father and his stupid will. If she and Therese were the only ones affected, she'd have kissed Jameson Steel good-bye and sold it to the highest bidder.

But there was Ellis. He would need the security it provided, not necessarily financial (for when she found Therese the money would be available) but for the hard work and challenge it would give him once he was strong enough to take over the load. Lord knew he felt as if life had nothing else left for him, and that scared her. He had always been so strong, a protective older brother to whom she had always run with every problem. He'd been her parent in a way, since her mother had died when she was a toddler and her father had always been so busy. And now it was her turn to do everything she could for him.

Ellis, thirty-eight years old, was paralyzed from the waist down, all because of the hard work and late hours he and her father had spent trying to win a government bid. If they hadn't been driving home so late, her father wouldn't be dead, Ellis wouldn't be in a wheelchair, and she wouldn't be on this wild-goose chase.

Dammit, Therese, where are you? At moments like this, Carly felt extremely frightened. Her father's death had been a statewide news event. Carly knew that if Therese had been in Texas she would have heard and been home. That left Carly believing that Therese was nowhere near the Gulf Coast. Had something happened to her?

Carly began to shiver all over, hating herself

for allowing her fears to take root, but she finally accepted the very real possibility that Therese had met with disaster.

"Are you cold?"

She turned abruptly at the sound of Tanner's voice. "Yes. Yes, I am. It must be the sunburn. It tends to make you feel hot and cold at the same time."

"Do you want to go below?"

"And miss seeing you land Moby Dick? No way." She couldn't tell him that she had to be around someone whenever she felt this way. Lying in a dark room by herself was the last thing she wanted to do.

"Hold on, then; I'll be right back."

She watched Tanner until his head disappeared, then she turned back to the water. Tomorrow she had to pick up where she had left off today, but she'd already decided not to try to catch Lisa Curtis at her apartment. In the morning, after they docked, she would climb on her bicycle and find the Diamond Lounge, but she'd wait until tomorrow night before she'd attempt to approach Lisa. Mainly, Carly wanted to see what it was about the place that appealed to Therese. Carly still had trouble believeing that Therese had enjoyed working as a cocktail waitress.

"Here ya go."

Carly jumped, then laughed. "I didn't hear you coming," she said. "Mmmm, thanks. This is just what I needed." Tanner wrapped a fluffy blanket over her and tucked it securely beneath her thighs and feet. Carly felt a warmth creep up the back of her legs when he gently squeezed her knee from his crouched position.

"You're welcome. I brought one for myself as well. It's gotten nippy up here."

Carly snuggled deeper into the folds of the blanket and curled her feet up beside her. "What about you, Tanner?" she asked as he settled back into his chair. "How long are you going to hang around the island?"

"My time's my own. Whenever I get tired of it here, I'll move on."

"And are you getting tired yet?"

"I was . . . until yesterday. You see, I saw the cutest girl yesterday wrestling with this bicycle, and . . ."

"Oh, hush!" she said, feeling her cheeks flame with embarrassment. He chuckled, and Carly felt her lips breaking into a wide smile. "I like you," she said spontaneously and felt her face grow hotter.

"I like you too, Carly. Very much." Tanner shook away the tight feeling in his stomach. He realized that what he had said was the truth, and it angered him.

Damn, he knew better than to allow this to happen, but somewhere during the evening he had recognized the fact that when this was all over Carly was going to hate him. Therese would too. But

Therese would get over it. She would understand why they'd had to take such extreme measures. Carly, however, would never forgive him. This had already been hell on her, he could tell. In her young face there were new lines of fatigue that hadn't been on the photograph he'd been given.

He suddenly wanted to laugh harshly. She didn't know what hell was. He doubted she could withstand even the most minor skirmish he'd been in. Yet he'd never want to see her placed in a dangerous position. Protectiveness? *You crazy son of a bitch, this is the last thing you need to be feeling right now.* He was losing it—really losing everything that had ever appealed to him about working undercover. The double-talk, the head games, and playing both ends toward the middle were tiresome. When had it happened? Every move seemed to be a rerun of the last. Find the right connections, make the right moves, and be the first to outmaneuver the opponent. The risks and danger were still there—they'd always be there—but his appetite had waned. He no longer felt the challenge, and that in itself was bad news. To be too confident was deadly.

He twisted the reel a little faster. He had been right in his decision to hand in his resignation; these feelings only reinforced it. Tanner wondered if Omi had sensed it. Was that why he'd been given this Mickey Mouse assignment as his last?

It would have been so much easier just to sit Carly down and tell her the truth, that he worked for a service trying to control drug smuggling and so did her sister Therese. That Therese was on a detail that demanded total silence from her. It was she who had to contact them and did periodically, but that his superiors had withheld the knowledge of her father's death from her because they couldn't risk losing three years' investigation when things were just about to go down.

Yes, he knew that would have settled everything, except that Therese had been blessed with a little too much of her father's personality. She had made it a policy that regardless of what happened, the service would never inform her family of her double life. If she died, it was to set up a freak accident of some sort and have the local authorities or government handle it from there.

So, old buddy, that leaves you to handle all the minor details.

Gentle thoughts of Carly were shoved aside. He was on the verge of leaving this life behind, but he hadn't left it yet, and he'd be damned if he was going to depart on an assignment that was a soft deal. However, as soon as this case was over he was hightailing it to a new life. Somewhere out there— he glanced at the Gulf without really seeing it— something awaited him, he felt its constant tug, and nothing was going to keep him from pursuing it. Hank, Omi, and the rest could have this life, but for him it was only a matter of time before he'd be off to something better.

Tanner came awake slowly, stiffly, groaning at the crick in the back of his neck. He opened his eyes to see the sun glinting brightly off the Gulf waters, and slowly he lifted his head.

He saw her out of the corner of his eye, huddled, as he was, in a chair. Lord, he thought, stretching his cramped limbs, they had both fallen asleep on deck.

She was so still. He studied her as she slumbered no more than a few feet away from him. Too bad she wasn't next to him, he thought, but he knew she would be, eventually. He only had to bide his time, take it slower than he'd first planned. Carly wasn't his usual type, but that mattered little. The change in pace might even do him some good.

He stood, deeply breathing in the tangy salt air. The water was calm, peaceful, and called out for his company. Within moments he was stripped naked and diving soundlessly into its warmth, surfacing some thirty feet away from the craft, only to upend and plunge into it again and again. He swam with long, sure strokes, exercising the stiffness from his muscles, not the least bit concerned about the distance he was covering. Too soon, however, the weightless feeling the water had first given him left, and he began swimming back toward the yacht. Just before he reached the hull he realized that the boarding ladder had been hauled up the night before.

"Crap!" he muttered angrily as he treaded water. He'd removed it himself when they'd prepared to cast off.

Tanner eyed the anchor line and weighed his options. He could climb it or call out to Carly for the ladder—Hank would never hear him. He struck out for the chain. He was determined to begin on the right foot with Carly this morning, and somehow he didn't think she'd appreciate hauling a wet, nude male out of the water first thing upon opening her eyes. But what an eye-opener it would be! He chuckled at the thought.

He gripped the chain and pulled himself up hand over hand until he managed to gain a toehold on the wave breaker, a piece of trim that encircled the belly of the craft. From his precarious position he reached for the rail, pulled himself against the yacht and straightened up, coming face-to-face with a half-asleep Carly.

She jumped in surprise, blinked rapidly, then laughed as she focused on his soggy appearance.

"Good morning," he said.

She tossed the blanket aside and pushed herself out of the chair. "Good morning," she replied and sauntered drowsily toward him.

His toe slipped and he cracked his elbows on the rail as he fell back into the water. Carly doubled over in laughter until she realized he might be hurt. She scampered to the side of the craft.

"If you're quite recovered," Tanner called,

spitting out water as a wave washed over him, "would you be so kind as to toss the ladder over the side?"

"Are you all right?" she asked first.

"I'm fine, but shriveled. Carly, go get the ladder . . . please."

Spotting the aluminum aid, she waved down to him and quickly left. She returned just as quickly and placed the ladder over the side, attaching it to the rail.

"There," she said, planting her hands on her hips in satisfaction.

Tanner gripped the rung and hoisted himself up, not caring if Mother Theresa herself saw him at this point. Even Carly's gasp didn't stop him as he tossed his leg over the side and planted both feet firmly on the deck. He mimicked her earlier stance and planted both fists on his lean hips. The battle was won before it even began.

She turned her back to him and covered her heated cheeks with her palms. She was totally flabbergasted. She didn't know what to say. She heard him moving away but didn't have the guts to turn and see what he was doing. She hoped he was putting on some clothes.

She felt so . . . conspicuous.

Why am I just standing here! The entryway to the cabins was right in front of her, and she wasted no more time putting the stairs to use. She found the galley right away. Hank was standing at the stove, frying bacon.

" 'Morning," she said as she slid into a seat behind the table.

He saluted her with a large, pronged fork, then turned back to his chore. He must have sensed she didn't want to talk. It was rude of her to turn away from him, but she wasn't yet in enough control of herself to make idle conversation.

Why had she let it get to her that way? She knew she had overreacted, but the whole episode had gotten the best of her. Shriveled, indeed! she thought. He was lucky a ling wasn't around or he might be missing a very large part of his anatomy!

Still flustered, she turned around in her chair. Hank was leaning back against a cabinet, staring at her as if she'd lost her mind.

"Is there a problem?" he asked, lifting his brow in confusion.

"No," she answered, scratching her head as she thought quickly. "I was just surprised when I woke up and found myself alone on the deck. The last thing I remembered thinking last night was hoping I wouldn't catch a fish."

"You weren't by yourself. Tanner probably slipped over the side for a . . . Ah, I see." He turned to flip the bacon. "Would you like one egg or two, easy over or sunny-side up?"

She flushed, then laughed. "Sunny-side up. It seems that's the way my morning was meant to begin."

"Must have been," Hank said, craning his neck around to give her a lopsided grin. His black eyes sparkled.

Watching Hank expertly prepare their breakfast, Carly wondered if Tanner was going to join them. Her silent question was soon answered; Tanner entered quietly and took the seat across from her.

He looked deeply into her dark green eyes. She held his gaze, refusing to be the first to look away. Both broke into laughter. A lock of hair fell into her face and she suddenly realized how she must look.

"Hank, do I have time to freshen up?"

At his nod, she excused herself, returning a few minutes later looking and feeling much more presentable. With the strain between her and Tanner gone, she thoroughly enjoyed the meal laid out before them.

As she buttered a slice of skillet toast, she asked Hank why he hadn't fished the night before.

"I was too tired. We docked only an hour or two before you did."

"Really. Where'd you come in from?"

"Cancun."

"Cancun," she repeated almost wistfully, for it dredged up thoughts of Therese and the numerous things Carly had to do. "I haven't been to Cancun in a number of years. That's where my sister took me as a graduation gift. I loved it."

Neither Hank nor Tanner answered.

Carly chewed a bite of egg, then placed her fork down. "Are you planning on going in this morning?"

Tanner looked up. "I hadn't really thought about it. Why?"

Carly took a deep breath. "I told you last night I had things to do, and if it isn't too much of an inconvenience, I really need to be taken back."

Tanner wiped his mouth on a paper napkin. "I guess that can be arranged."

The harbor master met them at the dock and saw them landed and moored. Carly had her clothing bundled in her arms and her canvas bag looped over her shoulder. She was ready to go ashore.

She smiled at Tanner. "Thanks again. Last night was . . . different."

"And here I thought you enjoyed yourself," he said in an injured tone. Carly could tell he was teasing, even if she couldn't see his eyes through the mirrored glasses he wore.

"I did, even if your luck was poor with the fish."

"Ling."

"Ling, then." She laughed and he smiled, genuinely. "Seriously, Tanner, I do thank you for the fishing trip as well as for taking care of me yesterday afternoon."

"No problem. I'm just glad I was there for

you."

"Me too." She lifted on her toes and pressed a kiss to his cheek. He wrapped his arm around her, halting her quick retreat.

"I will see you later today?" he asked, using his free hand to push his glasses on top his head.

"I don't think so." She tried to step back, but his arm tightened.

"Tonight?"

"I'm sorry, Tanner. I have plans."

"Am I going to have to make an appointment?" he asked brusquely.

"I don't know when I'll be free." And that was so true, she thought, looking ahead at the days and weeks to come. "It depends on how things go tonight."

"What's happening tonight?" He began rubbing her back in small, circular motions.

Carly fought the urge to lean against him. "I have to meet someone."

"Meet me after that." He pulled her closer, her balled-up clothing the only thing separating them.

"I don't know . . ."

"Try."

Carly pressed against his shoulder. She had to stop this, now, while she could. It was impossible for her to contemplate a relationship with him.

"I can't," she said firmly. "If things go smoothly tonight, I'll be leaving tomorrow." She didn't add that she'd either be going home or on

71

another jaunt to God knew where.

"Then I won't wish you luck."

"I didn't ask you to."

His jaw clenched. "Is this it, then?"

"Yes."

Before she knew what was happening, Tanner's mouth swooped down and captured hers demandingly. Without a fight Carly parted her lips and accepted his deep kiss. If this was all she'd ever have, she was going to enjoy it thoroughly. She released her bundle, letting it fall, unnoticed, to the deck, and encircled his neck, pulling him down to meet her fully. She raised herself on tiptoe, opening her mouth even wider, and slanted her head to accommodate him.

Tanner groaned and embraced her as tightly as possible without hurting her. He, too, twisted his head, adding pressure to her lips. He cupped the back of her head, holding her in place until he was ready to release her.

The kiss continued endlessly; each time Carly thought he was prepared to stop he'd fool her and deepen it, more thoroughly than before. He was warm, solid, strong, and felt better than she'd ever dreamed a man could.

A breeze whipped at her hair. A sea gull screeched from above. Life was moving on around them, but Carly was frozen in time.

At last Tanner began to break the kiss. She moaned in protest, not wanting it to be over—it was too soon. She wanted it to continue. She, Carly Jameson, who never rushed into romantic entanglements, wanted to stay with him.

Tanner lifted his mouth from hers and eye contact took over. For moments they stared. Carly tried to record his every feature in her mind. She wanted to be able to recall his picture during the rough weeks and months ahead. It was very possible this would be the only pleasant memory she'd have of this period in her life. She touched his cheek, then stepped back. It was over.

"Good-bye, Tanner," she said huskily. He nodded. She turned, casting one last look at him as she climbed down the ladder. He was still standing there, his hands thrust deeply into his pockets. But he wasn't looking at her. He was watching the lone gull circling overhead.

Inside her own cabin, Carly frowned. She still had Tanner's clothing and he hers. Was that really so bad? She touched her lips. Could she stand another good-bye? She released a pent-up breath and sat down. She really didn't want to see him again. He'd already touched a tender chord within her, and she was afraid of what might happen if she allowed it to continue. Was it possible to fall in love overnight?

She shook the notion away. It would only end up in heartbreak. She sensed he wasn't a man who would remain tied to one woman for any length of time. Besides, she decided with belated logic, she might be mistaken in her feelings. Her insecurity and fears over finding Therese might easily be clouding her normal judgment.

Sighing, she stood up and stripped off the warm-up suit. Perhaps the best thing to do was just to hand Tanner's things over to Hank and forget about her own shorts and top as well as everything else.

Carly pedaled the bike with a steady rhythm. She was sore, but once she limbered up the going wasn't too bad. Before she'd exchanged the warm-up suit for a pair of loose denim jeans and a lavender T-shirt, she'd coated her dried-out skin with a moisturizer and a heavy sunscreen. She wasn't nearly as sunburned as she'd first thought and wasn't going to risk becoming that way.

As she rode along she realized she was still puzzled. It wasn't until she had studied the map of Galveston that it dawned on her, but for the life of her she couldn't remember any clubs of quality on or near the docks. The address of the Diamond Lounge was definitely down there; she'd checked it too many times to have made a mistake. In fact, Therese had even commented on it in one of her letters.

Carly used her foot to slow the bicycle to a stop, then pulled it to the curb near the huge brick edifice that was the University of Texas Medical

Branch. The direction she was taking was definitely toward the old section of the island. The homes and businesses were run-down. She remembered from her last visit several years before that a large part of the old section of town was undergoing restoration, but it bothered her to ride through this area to reach that restored part.

She was being silly. It was morning, everything was quiet and peaceful, and if there were any hoodlums they were sleeping in preparation for the night, when it was easier to mug someone without being caught. She took a deep breath and shoved off. This was probably a small area and she would soon be past it.

But that wasn't the case. It wasn't long before she was riding over rough, potholed streets, with railroad crossings every few blocks. Longshoremen were moving about, unloading and hauling crates in and out of warehouses. Carly felt goose pimples rise on her skin. Maybe it would be wiser to turn back and have a cab bring her down here. She didn't feel safe—but she was getting close. If her calculations were correct, she was within a street or two of her destination, and she couldn't imagine the area would undergo a magic transformation that quickly. If anything, the buildings and houses looked worse.

She gnawed on her bottom lip and slowed her pedaling. It was as if she knew what she was going to find but was hesitating as long as she could before being proven right. The street sign was there, nearly bent in half and rusty. She turned the corner and coasted. There it was, the Diamond Lounge, with cracked white paint and letters faded to a pale, bleached gray.

Without realizing it she braked. "Oh, my God!" she barely whispered. Surely there had to be another place with the same name on the island.

CHAPTER FOUR

Tanner watched through the porthole until Carly had bicycled out of his range of vision. He thrust his hands deeply into his pockets and rocked back on his heels. There was work to do, but he was sluggish getting started.

He turned from the circular glass pane and looked over the stateroom. This was his yacht, given to him many years before by his father. The privileges that went with being the only child of wealthy parents were things he'd taken for granted. But what if he was threatened with losing it all? Would he go to any lengths to save it?

He knew he would and with a ruthlessness Carly would never match. She didn't know what it was to step on people, to go to the extreme to reach a goal. That was evident in the way she'd reacted the night before. She should have been livid with him. He had expected her to be. But Carly had thrown him a loop. She had accepted his explanation, a stranger's explanation, and they had ended up sitting in the moonlight, talking quietly, with Carly occasionally teasing him about the fish he was going to catch.

I like you, Tanner. Her words echoed through his mind and settled like rocks in his stomach. He genuinely liked her too, but whether she'd eventually discover his deception or he simply walked away as he had planned, she'd hate him when this was over. Her emotions ran too deeply for her to react any other way.

He didn't like the turn his mind was taking. The sooner he wrapped this up, the sooner he'd be gone and free of any feelings of guilt. Jesus! Guilt?

"Hank! Get your ass in here," Tanner yelled.

Hank entered, carrying a mug of coffee.

"She's gone," Tanner said bluntly.

"Cornwall's on her trail," Hank answered, lifting the mug to his lips.

"What news did he have this morning?"

"None." Hank sighed, then sat down. "Tanner, Lisa is missing."

Tanner's jaw set. He felt the truth of Hank's words in his gut. "What the hell could have happened?" He jiggled the loose coins in his pocket. "All she had to do was meet Carly and set her mind at ease. Something else is going down. Something at this end of the investigation."

Placing the cup on the arm of his chair, Hank ran his hand over his face. "Cornwall said he waited half the night at the lounge, and when she didn't show up he drove out to her apartment. He said the place was a mess, but the mess was made by Lisa. There were no signs of a struggle, and it didn't look as if she'd been back since she left yesterday morning."

"What about her car?" Tanner began to pace.

"Gone."

"Damn! If Lisa's been wasted,"—he flinched as he said the words—"little sister could end up neck-deep in trouble. I ought to kidnap her ass and lock her up on board!"

"Sounds good to me," Hank said agreeably.

Tanner stopped pacing. "*You* know that and *I* know that, but Omi insists on doing things the hard way! He's probably clapping his hands at the mess this case has become!"

Hank slanted a look at Tanner. "Have you forgotten how much stock he puts in Lisa and Therese's abilities? If he's doing anything, he's wringing his hands over Lisa's disappearance."

"I need some coffee," Tanner said to avoid having to accept his friend's words.

When Tanner came back, Hank was still seated at the table, but then he looped his finger through the handle of his empty mug and stood up. "We've got to put out an APB on Lisa's car."

"You going down there?"

"Naw, I'll just call and report it stolen."

Tanner said, "It'll be up to us to find Lisa. If

she's just holed up somewhere, we can't risk exposing her cover. The last thing we need is the police snooping around the waterfront for her."

"Three years of work would go sliding down the drain," Hank agreed.

"A lot can happen in three years. I just hope like hell too much hasn't happened." Tanner's normal cut-and-dried outlook was ruffled. Lisa was top-notch as far as undercover investigation went. He was concerned about her, but she'd known the risks when she accepted this case. Carly didn't. He'd have to move faster with her to make sure she stayed out of harm's way.

He plopped his empty cup on a shelf. "This isn't getting us anywhere. I'll report the car and contact Omi."

"Twice in one week?" Hank said. "Man you *must* want this case over in a hurry. Or . . ."

"Stow it, Armand. Someone has to do the groundwork, and it can't be me."

"I wouldn't mind waiting here for baby sister," Hank said with a comical leer. "Wouldn't mind it in the least."

"She isn't Consuelo."

Hank lifted a brow. "And you aren't me."

"Thank God."

Hank smiled.

It was back to business. "Something more important than Carly must have sprouted up yesterday," Tanner said. "Find that gardener and wring something out of him. He could have seen more than he thought."

"He doesn't have enough brains to think," Hank said dryly.

"Then grease his palm, Armand. That always stimulates the brain's juices."

"And if that doesn't work," Hank added, "I'll crack his head."

Tanner laughed. "Naw, man, that isn't your style."

"Ma'am, do you have business here?"

Carly turned at the intrusion. A city patrol car was parked behind her, the driver's door left open by the officer who now stood beside her.

"Have I done something wrong?" This was the last thing she needed.

"This isn't the ideal place to be hanging around. Believe me, I know. I've worked this beat for the past three months."

He was young, blond, and looked as though he belonged on the beach with a surfboard instead of in a hot, black uniform.

"I'm not hanging around," she said defensively.

"Then you have business here?"

She shrugged.

"Ma'am, don't be difficult. If you have business, take care of it. If not, you're loitering and I want you to move on."

Who did he think he was? "I'm not loitering either."

He glowered at her, and Carly knew he wasn't going to budge until she made her move. She looked again at the run-down shack, sitting unevenly on blocks. Not wanting to enter the place, but not wanting to leave just yet either, she glared up at him. He was calling her bluff. Sliding off the bicycle, she kicked the stand down and briskly marched away from him. She'd taken no more than a few steps when the crash of metal against pavement stopped her cold. Knowing exactly what had happened, Carly clenched her hands into fists. Damn that kickstand, she thought angrily before twisting around to see the officer standing over the heap with his hands planted firmly on his hips.

Carly walked to the bicycle, leaned over, and picked it up, then wondered why she was behaving as she was. The officer was only doing his job, so why was she overreacting to his authority? She no more wanted to go into that lounge than she wanted to fly to the moon. Giving in, she faced the officer; her attitude and manner were much nicer than they had been only moments before.

"Sir, I think I've made a mistake." He lifted a brow. "You see, I was looking for a place called the Diamond Lounge, but I've obviously come to the wrong place. Could you tell me where the other Diamond Lounge is?"

He shook his head. "This is it."

"This can't be it." Carly pointed emphatically at the lounge. "My sister would *never* work in a dump like that!"

"I've lived here all my life. There isn't another Diamond Lounge on the island." He narrowed his eyes immediately at her distress. "Maybe you'd better tell me what's going on."

Carly felt sick as she briefly explained.

The officer listened patiently until she was through. "There's got to be more to this story than you're telling me," he said, lifting his cap and placing it further back on his head.

Carly glanced once again at the dilapidated building. "I haven't heard from my sister in over eight months."

Silence brought Carly's eyes back to the officer.

"If you want police help you're going to have to come to the station with me. There's nothing I can do here on the street," he said.

She'd been afraid of that. She wanted and didn't want his help. Everything suddenly looked as bleak as the Diamond Lounge. Massaging her temple, Carly nodded, then said, "What about my bicycle?"

". . . So you see," Carly said as she walked down the vanilla-colored halls of the police station with Officer Taylor—Jim, he had told her to call him—"I'm really scared to death that something awful has happened to Therese. She would have scrubbed floors before stooping to work in that place."

"You should have come to us immediately."

"I realize that now, but after all the rot that detective agency fed me about you, I felt it was a waste of time."

"I'm sorry you got the impression that we were unconcerned—but that's usually the way these agencies paint us. They make more money that way. Sometimes they're a real pain in the . . . rear. Once in a while we run into a good one, but that's rare."

"I understand. Is there any way you can check on the reports they made on Therese?"

"That's exactly what I'm going to do. Here." He stopped beside a door and opened it. "This is our lounge. Grab yourself a Coke and wait while I see what's on record."

"Jim"—Carly halted him with a hand on his arm—"thanks."

"No thanks necessary. I'm just doing my job." But he smiled all the same.

Tanner listened to his call letters being read across the radio line before he punched the button on the mike and relayed the letters back. It was Cornwall.

"We're having a little problem," was his message.

"Anything serious?" Tanner was cautious

about what he said even though they had a special scrambler on their channel.

"Possibly. She's gone for a ride with a black-and-white."

"Damn!" Tanner muttered under his breath before pressing the button to reply. Calmly, he said, "I never thought she'd go to them."

"She didn't. They came to her. She was standing outside the lounge and one stopped to question her."

"I see." Tanner scratched his head. "Stick with her until she heads for home. I'll see what I can do from this end."

"Roger. I'm gone."

Tanner set the mike down. He hadn't wanted to deal with the local authorities, but it looked as if he was going to have to. When he'd reported Lisa's car, he'd said he was her brother. Now he'd have to contact the local police and let them know who he was and why he was there. They'd have to put Carly off as long as they could. He suddenly wondered how much more time Therese would need before she wrapped it all up. Too much was at stake where she was concerned for there to be a screw up of any size. He'd simply have to do whatever it took to keep Carly happy.

Complications. Everytime he looked around there seemed to be a new one.

Huge, scalding tears welled up in Carly's eyes.

"I can't believe this. They told me they'd turned to you."

"I'm sorry." Jim Taylor felt her pain. "There's nothing on record."

"Maybe they went to the sheriff's department? Couldn't you check with them?"

"It wouldn't make any difference. We'd still have access to the data, and there's nothing on file."

"Dammit! They lied to me. I used every penny I had on those private detectives and they lied to me. How can they have such good reputations and be so highly recommended when they pull this . . . crap!"

"It happens more often than you know. It's a chance you take."

"Well, I'm not taking any more chances. I'm here now and I want to file a missing-person report on my sister."

"Carly, before we do that there's something else I have to tell you. Lisa Curtis has a record with us." Carly's stomach knotted. "She's a prostitute."

The color drained from Carly's face. A hooker! Good God, what kind of a mess was Therese in? "You're sure?" she asked in a weak voice.

"Yes. Her name sounded familiar, but I wanted to make sure. It's one of several she uses."

"Is it possible that Therese worked at the Diamond Lounge under another name too?" She laughed harshly. "What am I saying! Therese would never prostitute herself."

Officer Taylor didn't respond. Carly knew he was thinking that anything was possible.

"I have to find out what happened, Jim," she said in a desperate voice.

"We'll do all we can. Why don't you let me take you home now?"

Carly fought for self-control. "Not until I fill out a missing-person report." She wasn't going to lose another day simply because she didn't want to deal with it now.

"That's the spirit," Jim said, smiling.

"You bet it is." She stood up and wiped her palms down the front of her jeans. "From now on I'm leaving nothing to chance."

"I don't know how to thank you for all you've done today," Carly said, opening the door of the patrol car.

"How about coming to the beach with me tomorrow?" he asked.

Carly smiled wistfully. "It sounds like heaven, but I can't."

"You're not going to try anything foolish, are you?"

"No, I'm just going to sit tight until I hear from one of you guys. You can tackle the Diamond Lounge all by yourself." She stepped out of the car and shut the door.

Jim followed suit and came around the back of

the car to meet her. "If you're going to be sitting by yourself, why not . . ."

"I need to be alone for awhile," she said before he could finish. She moved aside to give him room to lift her bicycle from the trunk. Her mind was in a whirl with all the facts she'd been told.

"All right, but if you should need me, I want you to call." He scribbled his number on a scrap piece of paper and handed it to her. Carly crumpled it in her fist.

"Thank you." With her other hand she gripped the handlebar. "I hope I hear some good news next time I see you."

"I hope so too. Try not to worry, and don't be upset if it takes a few days," Jim added.

"I'll try not to do either. In the meantime, you know where I'll be." She swung her leg over the bicycle seat.

"I've got to get back, Carly. Just sit tight. We'll handle everything."

"I will."

She watched him climb into his car and drive away. My, God, she thought, forty-eight hours ago this was child's play. Look at the mess it's turned into now. She hung her head, resting her weight on the bike as she scratched in the dirt with the toe of her sneaker. Had she ever really known Therese? Carly placed her palm on her stomach, which was churning from the anxiety she was feeling. If not, did she want to find out about her now?

Then she leaned her head back and saw Tanner marching straight at her.

"What's going on, Carly?" he asked.

"You saw the officer?"

"What happened?"

"It's a long story."

"I'm all ears."

Carly sighed wearily. It would be so nice to lean on him. But she couldn't. "I'm in no trouble, Tanner." She shifted her weight. "The local police are just trying to help me find something, that's all."

He didn't believe her. Carly knew it, but at this point she didn't really care.

"It's no big deal, all right?" Even to her own ears her words sounded shallow.

His eyes studied her intently, making her nervous. She looked away, not wanting to be pressured into talking. "Tanner," she said, licking her dry lips, "I appreciate your concern, but there's nothing you can do. Things'll work out for me. It'll just take a little more time than I thought." Intending to make an excuse to leave, Carly turned to face him. What she saw made her stomach clench even tighter. His eyes were narrowed into slits, but not out of anger. She saw sympathy in the dark blue irises. But she didn't want sympathy! Dammit, she just wanted all her problems solved!

"I've got to run. I'll see you later." Pushing off, she rode the bike away from the basin. What she really wanted was to go aboard her yacht and let everything run through her mind. She wanted to find a logical explanation for Therese's possible involvement with Lisa Curtis and the Diamond Lounge. She wanted to find Therese!

She pedaled hard and fast and in no time she was on Seawall Boulevard. All six lanes were congested with traffic, forcing her to slow to a crawl, then finally to stop. It took several moments until she found an opening to cross the street, enabling her to get onto the seawall where she could see the beach. Riding the bicycle was impossible. People were everywhere, scurrying in and out of the tourist traps and wedging themselves in between sun worshippers who plainly didn't care that people were stepping over their prone bodies as they caught the sun's rays. On the rock groins people fished, crabbed, and walked.

It was chaotic, wild, free, but at that moment Carly hated it. It was the type of life-style her sister had craved, and it might very well have been her downfall. Why was it so hard for Therese to settle down? Carly wondered. No one had asked Therese to give up this sort of thing, but it was time she assumed some responsibility. Thirty-three was past the age for remaining a swinger. Carly finally understood some of the reasons her father had always been angry with Therese; right now, she was angry at Therese too.

She stood still, ignoring everything around her, and stared overhead. A man on a wind glider was soaring above, looking down at the craziness below. Apart, Carly thought. He was apart from it all. Sometimes that was how she felt. She was always an onlooker, never truly a part of anything. Father had never included her in his dreams for Jameson Steel, except in his will. And that was done only to make sure Therese's hands were tied. He wanted Therese, he had Ellis, but he'd never included her.

Before the accident, she and Ellis had been close, but she realized that until he'd been hospitalized, he'd never seen her as anything other than a kid sister. And Therese had always been so wrapped up in her own world that the time she gave Carly had been short and sweet. Why hadn't Carly seen this years before?

The sound of the crashing waves brought her head down. She'd never been an aggressive person. She'd been easily satisfied with her life before the death of her father and probably still would have been if her family's life hadn't turned into such a mess. She guessed she'd just been lucky. At least she'd had twenty-five years of easy living before being pushed into the real world.

She wondered what direction her life would take when this messy part of it was finally over, and one way or the other this episode would be over in four short months. Would she settle back into the old comfortable routine, or would she—once she learned the ropes at Jameson Steel—insist on keeping an active role in the company? Carly sighed. She didn't see herself ever going back to the way she had been. She liked the person she was becoming. But if she didn't resolve all her present problems, she wouldn't have any worries about how her life would go—there wouldn't be much to go back to.

She looked down the steps attached to the seawall. She'd love to walk out on the groins herself, but knew there was no way she could wrestle the bike down. If she left it parked where it was it would end up being knocked some fifteen feet down onto the rocks or stolen. The yacht's cabin came to mind and with it the realization of how tired she was. It seemed like heaven compared to the scorching heat pouring down on her now.

She gripped the handlebars and worked the bike back through the traffic. She didn't dwell on the fact that it was Tanner's cabin she'd thought of.

Tanner glanced at his watch again. She'd been gone for nearly two hours. He paced the open deck, keeping the parking area in sight. If she wasn't back soon, he'd go after her. Damn, but it was hot, he thought, pulling his T-shirt over his head and tossing it on a deck chair. He scratched the dark brown hair covering his chest, picked the shirt up again to mop away the beads of sweat, and dropped it back on the chair.

Waiting had always been his weak point. He

supposed that was why he and Hank had done so well as partners throughout the years. Each had strong points that counteracted the other's weaknesses. Tanner was always restless—Hank had the patience of a saint. Tanner made split-second decisions—Hank held back and weighed the choices. Tanner smiled, knowing he could shoot a line of bull a mile long, while Hank remained quiet, always quiet. But both were dangerous as hell when they had to be.

Miss Carly would run screaming if she knew even a tenth of the things he'd had to do in his chosen profession. But when it was do or die . . .

Now Therese, he thought, understood. She could be as deadly as any of them when push came to shove. He wondered what she'd do when all was said and done. Would she give up her double life and settle into the family business? He thought not. She'd give it up for maybe a year, but somehow he couldn't picture her in any other field than the one in which she was. She loved the challenge, the risk. He almost felt sorry for her.

Tanner leaned his hip against the rail. He again searched the area for a rusty-haired girl on a bicycle. There was no sign of her. He sighed, knowing she was beginning to get under his thick skin. Her large green eyes always managed to reveal her feelings. She hadn't yet learned to conceal her emotions, and he hoped she never did. It was nice to think that there were still people like her in the world.

A small dot appeared in the distance. He strained his eyes to make it out. Luckily, his yacht was near the end of the pier where he could see all around, on shore and off. After a few moments he was certain it was Carly. He began to relax but didn't move. Levering himself up into a sitting position on the rail, he idly swung his foot as he kept a vigil on her. He reached for his front pocket, then remembered his cigarettes were in his shirt pocket and he didn't feel like taking the trouble to get them. He watched her lock her bike in the storage room, then make her way toward her yacht. She stared at him without acknowledging him in any other way as she climbed aboard her craft. In a matter of seconds she was in her cabin and out of his sight.

Tanner remained seated a while longer until his craving for a smoke had him leaping down and sweeping up the shirt from the deck chair. He tossed it over his shoulder and left the deck for the comfort of the air-conditioned cabin.

Tanner was in the galley, seated at the table with his leg propped on its edge, when Hank returned.

"This heat is eating me alive," Hank said wiping at his forehead.

"I can take the heat. It's the humidity that's a killer," Tanner responded.

Hank grabbed a beer from the refrigerator and held it up to Tanner. At Tanner's affirmative nod, he tossed Tanner the can and took another for himself before joining his friend.

"Heard from Cornwall?"

Tanner nodded his head. "Unfortunately. Carly's visited with the local police."

Hank leaned his elbow on the table and rubbed his finger across his lips. "How'd that happen?"

Tanner explained, then lit a cigarette.

"This could be a blessing in disguise," Hank said.

"How so?"

"She could be afraid to go back down there now that she's seen the joint, especially if the police advised her not to."

"Possibly, but then again," Tanner added, "it might push her into digging in with both heels to find out what's happened. They'd already told her that no reports were made on Therese, but I emphasized the trouble they'll have if any other information's leaked to her."

"She'll be content for awhile if she thinks they're investigating for her."

Tanner agreed. "What'd you come up with?"

"Not a whole hell of a lot. I found Martinez Garcia, the gardener. He couldn't tell me much. Just a description of a man who's been around the last few weeks. Sounds like the sleazeball who owns the Diamond."

"I take it you didn't have to crack his head?" Tanner asked blandly.

"Whose, Garcia's?"

"Yeah. How much are you out of pocket for?"

"Too damned much. And we can't trust him even though I've paid for his silence."

Tanner frowned. "You think he knows more than he's letting on?"

"That, or he's damned good in the role of an imbecile."

Tanner laughed, then stubbed out his smoke. "Looks as if you and Cornwall get an all-expense-paid trip to the Diamond Lounge tonight."

"I can hardly wait," Hank replied dryly. "I don't suppose you'd like to trade places?"

"No. It's a tough job, but somebody has to stay with Carly," Tanner said with a stretch of his lean body, then laughed as Hank reached across the table to jab him in the stomach.

CHAPTER FIVE

T wilight glistened across the water as Tanner calculated the time total darkness would fall. It was already nine o'clock and still the sun's rays battled the impending night. Taking a deep drag of his cigarette, Tanner decided to set the evening's plans in motion.

He glanced at Carly's yacht and saw it was still dark in the cabin. She hadn't turned on any lights, but she was there; he'd kept a constant watch on her vessel since she'd returned. It was time to check on her. Enough hours had passed for her to absorb and deal with the worst of the information she'd learned. It was time for him to make his play.

Flicking the remains of the half-smoked cigarette into the water, Tanner left his position on the stern of the craft and went in search of Hank. He found him below deck, putting the final touches on his garb for the evening.

"Very waterfrontish," Tanner said, smiling at

the sweatband around his friend's forehead.

"Damn, and I was trying for dockish," Hank countered as he stuffed the tail of his worn chambray shirt into the waistband of his faded jeans.

"They're so close I'm sure no one will notice."

"And if they do," Hank said, pinning the loose sleeve over the stump of his arm, "I'm sure they wouldn't be so gauche as to point it out."

"I'm sure you're right."

"Surely."

Tanner folded his arms across his chest. "Better count on keeping the whiskers. I've a feeling you'll be making more than one trip down there."

"Better count on keeping yours shaved. I've got a feeling you'll be jumping ship more than once before you're through." Hank laughed. "Hell, before she's finished she might even have you jumping through hoops."

"Up yours."

Hank laughed again and stuffed a small pistol into the top of his boot. He made a quick check of his appearance, then moved to the door. "See you later . . . I'm sure." He closed the door before Tanner had the chance for a come back.

Tanner moved to the porthole and watched Hank until his figure was swallowed by the darkness. He hoped Hank was lucky in his mission, but intuition told him it was a hollow wish. It was all over for Lisa. She'd crossed the wrong person or been found out. The men she'd been investigating were hard-core drug smugglers, even down to the lowliest pusher. If they thought she was a threat, whether they had facts to back it up or not, she'd have been eliminated. And Tanner felt sure she had been. It was up to Hank and Cornwall to discover how and when.

Tanner rubbed the bridge of his nose. He hated the whole thing. He hated that Lisa was gone and he hated the racket. It was a never-ending battle—good against evil. Bust one ring and another one formed, even stronger and craftier than its predecessor.

God, he hoped Therese was using her wits. If his gut reaction was telling him the truth, her position was even more tenuous than before. And that gut feeling hadn't failed him yet.

He moved away from the window and stretched wearily. Concern at this point wouldn't help a damned thing, he thought. He had to concentrate on his end of the mission. Therese would take care of herself. It was baby sister who needed his attention.

Tanner left the cabin and locked the door. He stood motionless for a moment and allowed his eyes to adjust to the darkness, then moved to the rail and leaped over it as easily as he had the first time he'd laid eyes on Carly Jameson. His landing barely made a sound. With a few steps he was at her door and knocking firmly. It was still dark inside her cabin, but he doubted she was asleep. When she didn't answer, he knocked again.

"Carly? Carly, it's me, Tanner. Open up." He listened for a sound of movement, but the cabin remained silent. She has to be in there, he thought. Maybe she was asleep. He rapped again, more forcefully. Still there was no sound.

"Carly!" he shouted, rattling the doorknob. It was locked. He knew something was wrong. "Son of a bitch!" he bit out as he dug into his pocket for a small leather case that held various paraphenalia for picking locks. His pocket was empty. He slapped his front and back pockets, but he had nothing usable to jimmy the lock.

Quickly he jumped on th rail and balanced himself on the balls of his feet as he leaped for his own craft. Catching the taller rail, he pulled himself up and over.

"If she's in there after all this, I'll strangle her," he muttered as he stomped across the deck, going in search of the needed case. "And if she's gone where I think she's gone, I'll beat her!"

Carly sat in the back of the yellow cab trying to convince herself she was doing the right thing. After hours of going over all the facts, one thought had simmered in her brain. The police could very well be giving her the runaround too. The more she dwelt on it the more intense her suspicion had become. Wasn't that the reason she'd come to Galveston in the first place? Because she'd never gotten a straightforward answer from any of the men she'd hired to find her sister? It was the waste of time and money that had sent her on this hunt, and yet she hadn't been on the island more than two days and already she had slid back into her old habit of waiting for someone else to solve her problems. She was disgusted with herself. Well, no more, she thought with growing anger. As of one hour ago, she had finally realized she couldn't depend on anyone but herself to get to the bottom of things—and that included the police.

The more she thought about it, the more convinced she became that going to the Diamond Lounge herself was the best thing she could do. Her complaint to the police was probably one of a hundred they'd received that day. Even Officer Taylor had told her not to worry if it took them several days to come up with something. Well, she didn't have several days. She couldn't afford to sit on her butt and worry and wait. She had to see Lisa Curtis tonight. And if Lisa wasn't there, then she'd find the scum bag who managed the damned place. And he'd have to be a scum bag, she thought, picturing the lounge in her mind. No one else would run such an establishment.

Passing her hand over the neat braid she'd made of her hair, she again wondered, as she had while she was dressing, if she'd blend in with the surroundings at the lounge. Her main fear was that some jerk would try to put the make on her. She was suspiciously sure that the characters in the Diamond Lounge would be hard to get rid of once they set their minds on something or someone—like her. She'd deliberately played down her looks. No cosmetics or jewelry—she'd even removed the thin gold chain she always wore around her neck and stored it out of sight in her purse—and she still wore the same jeans she'd donned that morning. In one of Ellis's lockers on board the yacht she'd found a large navy blue sweat shirt that reached her knees and nearly swallowed her. She felt very plain and hoped that was the way she looked.

Becoming edgy, she leaned forward and tapped the cab driver on the shoulder. "I was wondering if you'd be able to wait for me once we get there?" she asked.

"If you got the money, honey, I got the time," he answered, turning his head and giving her a gummy smile.

Carly winced. Money. Why did everything revolve around money? She didn't know they charged a fee to wait. This was the first time in her life she'd ever been in a taxi. She'd always had her own car or a driver to take her any place she needed to go.

"How much?" she asked, staring at the back of the cabbie's grizzled head. He was a large, barrel-chested man of indeterminate age, and he looked as if he'd be quite at home in this seedy area of town, Carly thought.

"Depends on how long I hafta wait," he said. "It's not like I was gonna be sittin' in front of the best joint on the island." He reached beneath his seat and pulled out a large club. "Down here ya hafta be prepared. A man could get hurt sittin' in a parked car at this time of night."

His statement didn't make Carly feel any better. She swallowed. "I'm supposed to meet someone there. It shouldn't be any longer than thirty minutes to an hour."

The price he named made her flinch. She didn't have that kind of money to waste.

"Look, lady," he said when she didn't respond. "I don't usually care where my fares go or what they do, but I got a sneakin' suspicion you ain't aware of where you're goin'. Just look out the window. See all them warehouses? Ain't nothin' but bad happens in them places after dark."

Just then he hit a pothole, bouncing Carly around like a rag doll in the back seat. She gripped the seat more tightly, convinced there had to be a way to keep him waiting for her while she went into

103

the lounge. She'd feel a whole lot safer knowing she had a quick, easy way of escape.

"What if you came back forty-five minutes after you dropped me off?" she asked hopefully.

"I still hafta charge a few bucks. Company policy and all. You know how it is."

"What difference could it possibly make whether you come back for me or whether I call for another cab?" she said heatedly. "I think it would be saving your company a lot of time."

"I'm just followin' the rules, lady." But he fidgeted in his seat.

"All right," she conceded. "When you drop me off I want you to return after forty-five minutes. And if I'm not there, wait for me anyway."

He nodded and Carly sat back, heaving a deep sigh. She looked out the window at the docks and saw the warehouses the driver had mentioned. They looked even spookier than they had five minutes earlier. In her mind she saw all sorts of illegal activities going on behind the large sliding doors and it occurred to her that this section of town would make a perfect setting for a thriller movie. The Diamond Lounge fit in perfectly with the scenery.

They were nearing her destination, and the closer they got the more apprehensive she became. No, not apprehensive, she admitted—scared. She was terrified of going into that place. But somebody had to do it, and she was that somebody.

The cabbie drove right up to the front door of the lounge, and Carly sucked in her breath at the sight of the rough-looking characters standing around the entrance. *I'll have to walk right past them to go in there,* she thought, her fear growing.

"Can you pull up to that curve over there?" she asked through lips gone dry, trying to buy time before she had to leave the safety of the back seat.

While the cabbie complied, Carly opened her purse to give him his fee, and her fingers touched the gold chain she'd placed there earlier. She gripped it tightly in her fist as an idea came to her. She couldn't pay him with money to wait, but maybe . . .

"I've been giving some thought to what you said,"—Carly once again leaned over the front seat —"and you're right. I'm not sure what I might find when I go in there." She pointed to the lounge, then smiled as sweetly as her stiff lips would allow before dangling the chain in front of his nose. "I really would feel much safer if I knew you were going to be out here waiting for me—should the going get rough." She shrugged. "And this little trinket is worth more than any fee you might get." She lifted her brows hopefully.

"Lady, you just made yourself a deal. I'll be here as long as you need me," he replied, relieving her finger of the weight of the chain.

"Just a minute," Carly stated. "How do I know you won't leave the minute I turn my back—and with my chain?"

"You trying to say that Tiny Morrow would be dishonest?" His beefy fist went to his chest as if he were truly injured.

Tiny? Carly couldn't believe the big hulk was actually called Tiny. She cleared her throat. "No . . . well, maybe. Look, Tiny, I don't know you from Adam. And that's a valuable piece of jewelry."

Tiny lifted the club he had casually laid on the seat beside him. Carly jumped back, her hand going to her throat. "Don't! I mean, keep the chain. You can have it!"

He slapped the club in his huge, callused palm. "It doesn't matter," she said. "Really." All she wanted was to get out of the cab. He frightened her more right now than did the idea of being deserted.

He turned around in the seat and faced her. "I can understand you not believin' me," he said, lisping through the gap in his front teeth. "So I'll just hafta prove I'm an honest man. I'll be here, with my club, and if I see anybody givin' you any trouble I'll bust their head for you. Now you get in there and get your business taken care of. And don't worry 'bout nothin'. Ole Tiny'll be here when you're finished." He rested his arm along the top of the seat.

Carly reached for the door handle, stopped, and patted Tiny's arm. "I believe you," she said softly, and she did. Quickly, before she could lose her nerve, she opened the door and stepped out into the moist night air. A musty smell permeated her nostrils, and Carly knew it was coming from the lounge. She wrinkled her nose and prepared herself for the stale air she'd be breathing once she went inside.

The large, weathered-looking men still stood outside the entrance to the lounge, making Carly feel nervous about passing them. She stiffened her spine; she wasn't going to let anyone intimidate her. With quick, crisp steps she marched right by them and placed both palms on the dark-painted door.

"Hey, Gomez, get a load of this," she heard one of them say as he gripped the back of her shirt. Before she could think rationally about it, she spun around and slapped his hand away. He laughed, and Carly clenched her teeth—to keep them from chattering.

"Leave her alone, Melvin." She assumed it was Gomez speaking. "Can't you see the little senorita is in a hurry?"

Carly cast a quick glance in Tiny's direction and saw that he was looking the other way. Great, she thought. Some protector! Her heart was pounding so fast she was sure they could see her chest rising and falling. *How the hell am I going to get out of this?* she asked herself, backing up a step.

"Are you in a hurry, sweetheart?" Melvin bent down and asked.

Carly turned her face away from the fetid smell of his breath. "Yes," she said. Her voice was stronger than she thought it could be.

Melvin reached past her and opened the door. "Then you'd better get inside quick," he said, laughing in her face, " 'cause I might change my mind and keep you here for my own entertainment." He puckered up and made a kissing noise inches from her face.

Carly spun around and raced through the doorway, hoping desperately he wouldn't follow her. She'd barely gotten inside before she had to stop and get her bearings. The room was thick with cigarette smoke, too thick to see three feet in front of her face. With stinging eyes, she took slow, even steps, making her way toward a corner where she could avoid being spotted by some drunken long-shoreman and taken as easy target—a place where she could watch for a woman of Lisa Curtis's description without calling attention to herself.

A small, scarred table and chair were shoved into the corner. Carly gratefully sat down in the shaky chair and gripped her purse in her lap. At this level the smoke wasn't nearly so thick, and she could see her surroundings better. Opening her purse she pulled out a tissue and wiped away the stinging tears that blurred her vision.

Looking around she saw several women dressed in skimpy outfits that left little to the imagination, but serving their purpose—to entice men. A busty, red-haired woman wore cheap gold bands on her upper arms, and heavy gold loops swung from her earlobes. Her backless, shiny green halter top barely covered her breasts. Her short shorts were blood red and slit up the outer part of her thighs. Carly thought of Therese dressed in such a costume and felt sick. It just didn't make sense to her.

Pulling her gaze away from the redhead, Carly searched the room for some sign of a blond woman near Therese's age. There were plenty of women coming and going through the back door—and Carly didn't dwell on why they were using that particular exit—but none that fit the image she had of Lisa. She sighed. She was probably going to have to ask someone if Lisa was there, and she didn't want to do that. It would be her luck that the person she asked would tip Lisa off that Carly was there and she'd leave before Carly could say Mississippi.

"What'll you have?"

Startled, Carly jerked her head up and saw the red-haired woman standing over her with a cracked, gray plastic tray in her hands.

"Nothing. I'm fine."

"Like hell, nothing. Either order a drink or get

your ass out of that chair." Her blue eyes glittered with malice. "We don't like new pieces moving in on our territory, honey. So you'd better watch your step. Now, what in the hell do you want?"

A tall, sandy-haired man scraped a chair across the floor and leaned it against Carly's table. He slapped the barmaid sharply on the rump. "Whatcha' givin' this young lady hell for, Rosetta?" he asked, smiling. Carly realized beneath that stubbly beard was a very sexy man. He was tall and lean and had a smile that could melt anyone's heart. His effect on Rosetta was obvious, and Carly watched the action between them as she wondered how she was going to get rid of him if he decided to join her univited.

"I ain't giving her hell. I was just explaining that she had to buy a drink, that's all." Rosetta pouted and rubbed her body against his. He pinched her breast and grinned, wrapping a long arm around her. Carly averted her gaze, unable to hide the embarrassment she felt.

"Whatcha having?" He touched Carly's arm and she jumped. She scratched the back of her head, squeezing her purse tighter with her free arm.

"Coke. I'll just have a Coke."

He lifted a brow but didn't try to persuade her to have something stronger. "You hear that, Rosetta? She wants a Coke." Tightening his arm around the woman's waist, he turned her around and led her toward the bar. "Come on, I'll help you get it."

Carly's shoulders slumped in relief as she watched them move away; then she swung her legs around, finding a better position to watch the room. She gasped. There couldn't be two of them, she thought, squinting her eyes. Placing her palms on the table, she pushed herself slightly out of her seat. *What's he doing here?* she thought, knowing it had to be him. How many tall, black-haired, one-armed men could there be? Hank! Hank was there.

Carly eased her weight back down on the wobbly chair. She didn't know what to think. Hank was actually there, sipping at a brown bottle of beer. What was he doing in a dive like this? Did Tanner know his friend was hitting the beer joints?

Oh, God. What if he sees me? She slumped down in the chair and half turned away from where he was sitting across the room. She glanced at the furnishings in disbelief. What was there about this place that attracted people with money?

She didn't want to accept what her mind was screaming—drugs! But that had to be it. It was the only logical explanation she could think of; yet, as she cast a quick look in Hank's direction, she couldn't believe that someone as nice as he could possibly be involved in anything shady. But what other reason could there be?

Get with it, Carly! she told herself. Therese

must have been a frequent guest here too, or she'd have never been coerced into working in such a dump. Had she been involved in drugs too? Was that why she was keeping out of sight, because someone was after her? Carly wanted to place her head down on the table and moan. She was so frightened for Therese. But she had to bear up.

At the bar the sandy-haired man was still talking to the barmaid. Carly was glad he hadn't come back again to chat. She had to fight the impulse to get up and run, for she knew she'd die of humiliation if Hank saw her. Yet she had to find out if Lisa was still employed here. Perhaps the sandy-haired man might be helpful after all. He looked harmless compared to the ruffians she'd seen thus far—just a guy out for a good time. And if he tried to put the make on her, she was certain he'd take no for an answer. Carly sat back, her decision made. If he came back to the table, she'd ask him if he knew anything about Lisa Curtis.

She couldn't seem to control the drifting of her eyes in Hank's direction. She was having a difficult time accepting he was there. Why? she pondered again. Why would a man who lived in obvious comfort come to a raunchy place like this? She knew of a dozen other clubs she'd visit if she only had the time.

Three rugged individuals approached Hank's table, and he stood up to greet them. Their faces seemed carved out of stone; not one looked pleased to be there, Carly thought. Or was it Hank with whom they were displeased? Hank smiled as he spoke to the largest man; Carly's anxiety faded when she saw that Hank wasn't the least bit concerned about their presence. Still, when he laughed, not one of the three even cracked a smile.

Carly glanced around to see if anyone else was watching the exchange, but everyone seemed content to carry on their various activities. Several people were shooting pool, while a relic of a fan twirled the smoke around overhead. The fan blades were knicked and spun at an uneven angle. She wondered if a flying beer bottle or a pool cue had caused the damage. She imagined a brawl in this place would be a bloody battle and prayed that none would happen until she was safely out and on her way back to the yacht.

"Hello, gorgeous," a man's voice spoke at her side. She spun wide-eyed in her chair, then smiled as she saw the sandy-haired man holding a bottle of Coke. She couldn't believe they still sold cola in glass bottles. Maybe they had a supply left over from years ago. Beer seemed to be the main item on the menu.

She took the bottle. "Thanks . . . I didn't catch your name before," she said, indicating the chair he'd dragged over earlier.

He hooked his boot around the chair and

113

pulled it out to sit down. "That's because I didn't give it."

And he wasn't going to, Carly realized, wiggling uncomfortably. It was one thing to think about asking this man questions and another thing to actually do it. She gulped a large mouthful of the cola, then sat the bottle down on the table. She smiled, panicking inside because she couldn't think of a logical way to open the conversation.

"Do you come here often?" she asked, berating herself as a dolt. She fully expected his next words to be, 'What's a nice girl like you . . .?'

"Uh-huh. But this is the first time I've seen you here. Why's that?" He squinted his dark brown eyes.

Carly thought quickly. "I just arrived in town yesterday," she lied. "The real reason I'm here is to look up an old friend of mine. You might know her. Her name's Lisa Curtis."

"Yeah, I know her." He didn't elaborate any further.

Carly pressed further. "Has she been here tonight? I went by her apartment, but she wasn't at home, and I kinda need a place to stay while I'm here."

He seemed to be a shrewd man. Was he the manager of this place? she wondered.

"I haven't seen her." He leaned his chair back on two legs. Carly felt defeated.

"She does still work here though?"

"As far as I know."

What happened to the good-time guy he'd been moments before? Carly was suddenly leery of him. "Do you think she'll be in tonight at all?"

He shrugged. "One never knows." He lit a cigarette and kept it between his teeth.

"Gosh, I wish I knew if she was even in town. I'm really low on cash and need a place to stay."

He smiled, deliberately misunderstanding what she was getting at. "You can stay with me as long as you want." He dropped the chair back on all four legs and leaned across the table toward her. The swirling smoke from the cigarette made her eyes water, distorting his features until Carly thought he looked evil.

Carly swallowed hard. She had to get away from him, had to think of a good excuse to convince him she wasn't *that* desperate for a place to stay. It was then that she spotted a pay phone on the far side of the room. "Actually," she said, pulling her purse high up on her chest and clutching it like a shield, "I have one other number to call." She pointed at the phone. "Will you excuse me, please?" Not pausing for an answer, she stood up and left.

Keeping her head down, she crossed the room. It was too late to worry about Hank spotting her, he already had. His black eyes darted between her and the men to whom he was speaking. She looked down at the floor; she couldn't look him in the eye. He knew she was there, but he didn't have to know for certain that she was aware he'd seen her. She reached for the phone and pretended to slip a coin in the slot. It was as old as the rest of the building. The receiver was black and heavy; it only took a dime to place a call.

Damn, she wanted to cry as she held a one-sided conversation with the dial tone. Hank was moving toward the back door, which was only a few feet away from her. He was escorted by a goonie friend at each side, while the third walked mere inches behind him. The door was open, and Carly could feel a light breeze sway through it. She turned slightly away as they neared. She didn't want to acknowledge verbally that she saw him and was sure he didn't want to speak to her either. She just wished he'd hurry and pass her by. She wanted to get out of that place as quickly as she could. It no longer mattered that she hadn't discovered who managed the Diamond Lounge or that she still hadn't found Lisa Curtis. She just wanted to go back to the yacht—to safety. Tanner's face suddenly came to mind, and she wished now that she had taken him up on his offer for the evening. She wished he was there!

Glancing back at her table she saw that the sandy-haired man had moved and was casually leaning against the bar. From the angle at which his head was tilted, she couldn't tell if he was watching her or not. She took a deep breath and murmured something in the phone, so it would seem as if she was talking to someone.

Hank was a few feet away. She could feel his eyes boring into her. Before she could prevent herself, she looked around at him. His jaw clenched briefly. His eyes narrowed, but not in anger. . . . He glanced away.

The largest man casually swung his arm around Hank's shoulder. Carly thought it odd that the man was now acting so friendly when Hank was so grim. It was as though they had switched roles. They were so close to her now that she could smell the sweat on their perspiring bodies. She glanced back at Hank, but he avoided looking at her. He was acting as if she were as anonymous to him as were the others in the room.

The man shook Hank's shoulder and pulled him closer. Carly's gaze was jarred by the glint of light that flashed briefly at Hank's midsection.

She blinked twice, choking back a gasp. Her hand dropped to her side, receiver and all. She didn't move, didn't speak. All she could concentrate on was the vicious-looking blade being pressed into Hank's ribs.

CHAPTER SIX

C arly quickly jerked the phone back to her ear. "What did you say?" she asked in a voice meant to carry, doing her best to act as if nothing out of the ordinary was happening. "The phone slipped. I missed what you said." Hank cut his eyes at her, then winced as the knife was prodded deeper into his skin.

He's in trouble and he's trying to warn me to stay out of it. She desperately wracked her brain for a way to help him. She could make a ruckus, but by the looks of the people around her, they'd glance her way and continue to go on about their own business. She couldn't just stand there; she had to do something! She'd follow him. Once outside she was convinced she could draw their attention away —somehow.

The sandy-haired man suddenly came to mind. She had to make sure he wasn't going to trail after her. She turned her head slowly, looking at the bar.

He was gone. Scanning the room quickly, she relaxed just a fraction. He was going out the front door.

Carly took a deep breath. She didn't have to look to know that the three men and Hank had disappeared out the door. She placed the receiver in its cradle, then slipped out the back door, nearly falling when she missed the step she expected to be there. She landed hard on her feet but didn't stop to check for an injury—she wanted to get away from the dim light shining through the doorway. Carly moved behind an overgrown oleander bush and watched Hank being pulled around the corner of the building. Stealthily she crept to the edge of the lounge and peeked around; they had stopped in a darkened alley.

Everything broke loose at once. Hank spun around, taking all three men by surprise when he jump kicked and hit one of the men in the jaw. Before either of the other two men could react, Hank's foot whirled through the air again and cracked the hand of the man clutching the knife. The knife fell harmlessly in the dirt. It became a free-for-all. It was hard to see who was doing what, but Carly knew by the sounds of punches, kicks, and groans that Hank was not making it easy for them to overcome him. She caught herself hopping up and down; her clenched fists swung through the air as she mentally helped him defeat the three thugs.

A wild punch connected with Hank's mouth and he staggered back, stunned. Carly gasped, then pressed her hand over her mouth. In a matter of moments Hank was on the receiving end of the abuse. He was grabbed from behind by the two large arms that looped beneath his arm pits and clasped him behind his neck. But Hank used the man holding him to his advantage. He lifted his feet and kicked out, knocking one of his enemies flat. He just wasn't quick enough to take down the third one.

Hank took a hard punch in the stomach. He was held upright, unable to bend over, as Carly saw his body wanted to do. She bit the palm of her hand to keep from screaming, praying desperately that they wouldn't remember the knife and stab him. One of the men grabbed a handful of Hank's hair and jerked his head back. His grunt of pain sliced through her, jarring her out of her frozen stance.

But what can I do? she cried in silence, thinking of a million things to try, knowing none of them would work. Then it suddenly hit her. Tiny! Tiny and his club. Without caring if she made any noise, Carly ran as fast as she could around the opposite side of the building and into the street. The cab and Tiny were exactly where she'd left them. She ran right up to his door and jerked it open. Startled, Tiny, with the club already in hand, reared back to use it.

Carly grabbed him by the arm, heedless of any danger to herself. "Hurry, Tiny! They'll kill him. Hurry!" She tugged his big bulk with all her might, and Tiny, not knowing who or what she was talking about, followed her as swiftly as his legs would carry him.

"Where are they, little lady?" he asked, panting. She was still a good ten feet ahead of him. "Hey, wait. I'm the one with the club, remember?"

Carly stopped, her heart thumping in her chest. She found herself wanting to grab the club from his hand and go after the men herself.

"Hurry, Tiny. This isn't a game. They're going to kill him!" Her voice was laced with panic and fear.

"I'm comin', I'm comin'. Where the hell are they?"

"In the back alley."

Tiny grabbed her by the arm and thrust her behind him when they reached the point she'd indicated. Carly shoved him each step of the way, hoping she could make him move faster. They rounded the building and came to a dead halt. All was silent. Hank's body was sprawled on the ground, with a lone figure leaning over him—the sandy-haired man from the bar. An angry sob escaped Carly's throat as she saw him, like a grave robber picking over a corpse, searching Hank's lifeless form.

A bellow, loud and threatening, came from deep within Tiny's chest, jarring Carly into action. Carly stayed at his heels when he swung the club over his head and charged like a raging bull. This one man was not nearly as threatening as the three who had beaten up Hank.

Tiny's roar made the man aware he was not alone. Looking up, he saw Carly and jumped to his feet, then ran down the opposite end of the alley until the darkness swallowed him.

"He'd better be glad he ran," Tiny said between gasps. "Otherwise I'd've cracked his head a good 'un."

Carly knelt down, checking Hank for injuries. "Grab his arm and we'll lift him," Tiny ordered. He went around to the opposite side of Hank and reached down for Hank's other arm. He stopped in his tracks and cursed mildly. A puzzled look came over his features.

"Don't," Carly ordered, understanding his confusion. "We could hurt him worse than he already is. I'll stay here with him and you go get the car."

"Are you nuts? Do you want to be standin' here with them mugs come back to finish off the job? Grab his arm and help me. We ain't got time to dillydally." Tiny grunted as he reached around Hank's body to lift him.

Carly saw his point and gave in. Hank was unconscious and dead weight. His breathing was shallow, and he rattled with every breath. Fearing he had broken ribs, Carly couldn't control the tears that ran down her face. He was badly hurt, and no matter what business he'd had down here, she felt horrible for him.

It seemed as if hours had passed by the time they dragged him to the cab. As Tiny held Hank's limp body, Carly crawled into the back seat, and together they worked his body in. Tiny slammed the door and hurried into the driver's seat, while Carly used the sweatband from Hank's head to stop the flow of blood oozing from a deep gash on his forehead.

"Oh, hurry, Tiny. He's in terrible shape."

Tiny stepped on the gas and spun the old car around with the finesse of a stunt driver. The squeal of the tires was the only thing that alerted a drunk to jump out of the way or be plastered to the street.

Tiny laughed. "It always 'mazes me how fast them ol' coots can move when they have to."

Carly saw nothing humorous in the situation. She felt that every moment counted if they were going to save Hank's life. She made him as comfortable as she could, then settled on the edge of the seat, willing Hank to hang on.

"Where's the nearest hospital?" she asked Tiny.

"They're all in the same area. Near where I picked you up this evenin'."

It would take them awhile, Carly thought, knowing Tiny was pushing the old cab to the limit.

Hank groaned and tried to lift his head; Carly pressed her weight on his shoulders to keep him flat. He swung his fist wildly, clipping her on the chin. The force of the blow knocked her back. At the sound of her head cracking against the window, Tiny braked the car to a screeching stop.

"Ungrateful bum!" he muttered, already swinging his door open and jumping out.

"Tiny, get back in the car!" Carly screeched, then wished she hadn't. Her jaw hurt terribly.

He swung her door open and jabbed a finger in the air. "I told you I wasn't gonna let nobody mess with you, and I meant it."

"Tiny, *please*! Just get back in the car and let's go. He doesn't know what he's doing."

Seeing the desperate look on her face, he slammed her door and begrudgingly climbed back behind the wheel. "If he wasn't already so busted up, I'd bust him myself," he mumbled under his breath as he threw the car into gear.

"He didn't mean to," Carly said defensively.

"I was just lookin' out for you," Tiny countered. He adjusted the rearview mirror so he could keep an eye on everything that happened in the rear seat.

"I know, and I appreciate it. I don't know what I would have done without you this evening. I mean it, Tiny. You were wonderful."

He sat up taller in the seat. "Aww, it wasn't nothin'," he said, suddenly sounding bashful.

Carly smiled at his reflection. "Yes, it was. Very few men would risk their lives to help a complete stranger the way you did."

Tiny shrugged. He seemed at a loss for words.

Hank groaned again, but this time Carly moved out of his way. He didn't try to get up but managed to open his eyes and blink several times.

"Hank? Hank, you're all right. We're taking you to the hospital. Just keep still. We're almost there," she said and patted his cheek.

"Miss Jameson," he whispered through his split upper lip; then he tried to laugh but started coughing.

Carly had no idea what had tickled him and didn't care. She was more concerned that his wheezing had become worse. Not wanting to alarm Hank, she asked Tiny in a casual tone how much longer they'd be. The ten minutes he told her it would take seemed like a lifetime.

Finally the University of Texas Medical Branch came into sight, and she relaxed a fraction before tensing again as Tiny drove through the emergency entrance. With his head stuck out of the window, Tiny began yelling for nurses and orderlies. Everyone in the vicinity soon knew they had a man in the cab who'd been beaten by a mob. But Carly didn't care. They had made it to the hospital.

Tanner paced the floor, cursing one moment and worrying the next. He stopped long enough to take a hefty swig of the beer he held, then decided to go on deck and wait for Carly's return. Where in the hell was she? he thought, not for the first time. When he discovered she was truly gone, he'd been madder than hell, but now so much time had passed, worry was replacing the anger.

What was she doing to him? he wondered as he opened the cabin door and closed it again. His anxiety was completely different from anything he'd ever felt before. He began to understand what his parents must have felt when he was a teenager and he'd been late getting home after a night out.

He threw himself down into a lounger and gazed at the stars. The night was clear, the moon full. It was a crying shame that the evening he'd planned for Carly and himself had never gotten off the ground, he thought. He had to hand it to her though. She had a hell of a lot more guts than he'd ever have given her credit for. Maybe old man Jameson's blood ran thicker in her veins than any of them had thought. Either that, or she felt she had no other recourse. If he'd just had time to win her confidence, perhaps she never would have tried to

127

go to that damned dive in the first place.

He squashed the aluminum beer can. She was wringing feelings and emotions out of him he never knew he had. Why? And for what! Hell, he hadn't even made love to her yet.

He pitched the empty can against the cabin wall. At least Hank and Cornwall were at the lounge, he thought as he stood up and paced along the deck. He knew they'd have spotted her the moment she set foot in the place. But that knowledge didn't make him feel any better. Childishly, *he* wanted to be the one to keep her out of trouble.

"Tanner, you've drunk too much beer," he told himself as an excuse.

His attention was caught by the headlights of a car pulling into the marina's circular drive. Curiously he watched as it parked. The street lights lit up the area clearly, and Tanner immediately recognized the figure that climbed out of the car.

Cornwall! Tanner's stomach muscles tightened, but he made no move to greet the third man in their investigation. He watched Cornwall walk slowly around the car, then stop to scope out the area. Cornwall, Tanner knew, wasn't exactly certain where the yacht was docked.

He also knew that Cornwall would never show himself there unless it was absolutely necessary—a life-or-death situation involving Hank or Carly.

Tanner barely controlled a shudder. If Cornwall had discovered what happened to Lisa he'd have contacted Tanner differently. So who was it? Hank or Carly?

Tanner went to the bow of the boat and stuffed his hands in his rear pockets. His movement was enough to draw Cornwall's attention. In a matter of moments Cornwall was climbing on board the yacht.

Neither said a word until they both were inside the cabin and the door was securely shut behind them.

"What happened?" Tanner asked immediately.

"Hank was worked over pretty badly," Cornwall answered.

"How badly?" Tanner asked.

"I didn't have time to see—"

"Damn it, how bad was he, and where is he now? Where's Carly?"

"The emergency room at UTMB—"

"What about Carly?"

"She's fine," Cornwall stated, intentionally evasive.

Tanner gritted his teeth. "Where is she?"

Cornwall ran his fingers through his sandy brown hair and swore. "If you'd stop interrupting me you'd know by now."

Tanner had the grace to flush. He was acting

like a fool. "The floor's yours."

Cornwall briefly explained the night's events to Tanner, knowing there wasn't time to give him full details on everything.

"Let's go," Tanner said as soon as Cornwall filled him in. "You can drop me off at the hospital and then get back to that lounge and dig around to find out why Hank was hit on."

"I already know," Cornwall said as he followed Tanner over the side of the craft and onto solid ground. "Hank asked the wrong person about Lisa. Rosetta, one of the barmaids, turned the information over to that weasel who manages the place, and before I knew it three giants were leading Hank outside.

"How'd Carly get involved?" Tanner asked as they reached the car. He had to wait for Cornwall to get in and unlock the passenger door before he learned the answer.

Cornwall grinned at Tanner, then started the engine. As he drove out of the parking lot he began to explain. "She was at a pay phone and must have seen that Hank was in trouble. I don't know what happened after that, because I went out the front door to circle around. When I got there Carly wasn't in sight. I pulled a gun and ran the men off. About that time she comes running up with this bear of a man in tow. I knew she'd take care of Hank, so I beat it to the car and followed them to the hospital. What'll you do now?"

"I haven't the faintest idea," Tanner said. All he knew was that he had to see how badly injured Hank was.

"How'd she get away from you?" Cornwall asked, breaking into Tanner's thoughts.

"I'm not sure."

"I never expected to see her down there," Cornwall stated.

"I never thought she'd go," Tanner countered.

"I spotted her when she first came in and decided to make a move on her before anyone else had the chance. Lucky thing I did too. As soon as she could work it into the conversation she asked about Lisa. I'm telling you, everyone down there seems geared for any questions about Lisa. We might never find out what happened to her."

Tanner lit a cigarette. He couldn't believe what a mess this case had become.

"Right now I'd give my eyeteeth to know," Tanner said in a low voice, almost to himself.

Cornwall pulled the car up to the curb near the hospital. "They're probably still in the emergency room."

Tanner opened the door and stepped out. "Where will you be?" he asked.

"I'm not sure. I'll let you know."

Tanner nodded, then took off across the sidewalk, tossing his cigarette on the ground as he went.

Carly, seeing Tiny grab the end of the gurney to help push Hank into the hospital, did the same, even though she thought it odd that the hospital staff would allow them to do so. But her wondering was quickly dispelled once they were inside and she saw how rushed and busy everyone was. The waiting room was filled with sick and injured people, crying babies with mothers begging that their child be examined next. It was bedlam, and Carly began to worry that Hank would be left unattended until someone had time to take care of him.

Her fears were laid to rest almost immediately. At the shout of one of the nurses, hospital personnel swarmed all over Hank, snipping away his clothes, checking his pulse, and inserting an IV while they rolled him even faster to an examining room. Carly was shoved out of the way, and when she heard the word "shock" she wasn't quite sure whether they were talking about her or about Hank.

She followed a few paces behind the gurney, knowing she'd only be in the way if she got any closer. But she made sure that when they took Hank into an examining room she was with him.

Tiny pulled her by the arm. "Stand over here by the wall," he whispered, "and they won't make you leave."

"Sounds as if you've been through this before," she whispered back.

Tiny nodded. "If you don't get in their way they never notice you." He suddenly looked at her suspiciously. "You ain't the kind that'll get all queasy, are you?"

"No," she answered, feeling a rush of anguish as she recalled going through the horror of her father's death and Ellis's long ordeal at the emergency room in Beaumont. Ellis! She suddenly remembered that she was supposed to have called him. As she watched the group of nurses and doctors examining Hank, she wondered what on earth she would tell her brother.

"Uh-oh!" Carly stared apprehensively at the small handgun a nurse had pulled from Hank's boot. For a long minute the room was filled with silence as all eyes stared at the weapon dangling from the woman's fingers. Then, as if nothing out of the ordinary had happened, she placed it in a plastic bag and the chaos began again.

A gun. Carly's head began to ache. In her heart she wanted to believe that Hank had as good a reason as she for being at the lounge, but in her mind the evidence seemed against him. He had to be involved in something shady. Why else would he have a pistol hidden in his boot? she silently cried.

Hank was stripped of all the tattered remains

of his clothing and a sheet was placed across his torso. An oxygen mask covered the bruises swelling his lips. The overhead light clearly emphasized how badly beaten his face was. The gash on his forehead bled steadily until a bandage was placed there temporarily to stop the flow. Carly knew the cut would have to be stitched. A young Oriental doctor flashed a small light into Hank's eyes, all the while talking and asking questions of the staff.

"Let's get him to X-ray," an older doctor ordered, removing a stethoscope from his ears. "His lungs are fine, but he has several broken ribs."

No sooner was the order given than they were wheeling Hank out. Carly and Tiny followed them into the hall, but Tiny grabbed her by the arm when she moved to go any further.

"They ain't gonna let you go in there," he answered her questioning look.

Blood coated her clothing and her arms, but it didn't seem to register in her mind. She saw it—so what? It was Hank's blood; he was the one who was hurt. She hadn't suffered at all, compared to what he'd gone through. Carly pictured in slow motion, the scene at the lounge—the huge fist of the big man swinging at Hank. She jerked back at the imaginary impact and had to stifle the urge to groan. What had the three goons done to him while she had run for help? she wondered, then shook her head. She didn't really want to know.

134

"Now that we got a minute to breathe, would you mind tellin' me how you got linked up with somebody like him?"

"Hank?" she asked, still in a daze.

"If that's his name," Tiny answered, jerking his thumb over his shoulder.

"He's staying next door to me."

"And where's that?" Carly thought Tiny sounded like an enraged father who had just found out his daughter was running with the leader of a motorcycle gang.

"Down near the waterfront."

"Where you shouldn't be. Listen, little lady. My place ain't much—"

"Tiny, you don't understand," she interrupted him, only to be interrupted by him in turn.

"Yes, I do. I don't know where you got that chain, and I ain't 'bout to ask. But it's as plain as the nose on my face that you got trouble with no easy way out. I just wanna help you."

"I appreciate it, Tiny, but things aren't as bad as they seem." But she knew that wasn't true.

Tiny gummed his bottom lip. "All right. I'll leave you alone." He pointed a thick, stubby finger at her. "But if you run into any more trouble, you call the cab station and tell 'em you need me on the double. Wherever I am, they'll find me."

She could feel tears welling up in her eyes. She must have finally done something right, she thought, realizing how lucky she was that Tiny had been the one sent to drive her tonight.

"I could sure use a cup of coffee right 'bout now," Tiny said.

Carly glanced up at him. "So could I."

Tiny pointed down the hall. "There's a coffee machine down around that corner and to the left."

Carly sighed, but knew she should go get it. After all Tiny had done he deserved the royal treatment—even if the best she could do was a rank cup of coffee out of a vending machine.

"Cream or sugar?" she asked.

"Black."

"You'll wait here?"

"I won't move."

She nodded. "I'll be right back."

Tiny smiled gratefully.

Carly didn't realize how tired she was until she started walking. She felt as if she had ten-pound weights attached to each of her ankles. Her bloody shirt was sticking to her stomach, and she plucked it away from her skin as she turned the corner. She walked down a corridor that looked endlessly long. There was no vending machine in sight, and Carly couldn't see if there was a cubbyhole further down the hall. But there had to be one; Tiny had said the coffee machine was nearby. Or had he? She couldn't seem to think straight. She stopped and rubbed her eyes. If she could just find a rest room she could wash her face and get rid of some the sticky blood. She resumed her walk, looking at each door she passed, and it finally paid off. Near the end of the hall she saw a public facility.

Carly had to double her effort to push the heavy door open. Going straight to the sink, she was shocked at the sight of her image in the mirror. She was pale except for a streak of crimson on her cheek and a red welt on her chin where Hank had hit her. She moved her jaw slowly; it felt stiff, but she wasn't hurt very badly. Twisting one of the sink taps, she scooped a handful of water into her hands and splashed it on her face. Her breath caught. It was cold—and reviving.

She braced her hands on each side of the sink and leaned over until her face was over the white porcelain basin. She couldn't believe all that happened. On the one hand she felt she had failed in her mission. She knew no more about Lisa Curtis's whereabouts now than she had before she'd gone to the lounge. But on the other hand, she consoled herself, if she hadn't been there, there was no telling what would have happened to Hank. He might have lain in the alley until he'd died.

She shivered. It was all beginning to sink in. The reality that she had actually saved a man's life hit her fully. She, Hank, and Tiny might have all been killed. Yet she had done everything in her power to prevent it—and she had succeeded. But the lingering fear of what might have happened was too real to be ignored.

Trying to get hold of herself, she splashed more water on her face and briskly scrubbed the red stains off her arms. The trembling continued. She really should rinse off the front of her shirt, she thought, knowing she had to keep occupied or she would lose her grip on herself. Without removing the shirt she leaned over and placed as much of it as she could get beneath the water, swallowing the nauseating lump that rose in her throat as the water ran red. After a few moments, she felt as if her knees were going to buckle. She shut off the water and wrung out her shirt. If she just had that cup of coffee it would help, she thought. Coffee was supposed to be good for people under stress. She knew she wasn't far from falling on her face.

She pulled several paper towels out of the holder on the wall and wiped her hands. As she left the rest room she blotted the front of her shirt, trying to keep her mind busy in order to block out how weak she was becoming.

Several feet down the hall she finally found the cubbyhole containing the vending machines. She tossed the wet towels into a nearby garbage can, then slid her hand in her pocket for some coins. It didn't take long to get one cup of black coffee and another heavily laced with extra sugar. She began sipping it as she moved to return to Tiny. It wasn't very hot, but to her it tasted heavenly until the syrupy sweetness hit her empty stomach and began churning there.

I can't be sick now, she repeatedly told herself as she reached the end of the hall and made the turn to go back to Hank's room. Her legs were beginning to feel as useless as limp noodles. Tears started running down her cheeks even though she wasn't actually crying. She did her best to concentrate on keeping the paper cups from slipping through her fingers. *What's wrong with me?* she silently asked, as if by some miracle someone would hear her and help her.

The coffee sloshed over her hand. The tears were now a steady stream, flowing down her cheeks. She felt foolish, but she was unable to help herself. She looked up and a sob tore from her throat. Tiny was no longer standing there. But Tanner was.

She stopped in her tracks, unable to take another step. The splash of coffee as the cups slid out of her hands and hit the floor didn't even register. Tanner was there, moving directly toward her. Nothing, no one, had ever looked so welcome.

He reached her, encircling her body with his warmth. Carly couldn't think; she just absorbed the heat and held on tightly to him. Tanner. Tanner had her. Everything was going to be all right.

CHAPTER SEVEN

Tanner watched Hank being rolled from the examining room to the X-ray department and then to another room but didn't move from his place in the waiting area. From the pace at which the nurses and orderlies were working, he knew that Hank's condition wasn't as serious as he'd thought. In fact, Hank's consciousness was a sure sign that his partner was going to be fine.

Tanner had just narrowly missed running into Carly several minutes before, and he wanted to make sure she was a good distance away before he approached the large man standing by the door to Hank's room. Tanner assumed he was the cab driver but didn't want to arouse any suspicion by just walking past him and into the room. If Tanner could get away without Carly knowing he had been there, he would do it.

Tanner shifted his weight from one foot to the other and was about to lean against the wall when he saw a policeman enter and go to the desk. Standing up straight, Tanner moved toward a magazine rack near the desk in order to hear what the officer's business was.

"Which room is he in?" the officer was asking the receptionist.

"Third room on the left. He was unconscious —still, when he comes around there's no telling what he'll do. They found the gun in his boot, you know."

Tanner didn't need to hear any more. He tapped the officer on the shoulder. "I'd like to speak to you privately."

The officer frowned. "Sir, I have a more pressing problem at the moment."

Tanner reached into his back pocket and pulled out a leather wallet. He flashed a badge before the officer's nose. "Now," Tanner said, and the officer followed him immediately.

He made it brief as he talked to the officer, and after a few moments the policeman left to make a phone call. Tanner didn't bother to see what the officer would do next. He knew everything would be settled and the young man would leave well enough alone—if he knew what was best for him, Tanner thought, smiling. He moved to see what was going on near the room Hank was in. The cab driver was still there, but Tanner couldn't afford to waste any more time if he was going to see Hank before Carly returned. He approached the man.

"Are you the one who brought in the victim?" Tanner asked, pointing at the closed door.

"Yep. Name's Tiny."

"Well, Tiny, there's a lady looking for you to answer some questions. She's walking around with a clipboard in her hand, asking where you are."

"Wonder what she wants?" Tiny asked.

Tanner shrugged. "Probably needs some forms filled out. Insurance claims and such."

"*I* don't know nothin' about this fella." Tiny said, scratching his head.

"Just find her and tell her that. Then she won't bother you."

"Yeah. You're right. Where she's at?"

"In the waiting area. You can't miss her." Tanner patted him on the shoulder and pointed him in the direction of the fictitious woman, hoping he'd be occupied for awhile before he came back to ask questions of his own.

"Thanks, buddy," Tiny said as he walked away.

Sighing tiredly, Tanner shook his head before going to the door of Hank's room and pushing it open.

"Some people just can't handle a simple problem," Tanner said, walking in. Hank jerked a white cloth from his face and turned toward Tanner, upsetting the elderly gray-haired doctor who was about to add another stitch to his forehead. A young Oriental doctor was assisting

143

him.

"You're not supposed to be in here," the older man reprimanded Tanner, then turned to Hank. "And if you don't want to end up looking like the son of Frankenstein I suggest you don't make any quick moves in the next few minutes. I'm almost finished." He lifted the needle for another suture, then paused to looked pointedly at Tanner. "Sir, you can wait in the hall."

"That's all right, Doc," Hank interrupted. "He's here to take me home."

"Yeah," Tanner said, folding his arms over his chest. "His mother was too busy to get away. Seems she's tired of getting her son out of these scrapes—"

"Like hell," Hank muttered as the nurse covered his face again with the sterile-looking cloth.

Tanner grinned. "—so she sent me to do it for her. Poor thing's eighty if she's a day. Can hardly see because of the cataracts."

"Can it, will you!" the doctor stated. "This emergency room is full of people tonight. People waiting to see a doctor. The last thing I need is to listen to a clown. I must ask you to wait outside."

Tanner looked down his nose at the physician but refrained from making a wisecrack.

"Sorry, Doc. I get sorta punchy in these places." Tanner was anything but contrite. "Listen, Hank. I'm tired. Why don't you grab a cab when you're through. I'm going to head home."

"I knew I could count on you," was Hank's muffled reply.

The door opened and all turned to see the policeman walk in. Tanner listened as he briefly explained to the doctor that Hank had a permit to carry the gun and that he had been doing some investigation work for the authorities. Tanner refrained from smiling at the doctor's frown, but he thanked the officer and watched as he left. The doctor lifted the needle once more to try to finish his work.

"Don't do too neat a job, Doc," Tanner said. "I know a little señorita who's wild about the son of Frankenstein."

The doctor stood up straight, pointed toward the door, and looked as if a vein were about to burst in his purple face. "Get out!"

"I'm going," Tanner muttered. "Hank, I'll see you at home." He let himself out of the room, knowing he had been aggravating but not caring. He'd been under the care of too many cranky old doctors; he decided they should have a reason to gripe.

The door swished closed behind him, but Tanner couldn't leave. Carly was walking right toward him.

Damn! He had hoped to be long gone before she saw him. Now he'd be forced either to tell her the truth or to make up a reasonable explanation of why he was there.

Before he could manage either, Carly halted abruptly. Tanner squinted his eyes; tears were running down her face. He moved quickly toward her, but not fast enough to save the two cups from sliding out of her fingers and onto the floor. It hit him hard to see her this way. It dawned on him she must be feeling she had been through hell. He reached for her and she nearly fell into his arms, clinging to him with all her strength.

God, he thought, feeling her soft body against his, *she's shaking all over.* She must have been scared to death. He felt guilty for what she had been through, yet extremely relieved that she was all right.

He pulled her even tighter against his chest and pressed his lips to the top of her head, just holding her. Yes, he was relieved, he admitted, relieved that Carly was safe and Hank was doing fine. So what if he had to level with her? This was his last assignment; what could Omi do to him if he told her the truth about her sister? Fire him?

"Oh, Tanner, I'm so glad you're here." Her breath was warm against his throat, but he steeled himself against it, waiting for what he felt sure would be her next words. When she didn't ask him how he'd found out about Hank, he relaxed a little.

"Everything's all right, Carly. I just saw Hank, and except for a few stitches, he'll be fine."

"Thank God. I was so afraid."

Tanner rubbed his hand up and down her back

in a soothing motion. "Shh, it's all over now."

"I know, but I thought they were going to kill him."

"Hank's tougher than boot leather. He'll be fine." Her moist shirt damped the front of his. No wonder she was chilled, Tanner thought, and wondered how she'd gotten wet. It hadn't been from the coffee—he'd seen that drop to the floor without touching her. "We'll go home in just a few minutes. The doctor's almost finished."

Carly didn't reply; she just strengthened her hold on Tanner's waist. Tanner simply stood and held her for endless moments. He knew it was only a matter of time before she started hurling questions at him, questions he suddenly didn't feel like answering.

Tanner saw Tiny approaching rapidly. He mentally braced himself, knowing all hell could break loose very soon.

"Hey," Tiny said, a sad look on his face. "Did he take a turn for the worse?"

"No, he's going to be just fine," Tanner said.

Carly peeked up from Tanner's chest but didn't relinquish her hold on him.

"I never did find that lady," Tiny said. "But some other woman took down everything I had to say."

"How strange," Tanner replied, lifting his brow.

"Ain't it? Why didn't you tell me you knew

147

her?" Tiny asked, pointing at Carly. He scratched the whiskers that were beginning to show on his chin.

Tanner shrugged. "She wasn't here at the time."

Tiny nodded as if he should have thought of that himself.

"Tiny," Carly said, "this is Tanner . . ." She looked up at him. "I still don't know your last name."

"Barnes," Tanner answered, extending a hand to Tiny. Tiny frowned, then shrugged and accepted the handshake.

"Tiny Morrow. I was drivin' the cab," he said. Tanner assumed Tiny thought Carly had explained everything to him and left it at that.

"Man, if you're not in a hurry, I'd sure be grateful if you'd wait around and give us all a lift home," Tanner asked.

"No problem. I kinda wanted to wait and see how things turned out anyway."

The door opened and the doctor walked out. "Don't leave with the patient until I've written out several prescriptions," he told Tanner. "One of the nurses will bring them to you."

Tanner nodded and the doctor walked away. "Tiny, why don't you take Carly and go get the cab? I'll help Hank get his things together."

"I want to stay with you," Carly stated, tightening her arms around Tanner.

148

He hugged her close. "I'd like nothing better, Carly," he whispered to her. "But Hank'll need some help getting dressed." He reached for her shoulders and eased her away. "Go with Tiny. We'll only be a few more minutes."

He watched Tiny lead Carly away; then he went in to see about Hank. Hank lay on the gurney with nothing but a sheet covering his body and a white patch on his forehead.

"What are you doing here?" Hank asked.

"I didn't leave in time. Carly was coming down the hall when I went out.

Hank sighed. "What have you told her?"

"Nothing yet. She was pretty shaken up and hasn't asked how I found out about you."

"Sixteen stitches," Hank said, pointing to his head. "Damn, my lip hurts."

"What happened?"

"I'm not sure. Somebody set those goons on me."

"Cornwall said it was the barmaid. He said everyone down there was primed and ready for anyone looking for Lisa. Where are your clothes?"

"I don't know. I was out of it when I got here." Hank tried to sit up but flinched. "Damn! I hate having cracked ribs."

"How many did they get?" Tanner asked, looking at the binding around Hank's middle.

"Two, but they aren't too bad. I'll be sore for a few days."

"Should have had them sew your lip."

"Hell, no. That would hurt worse than the ribs."

Tanner shrugged. "It would heal faster."

"I'm in enough pain already."

Tanner looked around the room and spotted the remains of Hank's clothing in the trash bin. He laughed softly, then turned to look at his friend. "I've got some bad news, Armand. . . ." He lifted up a piece of the shirt with his finger. "Looks as if you'll have to wear a gown home."

"I'm not surprised," Hank said, then closed his eyes.

The nurse entered with the written prescriptions in one hand and a hypo in the other.

"Roll over," she ordered brusquely.

Hank did, obviously in pain.

"That'll make him sleep through the night," she said, handing Tanner the prescriptions and telling him what to give Hank and when.

"Before you leave," Tanner asked the nurse, "would you mind bringing a hospital gown—"

"*Two* hospital gowns," Hank cut in.

Tanner cleared his throat to keep from laughing. "Two hospital gowns. There's not enough of his clothing left for him to wear."

"I can, but they'll have to be added to his bill."

"Whatever," Hank muttered.

Tanner turned on his winning smile. "We'd appreciate it. And can you hurry? We have a cab waiting."

With one gown covering his front and the other covering his rear, Hank eased his weight into a wheelchair so the nurse could push him out of the room and down the hall to the exit door. Through the glass pane of the door Tanner saw Tiny's cab parked right in front. Tanner went on ahead of Hank to open the front door of the cab for him. But as he grabbed the handle, Tiny placed his finger to his lips and motioned with his head to the back seat. Carly was curled up against the door sound asleep. Tanner nodded back at Tiny, then moved aside to allow Hank to get in. Once Hank was settled, Tanner closed the door, then climbed into the back seat, cautious not to awaken Carly.

The foursome remained quiet as Tiny drove them to the boat basin. Once there, Tiny helped Tanner get Hank out of the cab and on board the yacht.

"Tiny, will you help Hank get to his bunk while I run back and get Carly?"

Hank frowned at Tanner. "I can manage well enough on my own."

"You might think so until you try getting out of your evening apparel, Cinderella. Those gowns look awfully tight across your shoulders."

"Yep. Better listen to him," Tiny added. "Ain't nothin' worse than busted ribs."

"I'll manage," Hank said more sternly.

"I haven't got time to argue with you," Tanner said. "I want to get Carly before she wakes up. Tiny, just wait outside the door. He'll shout if he needs you."

Tanner left the yacht and went to the cab. The hinges on the old automobile squeaked as he eased the door on Carly's side open. With infinite care, he lifted her against his chest and walked back to the craft. He hated to wake her, but there was no way he could climb on board the way he was holding her.

"Carly."

She stirred, barely opening her eyes. "Tanner?"

He smiled at her sleepy look. "Honey, you're going to have to climb up by yourself."

She nuzzled his neck and Tanner knew she wasn't awake enough to be aware of exactly where they were. "Carly, baby, wake up."

She kissed his neck; her lips were warm. Tanner felt himself growing weak. He fought it by placing her feet on the ground.

"What?" Carly muttered, opening her eyes wider.

"Carly, you've got to climb up the ladder. I can't carry you." He turned her toward the ladder and gave her a little shove up the first rung. Slowly, and with his encouragement, he managed to get her on board. He led her into his sleeping quarters and laid her down on his bunk.

"I'll be right back," he said as she protested his

leaving. "I just have to lock up." He hesitated a moment to make sure she didn't try to rise and follow him before he left.

Tiny was waiting for him in the stateroom. "I didn't wanna leave until I made sure she was all settled," Tiny said, digging in his pocket. "Here." He handed Tanner a small gold chain. "Tell the little lady that I don't want it. It felt good to be able to help her."

Tanner took the chain. "I want to thank you for all you've done, Tiny. Hank and Carly both mean a lot to me."

Tiny shuffled his feet. "She's a sweet little thing. Be glad you got somebody like her."

"I am." He didn't allow himself to put any meaning into the words.

Tanner couldn't let Tiny leave without some compensation for all he had done. He reached into his pocket and took out his wallet.

Tiny's eyes widened at the size of the bill Tanner handed him. "Man, I can't take that kinda money from you."

"You deserve it. Break it before you return the cab, okay?"

Tiny extended his hand and Tanner shook it with genuine pleasure. "I know if Carly were awake she'd want to thank you herself," Tanner said as he led Tiny to the door.

"She sure has a lotta guts. Tell her it was a pleasure doing business with her. And, hey. If you ever need a cab, call for me."

"Will do. See ya, Tiny." Tanner closed the door and secured it before he went to check on Hank.

Hank was already sleeping; Tanner knew it was from the injection he'd gotten in the hospital. Tanner would have to get the prescriptions filled first thing in the morning. But right then all Tanner could think about was Carly sleeping in his bed.

He ran his fingers through his hair and backed out of his friend's room. Quietly he walked through the stateroom and galley and into the radio room. Everything checked out all right. He turned the frequency down so he'd still be able to hear it—but just barely. He would have shut it off completely, but he was waiting to hear from Cornwall. As he went to his bunk he unbuttoned his shirt and shrugged it off. Tossing it on the floor, he turned to watch Carly sleep.

Soft, warm, and vulnerable. Tanner hated that last thought. He took a deep breath. How would she react to the news of her sister? he wondered. His previous doubts about how Carly would handle it had now almost disappeared. She looked vulnerable, yes, but she had proved she was a strong person tonight. She'd gone into the Diamond Lounge not knowing what she'd find, watched Hank being beaten to a pulp, and managed to save him from being killed. And Tanner was very aware Hank might have ended up dead otherwise. Still, Carly had waited until it was all over and Hank was in the hands of a doctor before allowing reaction to set in. Considering she'd never been in such a position before, she'd handled everything like a pro, Tanner decided.

But how would she accept the news of Therese? Would she be grateful to have her fears put to rest and go home and await her sister's return? Damn, he wished he could believe that. But Carly had ever right to become angry. Tanner slid off his shoes and nudged them out of the way with his toe. He had deceived her. He had planned to play on her emotions to keep her out of the way, a suddenly distasteful idea. Would she understand? Or would she place all her anger on him—her anger about everything, including Therese's wish to keep her two lives apart?

Tanner unsnapped his pants and stepped out of them. There was no reason for him not to lie down in his bunk—except for all the thoughts of what might happen between him and Carly if he did.

Carly was vulnerable, overwrought, under tremendous stress. He'd sleep with her, but he wouldn't make love to her, regardless of the fact that his body cried out to fulfill that need. She'd hate him for sure if he did. She had to be told the truth. And when that happened, he'd be free of her, on his way to living life the way he had planned, taking each day as it came wherever he happened to be. He stepped to the edge of the bunk, admitting that even if everything was aboveboard between him and the young woman sleeping in his bed, he would not make love to her. If he did, he was sure the memory of that event would always be a silent magnet beckoning him to return for more.

Tanner eased his weight alongside Carly. She rolled toward him and he immediately felt the dampness of her shirt. He closed his eyes tightly, not wanting to undress her but knowing he couldn't allow her to sleep in discomfort. Sitting up, he lifted her limp form and eased the too-large shirt off her. Thank heaven she was wearing a bra, he thought. Then he noticed her shoes and moved to the end of the bunk to take them off. But he wasn't about to strip her of her jeans.

The night air was chill and he lifted Carly again to pull the sheet from beneath her. He lay down and covered them both with the sheet, hoping Carly would remain on the side of the bunk where he'd placed her. Sleep was long in coming, but finally Tanner's mind settled down and he dozed.

Soft skin rubbed against his naked chest; a hand moved across his shoulder, pulling him closer. Tanner automatically complied and turned on his side toward her. His arm encircled her warm body and he rolled half on top of her, moaning sleepily as his lips found hers and he kissed her deeply. He adjusted his weight until he was pressing her into the mattress, covering her completely. His hand moved up her side until he cupped her full breast in his palm. Annoyed by the material covering it, he removed his hand, slid his fingers beneath the elastic, and pulled it over, freeing her flesh to his touch. She wrapped her arms around him, encouraging him.

Tanner ground the lower half of his body into hers, then frowned at the rough feel of material pushing back against him. He raised himself up, away from her, now wide awake. Carly blinked at the abrupt stop. Her chest heaved against his from her quickening breath, and Tanner was barely able to stop himself from falling back on her to finish what had barely begun.

"We can't," he whispered raggedly, gently kissing her forehead.

"Yes," she murmured, trying her best to bring him back down to her.

"No." Tanner took a deep breath and rolled away. Lying flat on his back he placed his arm over his head. "There's too much that's got to be said. You may not feel the same about this after we've talked."

Carly moved back to her side of the bunk. "When do you plan to talk to me?" she finally asked after a lengthy silence.

"In the morning." Tanner rolled to his feet and slipped into his pants. "I'm going to check on Hank." He left without looking at her.

Tanner went to the stateroom and poured himself a drink. The whiskey burned nicely down his throat, and he decided to have another. As he twirled the dark liquid around in the glass, he cursed himself for a fool. Why did he allow her to get under his skin? How had she managed to affect him the way she did after they had known each other such a short time? He realized that her reaction to him after he confessed—Damn, why did that word come to mind?—confronted (he liked that word better) her with the truth would matter to him. And he'd never before really cared how his work affected people.

But Carly wasn't just an assignment anymore. She had become real to him. Perhaps it was because of his association with Therese. He didn't know if that was the true reason, but it made as much sense to him as anything else he could think of.

The crackle of static filtered through his thoughts and he hurried to the radio to check it out. Closing the door securely behind him, he listened to determine who, if anyone, was trying to reach him. The radio crackled sharply again, and Tanner adjusted the knobs to fine tune it to the right frequency. Settling down in the chair, he waited.

A few minutes later his call letters came through and Tanner replied to the summons. It was Cornwall.

"We got trouble," Cornwall stated through the static.

"I read you."

"Lisa's been found."

Tanner shut his eyes. "Where?"

"In the bay about two hours ago."

Tanner didn't speak for a moment. Finally, he pressed the button on the mike. "Where are you now?"

"At the Coast Guard base."

"I'll be there as soon as I can get away." Tanner relayed his numbers again and listened as Cornwall did the same. He placed the mike on its stand and gave himself a moment to digest the news; then he went to work.

Like a thief in the night, he edged inside the doorway of his cabin to see if Carly was still awake. He relaxed. She was sound asleep. Picking up his discarded clothing, he returned to the stateroom to dress, and, without leaving a note as to where he was going or why, he crept out of the cabin and left the yacht.

CHAPTER EIGHT

Carly stared into the darkness almost wishing she hadn't awakened. Too many questions surfaced; too many jumbled thoughts raced through her mind. She shivered and rolled on her side, tugging the sheet over her bare shoulder. She was beginning to understand why Tanner had not come back to bed.

She couldn't believe it had taken so long for the truth to dawn on her. Someone had obviously notified Tanner that Hank had been hurt. But who could it have been? A hospital employee? Someone from the lounge? Carly shook her head, ruling out both possibilities. Hank had barely regained consciousness when Tanner arrived, and no one from the lounge could have known where she and Tiny had taken Hank. If only she'd had the chance to ask Tiny, maybe she'd have learned how Tanner had known to come to the hospital.

She slid her hand across the bed, touching his

pillow. He must have left her the way he had because he knew she'd eventually come around and demand an explanation. He could have made love to her; she wouldn't have stopped him. Tanner had made her feel sensations she had never dreamed were possible. Yes, Carly thought, it had felt wonderful, but now that her mind was clearer she was relieved that he had chosen to stop. In her heart she wanted to believe that Tanner had a logical explanation for everything that had happened during the night, but her mind was telling her to be prepared for anything. If Therese was into shady dealings, then anyone could be—including Tanner Barnes.

She wanted to groan. She had to understand the reason for Tanner's sudden appearance at the hospital. She had to know why Hank had been at the lounge. Tired of speculating, Carly rose on her elbows and flung off the sheet. Nothing was going to be settled this way. If she wanted her questions answered she was going to have to find Tanner and insist on an explanation. He was an honest man, she thought as she stood and dressed. He would level with her, at least as much as he could. And if he told her to leave well enough alone, she'd cross that bridge when she got there.

A lamp was on in the stateroom, casting just enough light for Carly to see into the galley. But Tanner wasn't there. Thinking he might be on deck, she left the cabin and stepped out into the damp night. The air was chill as she walked the length of the deck.

"Tanner?" she called softly. When there was no reply she followed the deck along the port side and around to the stern. Tanner was nowhere in sight.

"Tanner?" she called again, moving to starboard. She stopped, puzzled. Where could he be? she thought, then snapped her fingers. He had to be in Hank's room. Her sneakers squeaked as she reentered the cabin and went to Hank's quarters. She opened the door quietly, looking all around the small room for Tanner. But the far side of the room was dark and she couldn't tell if he was there.

Carly crept to the side of the bunk. "Tanner?" she whispered.

Hank snored, and Carly's hand went to her throat at the sound. Then she rolled her eyes back and sighed as she realized what had scared her. Before she could whisper Tanner's name again, Hank flung his arm off the bunk and moaned. Carly could do nothing but stare at his bruised, swollen face. He looked horrible. She cringed just thinking about the pain he'd feel when he awoke. A picture of his beating flashed vividly in her mind. Bumps prickled her skin as she thought of all that had happened at the lounge. It had seemed so cruel for those men to attack Hank, a man with only one arm. But they had meant to be cruel; they would have killed him if she hadn't intervened. A weak

163

smile lifted the corners of her lips. She was proud of herself. Tonight she had saved a man's life.

Hank groaned again and Carly knelt beside his bunk, tenderly brushing her hand across his face. She wished there was something more she could do to comfort him, but she was at a loss as to what that could be. Staring at the deep gash on his lower lip she momentarily became selfish enough to wish he would wake up. Then she could ask him what he had been doing at the lounge, but she quickly cut off that line of thought. She'd eventually get her answers, but not at the expense of someone's agony.

Hank's arm suddenly wrapped itself around her, pulling her down beside him. He was still asleep and didn't know what he was doing, she realized. Embarrassed, Carly knew she had to move away, but if she pushed against him she'd hurt him. When his cheek brushed against hers she went into action. Carefully she gripped his wrist and lifted it just enough to enable her to duck beneath it, then she placed his arm beside him and scooted out of his reach.

Carly backed out of the room and closed the door, her mind already back on Tanner. He had obviously left the yacht. But where had he gone?

A wisp of hair fell into her eyes and she brushed it away, accepting the fact that she wasn't going to learn anything until morning. Gnawing on her lip, she walked into the stateroom and sat down. She fidgeted, blaming her restlessness on the hard cushions of the sofa. But she knew that wasn't true. She was anxious. Even the luxurious furnishings bothered her. Had Tanner and Hank's wealth come from dealing in drugs? Was this craft used for running narcotics?

Stop it! she wanted to scream. She had no proof that Hank had been involved in anything illegal at the lounge. Wasn't everyone innocent until proven guilty? Perhaps Hank had just been looking for a woman. But she couldn't imagine Hank associated with anyone like Rosetta, the waitress. Still, Carly desperately hoped that Hank had been looking for female companionship. Everything would then be so easily explained.

Curling up on the sofa, Carly turned her cheek against the cushion and saw that the door to the galley stood open. A cup of coffee sounded good, she thought, rising to her feet. She walked into the galley and stopped. Was it just yesterday morning that the three of them had enjoyed a leisurely breakfast? Was it just the night before that she and Tanner had slept on deck? It seemed like a year ago.

Rummaging through the lockers, she found a teakettle and filled it with water. Before she placed it on the stove, however, she paused, hearing the static of a radio. She turned, wondering where it was coming from. A sliding door, which Carly had thought was a pantry, was slightly ajar. She slid it open. A small room, perhaps with enough space for two people, was revealed. Carly moved her hand along the wall, found the light switch, and flipped it on. It was a radio room, with all the latest equipment built into the wall or bolted onto a desk.

Intrigued, she entered the room. Placing the kettle on the desk, she studied the equipment. The radio was set on a channel that was rarely used. Wanting to try out the equipment, Carly found the selector and pressed the button, watching as the numbers raced down the scale to the channel she wanted. A man's voice came through clearly, followed by the faint sounds of someone responding. She smiled as she listened, for she realized it was the shrimpers she was hearing. But the smile soon left Carly's lips and she frowned. Something must have happened. The usual joking and griping that went on between such people was missing; these men sounded serious. Intending to find out what they were talking about, she pulled out the chair and sat down, carefully turning up the volume a little.

". . . makes me sick whenever this happens. . . ." a gruff voice stated ". . . Wish these young people'd take more care. . . ."

Carly placed her ear closer to the speaker, listening to the faint reply of the other man.

". . . Coast Guard fished her outta the bay about two hours ago. Young thing, she was. Her remains in terrible shape. . . ."

How awful, Carly thought, leaning back in the chair. There must have been a boating accident.

". . . I wished I'd been somewhere else. I 'magine I'll see that long blonde hair for a long time to come. . . ."

Bolting straight up, Carly gripped the edge of the desk. Long blonde hair! For a moment she couldn't seem to move. Young thing. How young, she wanted to know?

She shook her head, berating herself for overreacting. There had to be a thousand young, blonde-haired women on the island. But a feeling of weakness overcame her. With shaky fingers she turned up the volume a fraction more.

". . . Naw. As soon as I drag this 'round I'm movin' outta the bay. There's too much goin' on out here for my likin'. Let me cut ya loose. . . ."

"No!" Carly said emphatically under her breath. "Don't stop talking now." But her plea was futile. The man signed off. She pressed the selector, moving it up a few numbers. Men were talking, but not about the incident in the bay. Their conversations dealt with the shrimping industry.

Carly leaned back, aware that she was trembling. It couldn't be Therese, she thought. If Therese had been on the island she couldn't have evaded all the people who had been looking for her. Yet . . . Carly's mind raced through numerous possibilities. What if Therese had just returned? What if she had been hiding out and the people she'd been mixed up with had found her?

"Oh, damn," she whispered, pressing her palms

into her eyes. Carly wondered if she was looking for trouble where there was none.

She slid her hands down her face and looked out the porthole at the sunrise. If Tanner were here, she thought, he could help her. He would help her. But this wasn't his problem. She had to take care of things herself. Everything that had happened the night before suddenly seemed insignificant. Right now she had a more urgent problem on her hands.

Even though she knew she was probably overreacting, she had to take action or go crazy. The Coast Guard base wasn't that far away; it was next to the ferry landing. She had to know, had to make sure it wasn't her sister's body that had been found.

She quickly left the room but stopped in the galley. Her purse. She needed her purse. Moving swiftly, she went into Tanner's quarters and found it on the floor. She reached inside and grabbed the key to the storeroom, then slung the purse strap over her shoulder and left the yacht.

It seemed like hours had passed by the time she retrieved her bicycle and was on her way. Instead of passing the hospital complex, she cut through a subdivision of well-tended older homes and made her way toward the ferry landing. It was too early for the usual backup of traffic waiting for the ferry, Carly thought, knowing that by midmorning the line of cars would reach the seawall.

As she neared the landing, however, she saw numerous cars and official vehicles parked all around the area. The sight of the ambulance made her swallow. She silently prayed that her wild imaginings were just that.

Carly coasted through the parking lot until she reached the Coast Guard entrance. She looked at the two guards on duty and gnawed her inner lip, wondering if they would allow her to pass. The thought of being barred from entering had never crossed her mind. Still, she had to give it a try. She braked the bike and got off, wheeling it along as she approached the guards. One stood up straighter and looked very official while the other smiled and winked at her.

"I've got to speak to someone about the woman's body that was found this morning," she said, looking back and forth between the two men.

"Sorry, ma'am. No one but official personnel allowed on base right now." Apparently this man was a stickler for regulations. Carly looked at his name tag and saw "Reynolds" in capital letters, then looked toward the friendlier man whose tag read "Manning."

"But I must find out who she was. I'm afraid it might have been my sister." Carly's voice quivered.

The smile left Manning's face. "Someone's already claimed the body, ma'am. Do you have other family members on the island?"

"No." Carly sighed shakily. "It must be someone else," she said, feeling tears building in her eyes.

"That was guarded information, Manning," the stickler said.

"So what? I couldn't let this pretty lady worry herself to death. Man, that's too coldhearted even for you, Reynolds."

Carly interrupted before an argument began. "Don't worry. I wouldn't tell anyone even if I knew someone to tell." She blinked rapidly, but a tear managed to fall. She dashed it away. "Why's that ambulance still here?" she asked. The sight of the yellow and orange vehicle bothered her.

"We're still searching the bay, ma'am. Just in case. The ambulance is on standby."

"I see," Carly answered.

"Is there anyone I can call to come and get you?" Manning asked.

"No. Thanks just the same." Feeling weak in the knees, Carly rolled the bicycle out of sight of the guards and laid it on its side. Then she sat down on the rear bumper of a parked brown-and-tan pickup truck.

Sadness and fatigue crept over her. How much more was going to happen before she finally got to the bottom of things? she wondered, allowing despondency to overcome her. *Damn Therese for putting me through this!* she wanted to scream. But she didn't. Instead she placed her palms on her knees and leaned over, knowing that if and when she found her sister, all she was going to do was cling to her, hold on to her.

Carly heard footsteps nearing. Not wanting to be found sitting on someone's truck she pushed herself up and looked to see who was approaching. Her mouth fell open and she gasped.

"You!" she shouted. It was the sandy-haired man from the Diamond Lounge walking between two cars on the next lane. He swung his head around. A flicker of recognition glimmered in his eyes before he walked quickly away from her.

"Wait!" Carly yelled. In her haste to catch him she tripped over her bike but caught herself before she fell. "Wait!" she called again, skirting the cars in a run.

The man glanced at her over his shoulder, then opened the door of a light blue car. Before Carly could reach him he had the engine started.

She raced to the rear of his car and pounded her fist on the trunk. "Get out!" she yelled. "You're going to talk to me whether you want to or not."

The man twisted around in the seat. Before it dawned on Carly what he intended to do, he jerked the car into gear and jumped the esplanade, nearly causing Carly to hit the pavement.

"Damn!" she cried. "Damn, damn, damn."

Fragmented thoughts and ideas swam through her mind, but none of them would fall into place. She rubbed her forehead. The lounge, the death, the sandy-haired man. How did they all fit together?

What was he doing down here? Carly thought desperately. Who was the dead woman? Had it really been a family member who identified her body? Carly's throat tightened in fear. Was it possible that the dead woman really was . . .?

She massaged the back of her neck. Too much was happening. Too much had already happened for any of it to have been coincidental. There had to be a connection between this woman's death and the Diamond Lounge. Why else would that man have been there? Surely not out of curiosity!

Feeling as if she were about to shatter into a million pieces, Carly made herself calm down. No one was going to deal with a half-hysterical woman. She had to use her brain—had to discover the identity of the woman who had drowned.

Out of the corner of her eye she caught a glimpse of the guards. She moved quickly across the parking lot and back to the gates. Trying to smile, she addressed Manning. "I was just wondering—do you know where they took the girl's body?" she asked, making the request sound like idle curiosity.

"That's privileged information," Reynolds informed her, but Carly kept her eyes glued on Manning.

"Can you tell me who claimed her?" she asked.

"I'd love to tell you," Manning answered, "but I don't know who he is."

So it was a man, she thought. "It wasn't that guy I just saw walking through the parking lot, was it?"

Without Carly indicating it, Manning glanced in the direction the sandy-haired man had gone.

"I'm warning you, Manning. Keep quiet."

"No," Manning replied. "It was someone else."

So the sandy-haired man *was* somehow connected, Carly thought, not believing him.

"I see," she said, racking her brain for a way to separate the two men. If Reynolds was out of the way she was certain Manning would talk.

"Well," she said airily. "I've got to be on my way, but I have a slight problem. My bike fell over and is caught on something under that brown truck over there. Can I get one of you to help me budge it?" she lied.

"Sure," Manning said obligingly.

"No, you won't," Reynolds stated. "You stay right here. I'll do it."

"Oh, good!" Carly pointed out the direction to him. "It's just over there."

"You're coming with me," Reynolds ordered. He waited until she moved, then followed her.

Rats! she thought as she walked toward the truck. She was going to look awfully foolish when he saw that the bicycle was free and lying on the ground. She slowed her footsteps in an attempt to delay her embarrassment. But when she reached the area, she was stunned. The bicycle was gone. She raced to where she had left it, then spun around.

"It was right here," she said, her voice pitched high. "I left it right here." She looked up at Reynolds. "Somebody stole my bike."

Tanner felt like hell. The last damned thing he had needed was to come back to the yacht and find Carly gone. He threw himself down on the sofa and waited for Hank to get dressed and come out. It had been a long time since he had been this tired, he thought. Why couldn't things have gone as planned? The events of last night and this morning were just the kind of things he wanted away from.

He'd seen too many reruns, lived through too many episodes. Hank's injuries and Lisa's death only cemented his desire to quit. It couldn't happen soon enough. He leaned back and closed his eyes. Today was going to be hell; he was going to level with Carly, come what might—when he found her. Why couldn't she, just once, be predictable!

"Tanner?"

Tanner opened his eyes and watched as Hank stiffly eased himself into a chair.

"Sore?" he asked.

"That's putting it mildly." Hank winced as he adjusted his weight. "What's happened? I must have slept like a log the last few hours."

Tanner's back left the sofa as he leaned forward, bracing his elbows on his knees. "Lisa's body was found early this morning."

The only sign Tanner saw of Hank's true reaction was his hand knotting into a fist. "What happened?"

"She was shot and tossed into the bay," Tanner said bluntly. "She'd been out there some time."

Hank paused for a moment; his black eyes looked cold. "Where do we go from here?"

"I have to find Carly," Tanner said, standing.

"She's gone?"

174

"Yes. She must have heard something on the radio. I found the kettle on the desk, and the radio has been tampered with."

"Give me a few minutes and I'll be ready," Hank said, moving painfully to the edge of his chair.

"I can handle it. Cornwall's taking care of the details on Lisa," Tanner said, walking toward the galley. "You should be in bed."

"I'm not tired," Hank said, addressing Tanner's back.

Tanner returned and handed Hank a small, red-striped bag. "Here are your prescriptions. I had them filled before I came back. You won't be of much use after you take those, so just stay here and wait for Carly. If she comes back, sit on her."

The outer door to the cabin rattled, then flew open. Tanner poised for action. He recognized Cornwall instantly and barked, "What the hell are you doing here?"

"It sure as hell isn't a social call." Cornwall matched Tanner's tone. "I thought you'd like to know that little sister spotted me at the base."

"Great," Tanner muttered. "What did you tell her?"

"Nothing. I ran like a guilty son-of-a-bitch. How in the hell did she find out about Lisa anyway?"

"It doesn't matter," Tanner said, inhaling deeply. "I plan to tell her everything as soon as she returns."

"Therese isn't going to like it," Cornwall said.

"She'll understand. I can't allow Carly to go any

175

further. She'll end up in the same condition as Lisa if she isn't stopped."

"Then stop her. You have your orders."

"My orders suck."

"Making it with Carly Jameson is anything but distasteful."

A muscle ticked in Tanner's cheek. "She's just a kid."

"She's twenty-five years old."

Tanner shoved his hands into his pockets and stared at Cornwall. He almost hated Cornwall for bringing the facts of his mission back into focus. Damn him. But Tanner's decision to tell Carly the truth was set, and nothing was going to change his mind.

Hank intervened by extending his hand to Cornwall. "I'm sure glad you were at the lounge last night. I owe you one."

Cornwall clasped Hank's hand and replied with a sheepish grin. "I think we're even. Last time the shoe was on the other foot."

"Yeah, but that didn't have anything to do with work. If I recall correctly, you got a little too close to someone's babe."

"It wasn't as close as I intended," Cornwall said, quirking his eyebrows.

The two men's easy conversation made Tanner feel like an outsider, and he didn't like it. "Have all the arrangements been made?" he asked.

The grin left Cornwall's face. "I just left the

hospital. Lisa's body will be shipped home after the autopsy. Omi's handling the rest."

"It looks as if I'm finished here then," Tanner said.

"I wish Therese would finish and get out of Mexico," Hank said. "Things are too hot right now."

Tanner couldn't agree more. "What are your plans?" he asked Cornwall.

"I'll be investigating this end of the operation until Therese is through in Orizaba. With any luck she'll be able to wrap up both ends." He looked seriously at Tanner. "I understand what you're up against with baby sister, man. Do what you have to do." He paused. "You'll be missed, Barnes. There aren't too many of us old guys left."

"Old?" Hank muttered dryly.

"Unless you consider Omi."

"I still have another twenty years left in me. And so does Tanner, if he'd just give it a shot."

Tanner smiled. "Maybe. But I want to live those years in peace. I've had enough of the Bond/Rambo life-style."

"When do you think you'll be leaving?" Cornwall asked.

"That depends on what Omi has to say and how soon Hank can travel. We'll be around for awhile yet." Tanner looked at his watch. "You'd better get going. I imagine baby sister will be here any time."

Hank tried to push himself up but fell back, sucking in his breath.

Tanner was instantly at his side. "You all right?"

When Hank paled Tanner was certain he had hurt himself. He looked at Cornwall. "Get him a glass of water while I help him to his bunk." Tanner lifted the bag containing the medicine and stuffed it in his pocket before helping Hank to his quarters.

"You have to give those ribs time to heal," he said as Hank lowered his weight onto the bed. Tanner shook two tablets out of one of the plastic vials and into Hank's palm.

"No kidding," Cornwall added as he entered the room with the glass of water, "you'll be as stiff as hell if you don't."

Hank took the medication, then winced as he licked a bead of water from his cut lower lip. "Too bad I won't be around when everything comes down on those SOBs."

"From what I saw, you came down pretty good on them while you had the chance. You can bet they're still suffering," Cornwall replied.

"What happened? All I remember is hitting the dirt that last time."

"You were in pretty sad shape by the time I rounded the building, but before I could do much, little sister came and ran me off." Cornwall laughed. "I know one thing; that girl has guts *and* a temper. She beat the hell out of the back of my car a while ago."

Hank smiled, carefully adjusting the pillow beneath his head. "She sure surprised me," he said, closing his eyes. The grin remained on his face.

"She's just full of surprises," Tanner mumbled beneath his breath as he left the room.

Carly held her breath and crept away from the cabin door, feeling as if her heart were in her throat. She looked at her small yacht, wanting with all her heart to board it, start the engine, and race back to Beaumont. But that was impossible. Tanner would hear the engine and stop her before she could back the craft out.

Damn! she cried silently, brokenly. Tanner had known all along why she'd come to Galveston. He had taken an interest in her only out of duty! The son of a bitch! She had to get off his yacht before any of the three discovered she'd been listening to them. She couldn't face them now.

Therese! Therese was some sort of government agent. Carly gripped the edge of the rail and lifted her leg over the side. She'd found out things from her eavesdropping than she'd dreamed were possible. Now she wanted to get away. She *had* to get away, she thought, feeling her heart constrict painfully. She couldn't face Tanner again after the charade he'd pulled. Why hadn't he just leveled with her?

As her feet hit land she realized she had no place to go. She rubbed her brow and squatted down, needing a moment to straighten out her thoughts. She prayed it would take them awhile to get Hank settled, at least long enough for her to hide somewhere. She had to get home. There was nothing left for her to learn in Galveston. Therese was a government agent. Tanner was an agent. *Think, Carly! Think!*

Frantic, Carly looked for an escape route. Her eyes darted to the storeroom. If she just had her bicycle . . . The storeroom. It was the perfect place to hide. Tanner would never find her there.

She lifted the strap of her purse high on her shoulder and jogged to the shed, digging the key out of her pocket as she went. She shook her head slightly at the sight of the storage place. If her bicycle hadn't been stolen, if Manning hadn't had a friend bring her here, if, if, if . . . how long, if ever, would it have taken her to find out the truth?

Carly ran around the building, unlocked the door, and entered. As soon as she locked the door behind her, she took a shaky breath. It was pitch-black inside. She'd never gone any further than just inside the door, never realized how dusty and close the air was. She stepped forward, then stopped immediately. A spider web stuck to her cheek. Carly bit her lip to keep from screaming, wiping at her face until she was certain the sticky threads were all off. Maybe this wasn't such a good idea, she thought as she stood in the darkness. It had to be a hundred and twenty degrees in here. She might have a heat stroke.

She shook her head and mentally berated herself. She couldn't allow the heat to affect her. It didn't matter that she had on the hottest sweatshirt ever made, that hiding like a frightened child was a really foolish stunt. She had nowhere else to go. Tanner would never find her here, locked in the storage shed, suffocating.

Reaching out, she moved slowly across the tiny room, not wanting to trip or make any noise. Her hand touched an empty crate and she sat down. If no one had seen her on Tanner's yacht, she'd be all right. He'd be asking about her before long. He'd be looking for her too, ready to play his game. But now that she'd found him out the game was over.

She closed her eyes tightly. It was the familiar sound of the third man's voice that had stopped her from knocking on the yacht's door. When he'd told Tanner she'd seen him at the Coast Guard base, nothing could have made her announce her presence. Just as nothing could have prevented her from listening to everything they had to say. If she'd only arrived a few minutes earlier, she thought, she might have learned even more.

Now all she could do was wait Tanner out. Perhaps he'd think she was still at the Coast Guard base, or maybe even at the hospital. It didn't matter where he thought she was, she decided, just as long as he left the yacht basin long enough for her to get away.

Carly covered her face with her hands. Her chest constricted with pain. It was Lisa Curtis's body they had found. The woman Therese had roomed with was dead! But Therese was alive. The relief Carly felt was so tremendous it made her nauseous, forcing her to bend over and clutch her stomach. She'd nearly convinced herself that Therese had been the victim of that drowning; her mind had been ready to accept the worst. But Therese was alive and well.

Carly wrapped her arms around her waist. This was not the time to fall apart. Everything was all right. She had to keep her wits about her.

She concentrated on everything the three men had talked about. It was all falling into place. She now knew why Hank had been at the Diamond Lounge. She now knew how the sandy-haired man—Cornwall, Tanner had called him?—tied into all the events. He had obviously contacted Tanner the night before and told him where she and Tiny had taken Hank. And he'd definitely been the one to identify Lisa Curtis's body at the Coast Guard base. That must have been where Tanner had gone before dawn.

So much was suddenly clear now, Carly thought. She should have known a man Tanner's age wouldn't be interested in a young, unsophisticated woman like herself! How could she have been so naive?

But she hurt all the same. She shook her head—it didn't matter. Now that she knew where Therese was and what she was doing, Carly's purpose in coming to Galveston was accomplished. She had all the information she needed. There was no longer any reason not to go home.

Carly wanted to groan. Therese was an agent. For whom? On what sort of cases? Carly clutched her hands together, having trouble seeing her sister in that role. How had her fun-loving sister been able to give the type of concentration and devotion Carly assumed was needed to such an occupation? She shook her head. Surely Therese was working for the right side? The good old U.S. of A.?

Despite the ovenlike temperature, her hands were ice-cold. She tucked them between her knees. Therese was in Mexico. Orizaba, Mexico. Carly had never heard of it. No wonder Therese hadn't returned at the time of her father's death. She still didn't know of it. Or did she? Carly felt angry. Maybe Therese's job was more important than the death of her father. Perhaps her sister couldn't care less about what was happening to Jameson Steel or her brother, Ellis.

Ellis! Carly closed her eyes tightly. What in the world was she going to tell him? Was he strong enough to be told the truth? She desperately hoped so. She was tired of carrying this burden on her own shoulders. She needed Ellis—for his strength, his honesty, his ability to analyze and evaluate. Suddenly hot tears cascaded down her cheeks and she sniffed.

She might need him, but she couldn't load him down with any of this, not yet. She had to do her damnedest to find Therese first. And if that failed, then . . .

The doorknob rattled. Carly sat straight up, holding her breath. It was Tanner. It had to be Tanner. A loud rap was followed by a muffled "Damn"; then she heard the sound of retreating footsteps in the gravel-covered yard. Carly eased to her feet. Seconds ticked by; she fanned herself with her hand, feeling the closeness in the airless room even more. There was no sound of movement outside. The heat was getting to her. She couldn't remain inside indefinitely. If she could make it to the beach without being spotted, she could lose herself in the crowd, find a way home.

Patience. She had to have patience—had to give Tanner time enough to believe she wasn't there and wasn't returning. And if Hank happened to see her leaving, well, he wasn't in much condition to stop her. Tanner was the one she wanted to avoid—at all costs. He had betrayed her. The bastard.

Carly knotted her hands into fists. Again she thought of how close she had come to falling for him. What a fool he must have thought she was. She certainly felt like one. The bastard!

She moved back to the crate and sat down, tugging the neck of the sweatshirt away from her throat. She'd wait another fifteen or twenty minutes and then leave. As soon as she could locate a phone she was going to call Tiny. Tiny she could trust; Tiny would see her safely to the bus station and on her way to Beaumont. There was no reason to wait around any longer.

So why was a painful lump forming in her throat?

CHAPTER NINE

Carly felt light-headed and swallowed. It seemed her lungs wouldn't expand enough for her to draw a deep breath. She had to get out of the storeroom, away from the ovenlike temperature. Tanner had to be gone by now. Wiping the perspiration out of her eyes, she made her way to the door on wobbly legs. As she reached the door she flattened her palm against its surface and struggled to insert the key in the keyhole.

"Come on," she whispered as it slipped. If her fingers would just stop shaking! She gripped the key more tightly, then lifted it again and sighed as it slid easily into the slot and twisted. More than anything she wanted to shove the door open and race out into the fresh air. But she held back, cracking it open just enough to see if Tanner or anyone else was out there. The coast was clear.

Carly stepped out and inhaled, ignoring her body's desire to sink to the ground. Instead she closed the door behind her.

A light breeze touched her, making her pluck the sweatshirt away from her damp skin. The crunch of gravel beneath her feet seemed ten times as loud as normal, but Carly attributed it to the ringing of her ears. She shook her head, clearing it of the bothersome hum.

Several steps brought Carly to the corner of the building, and she peered around it. A few men were working on the grounds but none she recognized. Taking care not to draw any attention, she began a leisurely stroll away from the boat basin, holding her breath as she anticipated someone screaming her name.

Halfway down the block she looked over her shoulder and breathed a little easier. No one had paid her any attention.

She had to find a phone. It was too risky using the one at the dock. She had no idea where the bus station might be, but if she could reach Tiny, he'd make certain she got there. Somehow, Carly decided, she was going to get home today and leave for Mexico tomorrow. She hadn't come this far to find her sister just to stop. Therese was in Mexico, and once Carly had her passport in hand she was going after her.

And Ellis will have a fit, she thought, feeling a little scared. But she had to go, no matter how Ellis reacted to her leaving again. Maybe he'd think Therese was just lazing around some resort in

Mexico and that would be that—she hoped.

Spotting a small convenience store, Carly briskly quickened her pace. She was practically jogging by the time she reached the solid glass door and pushed it open. A small, strange-looking man stopped dusting the tops of canned goods and grinned at her.

"How you doing?" he asked, bobbing his head up and down.

Carly caught herself nodding back and stopped. "Fine. I was looking for a pay phone and a telephone book."

"Ahhh, this way, please." He gestured with a pink feather duster. From behind the counter he handed Carly the inch-thick book and pointed her toward the back of the store.

In no time at all she was ringing the cab service phone number. "Hello," she said when a gruff voice answered. "Is Tiny in, please?"

"He don't work til this evenin'."

"Could you give me his home number? This is sort of an emergency. You see, last night he . . ."

"You must be the little lady he was talkin' 'bout."

"Yes. Yes, I am. Is there any way you can reach him and send him after me?"

"Yeah. Just tell me where you are."

Carly had to ask the clerk the address, but when she hung up she felt considerably better. She returned the phone book to the clerk, then paced up and down the aisle as she waited for Tiny to arrive.

From her place in the store Carly could see the yacht basin and sighed tiredly. What was she going to do about the yacht? She couldn't just leave it there, but there was no way she was going back for it either. It would simply have to wait until she reached Beaumont; then she'd see what she could do about having it moved.

A horn blared, rudely interrupting her thoughts. Carly spun around to see who was making the noise. A smile came to her lips as she saw Tiny's big form perched behind the wheel of a rusty Toyota that tilted dangerously toward the driver's side. She waved at him, then hastily left the store and started for the passenger side of his car.

"Wait a minute, little lady," Tiny said, swinging his door open. Carly stopped in her tracks, puzzled. Had she been wrong in calling him? Had he changed his mind about helping her?

"Ya gotta get in on this side. That door don't open."

Carly sighed. "Tiny, right now I'd ride on the hood if that's what it would take to get me out of here."

He laughed and stepped out. "You'd make a mighty fine hood ornament too. 'Specially on this old clunker."

"Why didn't you bring a cab?" she asked as she crawled in and over one bucket seat to get to the other.

"That'd have been a waste of time," he said as he took his seat again. "After last night I knew better'n to give you a chance to stop and think."

"I'm not that bad," Carly said, laughing.

"Naw? Could've fooled me. How ya feelin' this mornin'? I was worried 'bout ya last night."

Carly stared out the window. "I'm fine," she said, wishing it were true. "Tiny, I've got to catch a bus to Beaumont. Can you take me to the station?"

He nodded and cranked the motor. The fumes from the exhaust burned Carly's eyes. "Are ya in trouble?"

"No. I just have to get home as quickly as I can."

"I'll have ya there in a jiffy."

Feeling sadness creep up on her, Carly turned her face away from Tiny and swallowed. It hurt to think that Tanner had deceived her. The memory of his smile, his easy touch, his kisses flooded her mind. He'd seemed so sincere. But it had meant nothing to him. She took a deep breath, attempting to block out her thoughts. She couldn't afford to dwell on that now. But her heart overruled her head and the thoughts rushed back in. Tanner had gotten too close to her, and she had allowed herself to feel too much too soon. She just hadn't realized it until the damage was done. Dammit, she felt humiliated.

Her train of thought changed abruptly. Maybe she had been too hasty. Maybe she should go back and hit him with the truth. Maybe he *had* come to care for her.

Stop it Carly! He was doing his job, his duty, and it made her sick. How many woman had fallen for him before she had? How many more would follow her? Carly rubbed the back of her neck. She had made a decision, and she was going to stick it out. Tanner Barnes was a hard lesson learned, and it was over. But it still hurt.

Tiny turned down a busy street and parked at the corner.

"We're here," he said, pointing at the bus station across the street. He climbed out of the car with Carly right behind him; then he stood on the curb, scratching his grizzled head. "I ain't gonna ask ya where your luggage is, but I do wanna know if ya got enough money to make it home?"

"Yes, I'll be fine."

"I just wanted to make sure. Come on." He took her by the arm and led her to the ticket office, standing with her as she made all the arrangements.

"You're pretty lucky, you know that?" he said when she was finished and had her ticket in her hand.

"How's that?" she asked, slipping the ticket into her purse.

"Anybody else would've had to wait a couple of hours to get a bus, but you just waltz right up there and get one right off the bat."

"I still have to wait twenty minutes."

"Big deal."

"That gives me time to buy you a cup of coffee —to make up for the one I dropped last night."

"Save your nickels. This one's on me."

Carly tried to argue with him, but Tiny was adamant as he led her to the small coffee shop inside the depot.

"Tiny, will you do me a big favor?" she asked after they were seated.

He gave her that gummy grin she found so endearing. "Do you even hafta ask?"

"The man who came to the hospital last night . . . if he calls you . . . will you tell him you haven't heard from me?"

Tiny folded his hands together on the table. "If it means that much to ya, I won't say a word."

"It does."

"Then my lips are sealed."

They talked idly as they enjoyed their coffee, then Tiny looked at his watch and shoved his chair back. "It's 'bout that time."

"Yeah, I guess it is," Carly agreed.

Tiny followed her to the door of the big bus. "Take care, little lady. I don't know what ya got yourself into, but it's a big, bad world out there, and people ain't as good as they usta be."

"I will. Tiny, you'll never know just how much I owe you."

"Not a damn thing. Now get your butt on this bus and take care. I'll be seeing ya again. You can bet on it."

Carly didn't look back until she was seated. Tiny was still there, leaning against one of the posts. Other passengers boarded the bus after her, and before the minute hand had passed the hour mark Carly was on her way. Through the tinted glass window she waved.

"*. . . Crockett! Come in, this is the Alamo . . .*"

Tanner smiled as he looked at the radio. For once it would be a pleasure to answer the summons, because he knew it would probably be his last. If he only knew where Carly had gone he would be able to sit back and enjoy what he hoped was the end of a not-so-great working relationship.

He lifted the mike. "Crockett here."

"About time!"

Tanner bit his lip to keep from laughing. "A man can only walk so fast, Alamo; you should know that. What's up?"

The line was nice and clear. "I hope you have your suitcase packed, Mr. Stewart," Omi said. Tanner's smile vanished and he stiffened, anticipating a problem the moment he heard Omi use that alias.

"You're needed in Mexico."

"Like hell!" Tanner squeezed the mike until his fingertips were white.

"You're not finished until this mess is cleared up." Omi spoke with authority. "We have a real problem, and you're the only man I have who can handle it."

Tanner pulled at his earlobe and frowned. Was he never to be free? "What the hell happened?" he asked.

"Therese's cover was blown. Her contact, a man named Rodrigo, called us this morning. He was in a panic. Therese was taken by several men."

"What about the *Federales*?" Tanner's muscles tightened in anticipation of the answer.

"Crooked bunch of . . ." Omi broke off. "Everything happened before the designated time for the deal to go down. We can't hold them responsible. Someone turned on Therese. Rodrigo thinks he knows where she's being held, but frankly I think he's going to bolt if one of us doesn't get to him soon."

"Which brings you to me," Tanner replied.

"Exactly. I want Therese returned safely to my office. Get her out of there any way you can."

"What about the deal?"

"It's aborted as of now."

"Where do you think the leak is?" Tanner asked, closing his eyes.

"Therese is the only one who knows."

Great, Tanner thought. It was bad enough stepping in the situation as it was, but it was even worse with the added problem of not knowing whom to trust.

"What are my orders?" he asked.

"I've chartered a small plane. It'll be waiting

for you at the local airstrip. I'll see you in my office this evening. Be prepared to fly out of here tonight."

"I have a slight problem," Tanner informed Omi. "Baby sister has flown the coop."

"Cornwall can handle her. You get your butt to the airstrip."

Omi signed off. Tanner remained unmoving for a few moments, wondering what in hell to do about Carly. He'd looked everywhere for her. At the Coast Guard base the shift had changed, and the new guards hadn't seen her. He'd checked with the hospital, but there had been no sign of her. She hadn't even contacted the police station. A knot formed in Tanner's stomach. Had she come to any harm? Had her snooping landed her in the hands of the characters who had dealt with Lisa?

Damn! He couldn't leave without knowing. He glanced at his watch. It was still early. If he hurried he could make a few last-minute attempts to find her.

Tanner went to Hank's room. "Wake up, buddy," he said, kneeling beside the bunk.

Hank peered at him with bloodshot eyes and mumbled, "This better be good."

"I'll make it short. I have to fly to headquarters within the next two hours. Therese is in trouble. I don't know how bad it is yet, but if you can manage to throw my things into a duffle bag, I'll be back in time to pick it up and leave on schedule.

Meanwhile, listen for Omi."

Hank rubbed his hand over his face so that his black hair fell over his forehead. "Where're you going?"

Tanner was already at the door. "To find Carly."

Tanner listened to the telephone operator relay the cab service's number, then disconnected the line and dialed it. A brusque voice answered on the second ring.

"I want to speak to Tiny," Tanner said.

"He called in sick."

"You get him for me," Tanner said, "and there'll be an extra hundred on your totals tonight."

"Damn. Tiny musta sure done well last night. This is the second time today somebody's wanted him."

Tanner paused, sensing his search was nearly over. "Was the other caller a woman?"

"Yep. Same one he helped last night."

"And did Tiny pick her up today?"

"Far as I know."

"What time was that?"

"Looky here, man. I probably told you too much already. If you wanna know anythin' else you're gonna hafta ask Tiny."

"Fine. How can I reach him?"

"Give me your number. I'll have him call you back."

"Never mind that. You have him meet me at the yacht basin where he let me off last night. He'll know who you're talking about."

Tanner hung up and studied the storeroom where Carly had been parking her bike. He had checked it once; might she have returned since then? He walked over to the whitewashed shed and pressed against the door. It opened when he twisted the knob; it had been locked earlier.

She had been there all right. And there was no telling where she'd gone or how long it had been since she'd left.

"Damn her," he swore under his breath. Didn't she realize she could be walking into trouble? He went into the storeroom and looked around. All he encountered were the horrible heat and cob webs. Why had she returned and then left again? Why hadn't she come to him? Tanner chewed on his inner lip and answered his own questions. She must have seen Cornwall here at the basin. His presence again so soon and so close must have sent her running.

All he could do now was wait for Tiny. He knew the cabbie held all the answers, if Tanner could just get him to own up to them. Tanner walked back to the parking lot and sat on a short piling, wishing Tiny would hurry.

After thirty minutes had passed, Tanner called the cab service and reached the same man again.

"What's keeping Tiny?" he asked.

"I had to track him down."

"But you did get him?"

"Yep. He should be comin' your way any minute."

"Thanks, man." Tanner hung up the phone and leaned against a pole. Just as he lit a cigarette, he spotted Tiny coasting into the parking lot in a beat-up Toyota.

Tiny pulled up beside him, creating a cloud of white dust and exhaust fumes. "How's it goin', man?"

Tanner waved his hand through the air. "That depends," he said, leaning his forearms against the top of Tiny's car. "Where'd you take Carly?"

"Huh?" Tiny tried to look surprised, but failed miserably.

"Carly. Where is she?"

"Carky who?"

Tanner leaned his head back, then forward again. He rubbed his cheek, feeling the growth of whiskers he hadn't had time to shave. "Tiny, I'm sure *Carly* asked you not to tell anyone where she is, but I have to find her."

Tiny stared at Tanner with earnest brown eyes. "I can't tell you, man." He shifted his car into gear but was halted by Tanner's firm grip on his beefy wrist.

"Dammit, Tiny, she may be in danger. There are men on this island who'd burn her in a second if they knew she was here."

197

Tiny put the engine in neutral. "I like you, man. But all I'm goin' to tell you is this; she's all right."

"Where is she?"

Tiny glanced at the hand cuffing his wrist. "She ain't on the island no more. And as far as I know she ain't comin' back none too soon neither."

"I have to know when she left."

"This mornin'. She left this mornin'. I promise ya she's okay."

Tanner released his grip. He could push Tiny further, even reveal who he was, but he didn't want to do that. Tiny had given him enough information, and he was going to let him leave it at that.

"I guess I'll have to take your word for it then. But do me a favor, will you? If Carly should return and contact you, get her the hell off this island. And if she won't go, tie her up and keep her until I contact you. It could mean her life."

Tiny nodded. "Like I told her, I don't know what ya'll are mixed up in, but whatever it is you can bet I'll take care of her. I gotta run. If you need me anymore, just call like you did."

"I'll be gone for a few days. I'll check in with you when I get back." Tanner stepped back and waved Tiny away. He had a hunch he knew where Carly had gone. Once more he went to the phone and, pulling out another number from his wallet, he dialed the operator.

Carly let herself in the front door of her home, wondering if she had half a chance of making it up the stairs and into her room without being detected. She closed the door softly and stood in the large entry hall, taking a moment just to absorb the comfort of being home. Had she only been gone a few days? It seemed as if a month had passed. She glanced at the large oval mirror that had hung on the wall for as long as she could remember and grimaced at the sight. Her skin was darker than it had been. The dry, cracked skin around her nose was going to peel. Dusty blotches stained the area beneath her eyes. She lifted her hand to her hair, trying to remember when she'd last had it styled. Then she decided it didn't matter. There was no one who really cared what she looked like and no one she cared to impress. Not anymore.

Wearily she tiptoed up the stairs and went directly to her room, relieved that she'd made it that far without having to give a lengthy explanation to Ellis, an explanation she still wasn't certain how to present.

The queen-size bed, covered with a light peach comforter, looked like heaven. She wanted nothing more than to fall across it and sleep for hours. But she couldn't. Everything had to be taken care of this afternoon so she could be on her way to Mexico by tomorrow. Stripping off her clothing, she dropped it carelessly on the plush beige carpet and entered her bathroom. For the next fifteen minutes she planned on doing nothing but letting the shower spray against her aching head.

Thirty minutes later Carly felt much better. Dressed in a cool pink-and-white sundress, she clipped on pink earrings and went to the closet for a pair of shoes. Selecting white sandals, she sat on the edge of the bed and lifted her foot, putting on one of the sandals but pausing before donning the other.

If only things were settled with Ellis, she'd almost feel excited about going after Therese, she thought. But Ellis was going to want to know everything that had happened in Galveston, and Carly still hadn't decided what she was and wasn't going to tell him. For a split second she almost felt it was her father instead of her brother she was about to face. She knew if Ellis learned of Lisa Curtis's death, he wouldn't let Carly out of his sight. She didn't want to run out on him again, but if he reacted the way she anticipated she wouldn't have any choice.

She stared blankly into space. She didn't like the scene that rose in her mind of Ellis sitting in a wheelchair, angry. She didn't like the image because it mocked everything Ellis had ever been to her. She blinked, and her mind snapped back to the present. If she could just have a few moments alone with him and approach him with the right attitude, then . . .

"Have a nice trip?"

Carly looked up to see Ellis's therapist standing in the partially open doorway. She was immediately put off by Tina King's snide tone.

"Don't you know how to knock?" was Carly's reply.

Tina stepped into the room, closing the door behind her. Carly could feel her facial muscles tensing.

"Obviously not," Carly answered her own question. Heaving an exaggerated sigh, Carly stood up. "What do you want, Tina?"

"Just your promise to stick around. You have no idea how traumatic it was for your brother to sit in this house and worry about you."

"Gee, that's really too bad. But the last time I looked, Ellis was a great big thirty-eight-year-old man. Maybe it's time he faced the fact that life goes on. There *is* a world beyond the four walls of this house, you know?"

"He's not ready for that yet."

"He's not? Or you're not?" Carly folded her arms across her chest. "It's been months since the accident. Jameson Steel needs him back. There's no reason he couldn't return on a part-time basis. More than likely it would be the best thing in the world for him. Why are you so dead set against it?"

Red stains blotched Tina's cheeks. "I'm not dead set against anything! I'm giving you my professional opinion. Your brother not only lost the use of the lower half of his body, he's lost his father!

The company he loved so is falling apart right before his eyes. . . ."

"Then push him into trying to save it."

"You still have no idea how much he has suffered," Tina stated, lifting her bright red hair behind her shoulder.

Before she knew it Carly was only inches from Tina's face. "I know this much. I think you and your so-called professionalism stink. And I have a mind to call another agency just to see what they think of your way of handling things. Maybe you're not all you claim to be. Maybe you want to delay his progress because you enjoy living here. Is that it, Tina?" Carly paused a moment, then added in a softer yet emphatic tone, "I can't imagine anyone in your field not wanting Ellis to become involved in something that would take his mind off all he has lost. Can you?"

"It would be a major setback if you fired me now."

"For whom?" Carly asked as she walked past Tina and out the door. With her back straight Carly descended the steps, silently fuming that she had allowed Tina to get to her. She had never liked Tina. The two women had struck sparks from each other from the first time Ellis's doctor had introduced them. But they'd always kept their feelings under control before this. Or maybe it was simply that Carly had never really stood up to Tina until now.

As Carly's foot touched the bottom step, she

stopped, hearing the whine of her brother's wheel-chair.

"Tina?" Ellis called out.

Damn, Carly thought, taking a step backward and moving against the wall. She wasn't prepared to face him yet. All during the bus ride home she'd tried to decide what she was going to tell him, but . . . Tanner, Hank, Therese—they'd all kept intruding on her thoughts. She'd had so much on her mind. And now Tina had upset her to the point where all she could think of was getting away from her.

"Tina!" he shouted again. She frowned as she heard the wheelchair nearing. He was definitely in a foul mood, Carly thought, steeling herself to face him. But suddenly the chair stopped.

"To hell with her," she heard her brother grumble. In a moment the chair started again, but he must have turned and gone back the way he had come, for the sound became fainter instead of growing louder.

Carly's shoulders slumped in relief. She pivoted on the ball of her foot, intending to go back for her purse. She needed a little more time to decide how much she was going to tell Ellis. But as she turned she saw Tina standing at the top of the stairs.

"Change your mind?" Tina said in a voice just loud enough for Carly to hear.

Carly ignored her as she climbed the stairs and

passed her. In her room she retrieved her car keys and purse, then left again. Tina was waiting for her at the bottom of the stairs; her arm was casually propped on the banister. Carly hadn't intended to speak to her, but the look in Tina's light blue eyes caught her attention. It was a look that Carly could have sworn said Tina knew everything that Carly had been involved in, a look that said Tina would use it all against her if pushed. Carly blinked and Tina smiled, a sly smile that barely lifted the corners of her thin mouth.

"Going somewhere?" Tina asked as Carly brushed by her.

Carly opened the door, then stopped. She looked over her shoulder and smiled back at Tina, who was visibly unsettled at the abrupt change in Carly's once meek demeanor.

"Bitch," Carly mouthed through the grin and closed the door behind her. Her smile grew wider as she rounded the house and went to the garage. From her expression, it was obvious Tina had read her lips extremely well.

CHAPTER TEN

A s Carly drove down the quiet streets of
Beaumont, she tried to decide what she
should do. Nothing, absolutely nothing,
was going to keep her from going after Therese.
Regardless of how hot—as she remembered Hank
saying—it was in Mexico, Carly had to try to reach
her sister. She hadn't even seen Ellis yet, but from
the sound of his voice she knew he was definitely
not improving—at least, not mentally. If only he'd
make an effort to become involved in Jameson
Steel again. Carly knew he could pull strings she
was helpless to reach. He had the clout to call in
favors. Ellis knew the ins and outs of the steel
industry better than anyone in the area. Why was he
avoiding it?

Did he feel guilty about their father's death?

Carly braked at a red light and gripped the
wheel. Ellis had been driving the night of the
accident, but it wouldn't have made any difference

if their father had been behind the wheel. The truck driver had been at fault. He had lost his life too. Didn't Ellis realize yet how lucky he was to still be alive, what a miracle it had been that he survived the impact?

Pressing on the gas pedal, Carly moved with the light traffic. Time was running out. Even if she did manage to bring Therese home, Carly wondered whether it would be too late to save the failing business. They had lost so many important bids she was afraid it would now take a miracle to pull the company out of the hole. If something wasn't done soon they would be lucky even to remain a part of the company her father and brother had not only owned but ruled as well. How could Ellis allow Jameson Steel to wither away, to fall further and further into debt without lifting a finger to try and save it? Maybe she was being a fool, Carly thought. Maybe she *should* allow the company to fold, leaving Ellis to live his life the way he seemed to wish. But it wasn't in her nature to give up that easily. If she truly believed Ellis was finished as an executive in the steel industry she would force herself to give in gracefully, but she wasn't convinced that was so. Ellis simply needed a good, solid push. Perhaps if he were threatened with the possibility of Therese taking over . . . ?

Carly sailed through an amber caution light, not quite beating it as it turned red. Looking into her rearview mirror, she waited to see if a patrol car was anywhere around, then sighed. She had to keep her mind on her driving.

Instead of going to the steelworks to check things out, Carly found herself pulling into the parking lot of the travel agency her family had always used. She sat for a moment thinking. Orizaba? She hoped that was the correct name of the town or village or place where Therese was supposed to be. She had been so rattled when she'd heard the name she wasn't sure if she'd caught it properly. Well, she thought as she opened the car door and climbed out, there was only one way to find out.

Orizaba was near an inactive volcano of the same name. The perfect place for Therese, Carly thought wryly as she clutched the travel pamphlets and ticket in her hand and walked back to her car. The volcano was the highest point in Mexico. Well, where else would Therese be?

Her thoughts became more serious as she climbed back behind the wheel of her red Corvette and started the engine. Orizaba was also a large city, popular with tourists, in the state of Veracruz. Carly frowned, wondering how easy it would be to find Therese in such a place. Carly had assumed Orizaba was a small village, with no running water and small huts scattered about. After all, weren't most of the trouble spots in Mexico in the less populated areas? She never dreamed it would be smack in the middle of such a highly industrialized area. By the time the travel agent had finished her spiel, Carly knew every plantation, fiesta, and orchard that thrived there. How was she ever going to find Therese, especially if Therese didn't want to be found?

Carly jerked the car into reverse and spun out of the parking space. The tires squealed as she threw the gear into first and sped into traffic. Dammit, she was going to find Therese if it was the last thing she ever did! Her sister might have had the best explanation in the world for keeping her life a secret from her family, but nothing was going to stop Carly from finding her and bringing her home —even if she had to drag Therese by the hair all the way. And Carly would make Therese stay long enough to get their family crisis settled and ironed out. By damn, Therese owed Ellis that much! No matter what, he'd always defended her against their father's anger and threats. In many ways Therese and Ellis had been the closest of the three siblings. They had clung together when their mother died; Carly had been so young she scarcely remembered anything but clutching her doll and sucking her thumb.

What an odd thing to recall, she thought, letting the vague memory play on. She remembered people crying, a few women trying to hold her, but all she wanted was her doll, Ellis, and Therese. And both had shunned her in their grief. She remembered standing next to her father's chair, then Father picking her up and squeezing her tightly, barking at the two older children for treating their baby sister so badly. And that was all she recalled, other than a few dim memories of the funeral.

The bad feelings had begun that far back, Carly realized. Even in the face of such tragedy, their father had expected the two older children to be strong. Carly began to see more and more why Therese had stayed away.

But Ellis had weathered it all. And he deserved to have the company he had worked so hard to make successful. Therese might harbor her anger at their father the rest of her life, but for Ellis's sake she would have to swallow her pride and come home. Carly knew that much at least about Therese. She also knew that when Therese discovered her father was dead, it was going to be a hard blow, regardless of how hostile the feelings between them had once been.

Why did life have to take so many dips and swirls? Fatigue crept up on Carly. The more problems she untangled the worse it became, new snarls and knots appearing every step of the way. She wondered if this part of her life would ever be resolved, if she would ever be allowed to move on to something else. She turned a corner and stopped.

What she really wanted was to level with Ellis. Tell him the truth from beginning to end, regardless of how badly he handled it. But she didn't know if what Tina had said was true. And she didn't have time to make inquiries of other therapists. She had to reach Therese before her wayward sister moved on.

Carly realized she was going to have to tell Ellis the basic facts—that even though she'd never met with Lisa Curtis, Carly had found a friend of Therese's—she wouldn't mention Tanner Barnes' name—who had told her that Therese was in Mexico. And Ellis would have to accept that. With her mind made up, Carly once again put the car in gear. She was scheduled to fly out of Jefferson County Airport at eight o'clock in the morning. And if Lisa's death made the *Beaumont Enterprise,* well, Carly planned to be long gone before Ellis had time to read the daily news.

Carly drove straight to Jameson Steel and pulled into the parking space reserved for her brother. When she entered the office building she smiled at Ann Gordon, the receptionist.

"Miss Jameson—I didn't expect to see you back so soon."

"I wrapped things up quicker than I'd anticipated. Is Jackie busy?"

Ann shook her head. "He's just going over the

monthly report."

Carly asked Ann a few questions about what had happened while she was away and wasn't surprised at the response. The small amount of work they had left was quickly diminishing. Carly refrained from sighing, but in her mind she knew that going to Mexico was the only recourse left. Ann's news simply reaffirmed her plans. She knocked on Jackie's door and entered at his muffled reply.

The gray-haired man widened his eyes on seeing her. He stood up and walked around his desk to embrace her gently. "You're back awfully soon." She heard the question in his voice.

"Therese is in Mexico, Jackie."

He looked immensely relieved. "For a minute there I thought, well . . ." He cleared his throat. "When will she be home?"

"I have to go after her." Before he could say anything, Carly held up her hand. "Please don't ask me to explain."

"Is she in trouble?" Carly knew how much Jackie loved the Jameson children and that he was more than a little concerned.

"No. She's in a remote area and can't be reached easily." Carly smiled weakly. "I'll have her home in a few days."

Stepping around Jackie, Carly went to stare at the nearly vacant steelworks through the large window behind his desk. A few of the old-timers, her father's friends, could be seen walking around, occasionally stooping to make a minor repair but mostly whiling the time away until the shift was over. It looked so sad. Carly could easily see the yard as it had been in its heyday, just a few years before. Now it was a desolate, depressing sight.

"Jackie, I left the yacht moored in Galveston. Will you take care of it, see that it gets back to our dock?" she asked, continuing to eye the grounds.

Carly heard Jackie sigh before he said, "Of course."

"I've decided to sell my car." She wrapped her arms around her waist and turned to face him. She was surprised by his lack of reaction. "It's the only thing I own that I can sell without having Daddy's attorneys breathing down my back."

"Ellis gave you that car."

"I know. But I have to have some money."

"I have plenty of . . ."

"I appreciate the offer, but I want to sell my car. Can you set it up today."

"That's awfully short notice. Can't it wait until tomorrow?"

She shook her head. "I'll be gone before the bank opens in the morning. I think the title is here in Father's safe." She stared pensively at him. "I need this done as soon as possible, Jackie."

He paused, as if wanting to say more, then

relented. "Let me make a few calls."

Carly opened the door to Jackie's car but didn't get out. Thanks to him the Corvette had been sold, the money placed in Carly's account, and all the details finalized.

"If things go well," Carly said, "all our troubles will soon be over."

Jackie reached for her hand. "Carly, I hope you realize that even with Therese back, it'll be a long time before things are straightened out, if ever."

"I know, but at least we'll have a chance of pulling through."

"If only Ellis . . ."

"As soon as I get back Ellis is going to shape up and Tina King is going to ship out. That I promise you."

Carly leaned over and kissed the older man on the cheek, then left the car. Determination filled her soul as she walked into the house. It seemed deathly quiet in the hall. She walked into the den, hoping Ellis was there, but found an empty room. He had to be in his bedroom, Carly thought, going directly to the downstairs room she had furnished for him after his accident.

Before she entered Ellis's room, Carly stopped and peeked into the one Tina was using. She wasn't there. The last thing Carly wanted was Tina

213

walking in while she was talking to Ellis. The house was so quiet Carly was beginning to believe everyone had gone. Stepping across the hall she knocked on Ellis's door. When no one answered, she pushed the door open and she saw her brother sitting in his chair with his back to her. Carly was certain he'd heard her enter, yet he made no move to see who was there.

"Hi," she said softly, placing her hand on his shoulder. His thick blond hair brushed her fingers. It was much longer than he'd ever worn it, she thought as she walked around the wheelchair and sat on a stool near his feet. He still looked terribly ill, she thought, seeing the unhealthy yellow cast of his skin.

"Carly," he answered, turning light blue eyes on her.

Somewhat cool and reserved, Ellis didn't hit her with the barrage of questions she'd expected. He remained quiet, as if he really didn't care to go into any details with her.

Carly didn't know how to break the ice. They had so much to discuss, yet he was making her feel . . . uncomfortable.

"How have you been?" she asked, aware that the question sounded inane. But she truly wanted to know how he'd done without her there.

"Fine."

"Good." She crossed her legs, adjusting the

skirt over her knees, then shoved the stool back a bit. Staring up at him, she noticed how slumped his shoulders were and that he hadn't yet gained back any of the weight he'd lost. She smiled at him. "I have some good news. I know where Therese is."

"Really?" He quirked his brow but made no move to further question her.

Carly made herself smile. "You'll never guess." Boy, was that an understatement. "She's on a volcano in Mexico."

"No kidding?" He drummed his fingers on his thigh.

Carly bristled. "All you can say is 'no kidding'?" She leaned forward again, placing her hand over his. "What's wrong with you?"

He looked blankly at her. "Nothing. So Therese is on a volcano in Mexico. That sounds like a good place for her."

"I'm not hearing correctly," she said out loud but more to herself than to Ellis. "This isn't the same brother who nearly had a fit when I took the yacht to Galveston." She looked at him. "Ellis, something *is* wrong. What is it?" Carly blinked. He wasn't paying any attention to her. "Are you in pain?"

"No," he said sharply, then sighed. "I'm sorry. Nothing's wrong. I guess I've finally realized that you're not a little girl anymore and that you have the right to do as you wish. But"—he smiled sadly

—"that doesn't keep me from worrying about you."

"Oh, Ellis," she said, reaching up and caressing his cheek. "You don't have to worry. Everything is going to work out just fine. You'll see."

He took her hand and kissed her palm. "Now tell me what volcano our beloved sister is on."

Carly sat back. "Orizaba. Well, actually she isn't really on the volcano itself; she's in the city of Orizaba. And the volcano is inactive. But that's rather exciting, isn't it?"

"It may be inactive now, but give Therese a chance. If anyone can stir up old rocks and ashes, I'm sure it's her."

"Ellis, really." Carly rolled her eyes and laughed.

He shrugged but had a grin on his face. It had been so long since she'd heard his dry wit.

"So when is she coming home?" he asked, some of the dullness leaving his blue eyes.

The smile left her face. "She isn't." She rushed on before he could draw his own conclusions. "What I mean is she doesn't know . . . *I* don't know how to reach her."

Ellis's eyebrows drew together, forming a light brown line across his brow. "You know where she is, but you don't know how to reach her," he repeated.

Carly nodded. "I know she's in Orizaba, but I

don't know where she's staying. That's why—and I know you probably aren't going to like this—that's why I'm flying to Mexico in the morning."

"Wait a minute. Why do you have to fly to Mexico? Why can't you just get on the phone and make a few inquiries? The Mexican government can surely find her and inform her that there's been a death in the family."

Carly gnawed anxiously on her bottom lip. Why hadn't she thought about that?

She cleared her throat. "I could do that, but wh . . . wh . . ." But what?

"Having a nice chat?" Brother and sister both turned at the intrusion. Tina King stood just inside the door.

"How was your trip, Carly?" Tina asked, having the gall to act as if this was were the first time she's seen Carly since her return.

"Short," Carly answered flatly.

Ellis looked strangely at his sister. "Carly was just telling me that she knows where Therese is."

"Really? How wonderful." Tina walked toward Ellis's bed and sat down. "Well, tell me everything. Where is she? When is she coming home? I can't wait to meet her."

I'll just bet you can't, Carly thought, then stood up. She had no intention of telling Tina anything. "I'll let Ellis fill you in."

Ellis reached for Carly's hand and pulled her

back. "How can I tell her when I still haven't been told everything?"

"There isn't much more to tell," Carly responded.

"I disagree. You haven't told me how your meeting with Ms. Curtis went." He was beginning to react the way she had originally anticipated.

"Ellis . . ." The phone rang, cutting her off. Taking a deep breath, she pulled away from her brother and moved to answer it.

"Hello, Jameson residence." There was no answer. "Hello. Is anybody there?"

The phone clicked; the dial tone hummed in her ear. "Well," Carly said, holding the receiver away from her ear and staring at it. "They hung up. How rude." She looked at her brother and put the phone down, wondering briefly who it had been. But her mind was becoming aware that this was the perfect time to make her excuses and leave. "I'd love to sit and visit some more, but I have some errands to take care of. I'll see you at dinner."

"Carly!"

She stopped at the door and turned to face him. "I'll see you at dinner," she repeated.

Tanner hung up the phone and leaned against the post. *So she's gone home,* he thought, relieved. That had definitely been her voice on the other end of the line. Now he could carry out the remainder of his duties without worrying about her. Carly was at home, under the watchful eyes of Tina King, and he knew Tina would keep close tabs on the Jameson family until notified otherwise.

Thoughtfully, he walked back to the yacht, wishing he'd had the chance to tell Carly the truth, since he imagined she was thinking the very worst. The sad thing was that so much of the worst was true.

In her room, Carly pulled out a suitcase and began to pack. No matter what Ellis had so say, she was going to Mexico in the morning. Even if she had to leave him mouth agape, without an explanation, she was going! Opening a drawer, she lifted out some undergarments and tossed them into the bottom of the case. Moving to the closet she jerked down several outfits and began rolling them into a ball; then she stopped herself.

She sat down on the bed and looked at the mess she had made in the suitcase. She wasn't leaving until morning; there was no reason to be in such a hurry now. She was agitated and knew she had to calm down. Smoothing out a pair of pants, she folded them neatly and set them aside. She wasn't even certain what to pack. It would be extremely hot in Mexico, of that she was sure, but did she need to dress clothes or jeans?

A chill of apprehension touched her and she

rubbed her arms, wondering with what type of people Therese was associating in Mexico. If they were anything like the people at the Diamond Lounge, she knew she'd best be prepared. Could she be walking into danger? she wondered. An image of the drowned woman came to mind, and Carly pushed herself off the bed and went to stand near her bedroom window. If she could just go to Mexico, find her sister, and return, she'd be extremely lucky. But if Therese was deeply involved in some sort of conspiracy or investigation, whatever people did in those situations, Carly knew she could be placing herself as well as Thesese in danger.

With the back of her hand she brushed aside the curtain and glanced at the backyard. For twenty-five year she'd lived in this house, had been safe and secure here. She'd had problems, a soured affair being the worst one she'd ever faced, but nothing came close to what she was going through now. Therese could obviously take care of herself, but her occupation was risky. What if Carly stumbled onto her at a critical point in her assignment? What if Carly ended up placing Therese in jeopardy?

Carly dropped her hand and the curtain fell back in place. She had to be careful. Finding Therese was not going to be easy. But Carly was going to do it! She refused to allow the less appealing aspects of the situation affect her decision.

"So, tell me, Ellis, what did Carly discover?" Tina King remained on his bed, her feet dangling over the side. The ringing of the phone had bothered her; could it have been Omi, or Tanner? Whoever had been on the phone would just have to wait. Until she knew exactly what Carly had learned, she couldn't relay any news.

Carly's arrival had been a complete surprise. Tanner was supposed to have kept her occupied for the next few weeks. Why had he failed? Tina did her best to keep from grinning smugly. Perhaps Romeo didn't have what it took to interest Miss Carly. What a shame. Also, Tina would have loved seeing Carly taken down a peg or two, especially after the way she had snipped at Tina earlier. Tina hated to admit it, but it looked as if Carly was finally growing a spine.

"Ellis, what did Carly find out?" Tina asked again, exasperation coloring her words.

Ellis turned the chair slowly. "I'm not sure," he replied, rubbing his brow.

"Not sure? Oh, come on, you just got through saying she knew where your sister was."

"Somewhere in Mexico," he answered, not really paying any attention to her.

"That's all Carly knows?" Tina asked in

disbelief.

"Yes." He narrowed his eyes and stared at her. It made her nervous, that way he had of silently studying her. She and Ellis had had their rounds with each other, and sometimes he even made her think twice before she pushed him. But she always stood her ground. In fact, she reveled in their disagreements, for if she couldn't put Therese in her place, then at least she could get to her brother and her baby sister, Carly.

Tina had clashed with Ellis's beautiful blonde sister from the first day she had begun to work for the organization. She hated the way Therese was treated like a princess by most of their male co-workers. *She* wanted to be the one of whom they thought so highly. *She* wanted their adoration, their respect. She'd worked and trained as hard as anyone for her position, and still she got stuck with the boring jobs, like baby-sitting this cripple. Granted, she *was* a therapist, and a good one. But that career had lost its appeal long ago. She had given it up in the hope of going places that were exciting, of becoming embroiled in special missions. Sitting here was not what she'd had in mind seven years ago when she'd started her training.

How did Therese always manage to be the chosen one? She'd only been in action one year longer than Tina.

Tina looked at Ellis. He was as handsome as

Therese was beautiful. Both were blue eyed blonds. Ellis was tall and slender, but his frame was muscular. She knew after the first few weeks of working with him that he'd pull out of his despondency and anger. He'd make it because he had the same strong will Therese had. At times he still believed his therapy was futile, but Tina had seen patients with much less strength of character come through to make a new life for themselves. And Ellis would too, just because he was stubborn enough to prove that he could.

If she could just prevent Carly from encouraging him to return to light duty at Jameson Steel, she'd be happy. A slight delay wasn't really going to affect his recovery one way or the other, but it would make things much rougher on Therese when she finally came home. And Tina felt Carly had just been too high and mighty with her. All three Jamesons had had things too easy. It was time they lived in the real world. Again Tina had to keep from smiling. Jameson Steel was suffering, but that was good. It would give Therese something to do once she returned. And maybe, just maybe, it would give Tina a chance to get the next major assignment.

"Are you still with me?" Ellis asked her, jarring her out of her reverie and back to their conversation. His expression hadn't changed.

Tina squirmed slightly. "Of course."

He ran his tongue over the front of his teeth.

Pressing the control on his chair, Ellis steered himself toward the phone. "If you don't mind, I'd like to be left alone now."

"Sure," she said, sliding off the bed. With a puzzled look she left. In the hallway she decided to needle more information out of Carly. She was almost certain the phone call earlier was meant for her, but Tina didn't want to report in until she had more facts. She walked to the bottom of the stairway, then stopped, hesitating only a moment before climbing it.

At the soft knock on the door Carly looked up from her packing. Draping a blouse across the bed, she went to answer the summons, surprised to see Tina on the other side.

Why'd you bother knocking? was the first thing that came to her mind, but she refrained from saying it. "What do you want?" she asked instead.

"May I come in?"

"No."

"Why?"

"Because."

Tina peeked over Carly's shoulder. "Where are you going?"

"What do you want?"

Tina shrugged. Carly sighed.

"This really is pretty silly," Tina said, narrowing her eyes.

"Isn't it."

"Are you going to Mexico?"

"That's none of your business. Now if you'll excuse me . . ." Carly knew it wouldnt' work, but she shut the door in Tina's face anyway. And just as she expected, Tina opened it and came in.

"It really isn't any of my business," Tina said, moving over to Carly's bed and looking at the clothes she was packing. "But I'd like to know where you'll be should Ellis suddenly become ill."

"Then I'll leave *him* a number where *he* can reach me." Carly slammed the suitcase shut, deliberately blocking Tina's sight of her belongings. "Is there anything else?" she asked.

Tina plopped down on Carly's bed. "Carly, I know we aren't exactly bosom buddies, but don't you think you can put the hostility aside where Ellis is concerned?"

"Just what exactly do you want, Tina?" Carly crossed her arms in front of her, tapping her foot angrily. "Is it Ellis you're so worried about, or are you just plain nosey?"

"I resent that," Tina said.

Carly didn't know why she was being so closemouthed with Tina, especially when Tina was going to hear everything at dinner that night anyway. It was just that she hated being pressed into giving an explanation by this woman. But she hated the hassle of trying to make her leave even more, so she relented.

"All right. I am going to Mexico, but I'll only be gone a few days. There. Are you satisfied?"

Tina's only reaction was to blink her eyes. "What part of Mexico?"

"That doesn't matter. I'm not certain where I'll be staying yet, but as soon as I know, I'll call and give you all the details. Now," she said firmly, "will you please leave?"

Tina crawled off the bed and walked to the door. "I hope you know what you're doing," she said, then departed.

Carly stared at the closed door for several moments. What was it about Tina that was getting to her? No, not just getting to her—this was different. Carly, however, couldn't put her finger on what it was.

"There's been a change of plans," Hank said when Tanner entered the galley.

"Already?" Tanner asked, taking a seat across from his friend at the table.

"Omi wants you to fly to Mexico tonight. The plane you were supposed to take to headquarters will now be flying you to Houston. There'll be another flight waiting to take you into Mexico."

"What's the rush?"

"He seems to think Therese may be in real trouble. Her informant has called Omi several times, and each time he sounds even more desperate than before. I've got all the details written down and placed in your files."

"Damn."

"What about Carly?" Hank asked.

"Don't have to worry about her anymore," Tanner responded. "She's hightailed it back to big brother."

"In Beaumont?"

"Yeah," Tanner said quietly.

Hank nodded. "It's best that way. She won't be in your hair anymore."

"Yeah," Tanner agreed.

"And you'll be working with Therese instead of baby sister."

Tanner stood up.

"It's not the bon voyage you'd anticipated, but . . ."

"Can it, Armand." Tanner walked out of the room. In his cabin he stood looking at his duffel bag but not really seeing it. He scratched the back of his head, remembering how he had felt about Carly just a few short days before. Hank had hit too close to the truth. This wasn't the way he had wanted it to end, but it was probably for the best. Perhaps when everything was over Therese would tell Carly the truth about everything, including himself.

Tanner hoisted the bag over his shoulder and grabbed the file Hank had prepared. Taking a last look around, he returned to the galley.

"It won't be the same without you," Tanner said to Hank. This was his last go-around; it would have been nice to finish up with Hank at his side.

"Duty calls." Hank reached across the table. Tanner took his hand and shook it firmly.

"It's been a great fifteen years, Armand," Tanner said quietly.

"The best. I'll miss you, *amigo,*" Hank responded.

"Don't start on the Spanish yet. I'll have enough trouble falling back into it once I get down south."

"I'll see you when you return." Hank was slow coming to his feet, but he followed Tanner up on deck. "Give Consuelo my regards."

Tanner grinned from ear to ear. "If I remember."

As he waved Tanner off, Hank smiled despite the pain it caused his lip. He doubted if Tanner would have much time for Consuelo anyway. He was fairly certain Carly Jameson was going to be occupying most of Tanner's thoughts, whether Tanner wanted her to or not.

CHAPTER ELEVEN

Tanner pulled his denim jacket close against the early morning chill and anxiously tapped his watch, wondering how much longer he'd have to wait until Rodrigo, Therese's informant, appeared. Dammit, he was already twenty minutes late. It wasn't as if Rodrigo had been called on the spur of the moment; the plan for him to meet Tanner here, behind the tobacco warehouses, had been made late the night before. What in the hell could be keeping him?

Cautiously Tanner looked up and down the narrow alley and saw that it was still vacant. He pulled a cigarette from his front pocket, then clamped it between his teeth. Had Rodrigo forgotten, he wondered as he lit the smoke, or had he been stopped before he could reach Tanner?

Tanner drew deeply on the cigarette, then swiftly exhaled. He hated waiting! He was too easily spotted in this area of Mexico. His wheat colored hair was too easily noted, his height and blue eyes uncommon. It was times like this he'd relied on Hank. Hank had been able to move among the people without drawing anyone's attention. Even his missing arm was no problem that way: he wore a prosthesis when necessary. Tanner wished his buddy was with him now. He didn't like the way he felt. Something wasn't right.

Again he looked at his watch. Something was definitely wrong. Tanner ran his hand through his hair; what would he do if Rodrigo failed to show?

Starting at the sound of footsteps rounding the warehouse corner, Tanner quietly ground out the cigarette, then stepped into the doorway behind him. He automatically reached into his jacket and pulled out a pistol, listening intently as the person neared. When the short, squat man walked slowly by, Tanner seized him from behind, swinging him around and against the warehouse wall before he shoved the nose of his pistol into the man's Adam's apple.

Black eyes nearly bulged from their sockets; a hoarse whisper tore from the man's throat. "Señor Stewart?" He arched his head back as far as he could manage, attempting to keep the gun from touching him. But Tanner refused to allow him that relief; the gun stayed exactly where Tanner intended, gouging into the man's fleshy throat.

"My name is Benito. Please señor, remove the

gun, I have no way to harm you."

Benito? Where in hell was Rodrigo? "The gun stays, Benito." Tanner cocked the hammer slowly; the action was calculatingly frightening. His eyes narrowed to slits as he stared down at the man. "Why are you here?"

"Rodrigo. Rodrigo sent me."

Tanner's body was tightly coiled, ready to strike. "Rodrigo?"

"*Sí*. He is frightened. Someone is after him. He can no longer help you."

Tanner slid the barrel up Benito's throat until it was pressed against the underside of his chin. "Where is he?" he asked, his lips barely moving.

"I cannot say, señor. Please, do not kill me."

"I asked you a question. Where is Rodrigo?" he whispered against the man's face.

Benito swallowed. "I do not . . ."

With his free hand, Tanner snatched Benito's collar and twisted it in his fist. Benito closed his eyes, silently moving his mouth as if he were praying for his life.

"I'm going to give you about three seconds to decide which you prefer: tell me where Rodrigo is, or suffer unthinkable pain."

Never releasing his grip, Tanner stuffed the gun back into the harness and pulled out a slick pearl object, not more than four inches long. With the slightest pressure from his thumb a razor-sharp blade slid out and clicked ominously into place. His aim was to find Therese; he didn't care who had to be roughed up along the way.

Benito opened his eyes even wider. Tanner, playing on the fear he saw there, waved the blade back and forth beneath Benito's nose. "It's as sharp on one side as it is on the other."

"Señor, Rodrigo is afraid. . . ."

Tanner pricked his cheek.

"The Mendez factory. Rodrigo works in the brewery." Benito suddenly gushed information.

"He's there now?"

The Mexican gulped. "*Sí*"

"What time does he get off?"

"Sometime late this evening." Benito swallowed. "I am not sure, señor."

Tanner cursed silently. Therese needed his help now; she couldn't wait till later. Damn that Rodrigo character, he thought as he shoved Benito in front of him.

"We're going for a ride, Benito. And if you make one sound between now and the time we get to my car, you'll be dead before your body hits the dirt. *Comprende?*"

Tanner stifled the urge to punch something, but the curses hurling through his mind could have formed a blue cloud around his head. It was bad enough having to depend on a man he'd never worked with before; to have this third wheel to deal with was even worse. But he didn't have any choice; he had to take Benito with him in order to catch Rodrigo before he left the brewery. Without Benito, Tanner didn't stand a chance of finding Rodrigo, since Tanner didn't have the foggiest idea what Rodrigo looked like: Benito did.

"Ellis, this is Carly. Hello? Are you there?"

"Where are you calling from?" His angry voice sounded as if it were traveling through a tunnel.

"Mexico. I'm in my hotel room," she replied, not surprised by his tone.

"You knew we had to talk. Why did you let me sleep through dinnertime last night?"

She closed her eyes and lowered her head. "Tina said you were exhausted." *Which was only part of the reason I didn't wake you,* she added mentally.

"That's a pretty lame excuse."

"Ellis, I don't need an excuse. I can do whatever I want to do."

There was a moment of silence; then Ellis said, "Have you found Therese?"

"Give me time. I just arrived a little while ago."

"I still don't understand why you felt the need to go to Mexico personally."

"Ellis . . ."

"What are you up to?"

"You know what I'm . . ."

"Knock it off, Carly. Jackie was just here with some interesting news. Would you care to explain why you sold your car?"

"I needed the money."

"That's absurd! You had plenty in your account." His tone of voice alarmed her. She hadn't intended him to find out how desperate their situation was, especially like this.

"I used it up a long time ago."

"On what?"

Carly closed her eyes and rubbed the bridge of her nose. Whether the time was right or not, she knew she couldn't continue to protect him from the cold, hard facts any longer.

"Jameson Steel," she said, her voice devoid of all emotion.

There was no reply for several seconds; then finally Ellis said, "I don't understand." The misery in his voice made Carly's stomach twitch.

"You were so ill. . . . I tried to keep things going for as long as I could, but . . . Jameson Steel is about to go under."

"That's impossible."

"It's the truth," Carly said.

"How in hell could this happen?"

She changed the subject. "Therese must be found as soon as possible, Ellis. Among the three of us . . ."

"Come home, Carly. Now."

"I can't."

"Carly . . ."

"I'm not coming home, Ellis."

"Dammit, Carly . . ."

She heard her father in her brother's voice and gripped the heavy black phone tighter. "We have no choice but to find Therese."

"Like hell we don't!"

"Talk to Jackie. Listen to everything he has to say; then you'll understand why—"

"Carly, I want you to come home now."

"I will, just as soon as I find Therese."

"We don't have time—"

"Exactly! We don't have time."

Ellis became silent for a second time. "I hate this as much as you do," Carly said, "but without Therese we're lost."

"Then find her," he finally said.

"I will." Emotionally drained, all Carly wanted to do was hang up the phone. "I'll call as soon as I know something. In the meantime, speak to Jackie and try not to worry about me."

"Easier said than done," he remarked, then hung up.

Carly took a deep breath and set the phone down. In a way she was relieved that Ellis now knew everything. But Tina King's words haunted her, and she worried that it might be too much for Ellis to handle.

She walked to the window of the hotel room and stared at the enormous volcano Orizaba. A chill raced over her and she rubbed her arms briskly, wondering if it might not be easier to climb that mountain than to find her elusive sister.

At any minute Rodrigo was going to walk through those doors, Tanner thought as he waited in his car across the street from the Mendez Brewery. The brewery was away from the main section of the city, and Tanner couldn't decide if that was good or not. Here he was a lot more noticeable than he was in a crowd. He reached for his navy blue baseball cap and tugged it low on his brow, then rolled his collar up and pressed as much of his hair as he could inside his shirt. Satisfied that he had played down his looks as much as possible, he hunched down in the seat to wait. It couldn't be too long before Rodrigo appeared.

"Benito," Tanner said without looking at the Mexican seated at his right. "You're certain Rodrigo will come out this way?"

"*Sí. Senõr,* will you release me after you have Rodrigo?"

"I can't make any promises."

"I am ignorant, señor. Rodrigo has never told me what he is involved in."

236

Tanner wanted to believe him, but he couldn't trust anyone until he knew the source of the leak. "Then you have nothing to worry about, do you Benito?"

"Señor Stewart, *mi padre*, he is old. I am all he has left in the world. . . ."

"Relax, Benito. Things always have a way of working out."

"*Sí*, I hope."

Putting Benito out of his mind, Tanner glanced out the car window and began to recall everything he knew about Rodrigo. Rodrigo hadn't been an informant for long; his picture wasn't even on file at headquarters yet. But he had played a major role in the success of Therese's investigation. Now he was running scared and had to be caught before anything happened to him. Otherwise it could be too late for Therese. Without Rodrigo's help, Tanner knew he had a snowball's chance in hell of saving her.

He'd studied the brief file Hank had drawn up. But there hadn't been a whole hell of a lot in it. Basic facts, nothing more. Therese was using the name Linda Montoya. She'd found Rodrigo, convinced him she needed his help, paid him handsomely, and felt he was as trustworthy as anyone she'd yet encountered. Rodrigo's connections had pushed the investigation ahead by months. But Tanner was leery. Until he discovered who had double-crossed Therese, he couldn't trust anyone but himself.

"Benito, are you sure the shift's about to change?"

Benito nodded.

"I want you to get out now and stand near the hood of the car. As soon as you see Rodrigo, nod at me, then call him over here. I'll handle the rest. But remember"—Tanner patted the gun strapped to his chest—"no tricks."

As soon as Benito was in position in front of the car Tanner felt the muscles between his shoulders grow tight and tense. He sank down in the seat, scanning the surrounding area. Everything seemed to be moving at a normal pace, but intuition told him to be cautious. He lifted a pair of field glasses from the seat, then placed them to his blue eyes, focusing on the doors to the brewery. There was no movement at all. Not satisfied, Tanner explored the surrounding area. Everything seemed to be calm, yet he couldn't seem to shake his unease. He turned in his seat, looking behind the car.

Tanner zoomed in on a row of bicycles parked at the side of the factory, and Carly instantly came to mind. The memory of how she looked the first time he'd seen her, cheeks red with anger, her temper ready to explode, brought a smile to his face. He would have helped her with the bicycle much earlier than he had if she hadn't looked so adorable wrestling with the heap of metal.

Tanner lowered the field glasses and stroked his chin, wondering if he'd ever forget her or the promise of what it would be like to make love to her. He couldn't remember any woman feeling as soft as she had when he held her just two nights ago. Maybe he'd been a fool to walk away from her as he had; if he had taken her, perhaps her memory wouldn't pull at him so strongly. But he knew he'd done the right thing, especially where she was concerned. He and Carly didn't really live in the same world. Tanner was used to walking away once an affair was over, and somehow he knew Carly would never be able to accept that.

The tense feeling struck him again. Once more he lifted the glasses, this time searching both sides of the street. Still he saw nothing out of the ordinary. Benito stood nonchalantly in front of the car, his hip resting against the hood, obviously unaffected by the tense vibes Tanner was getting. Was his imagination playing games with him? Was this edginess he felt something of his own making? Tanner told himself repeatedly that this was it, this was his last assignment, that he could relax, everything was running fairly smoothly. Rodrigo would come out and Tanner would grab him, then wrench the truth from him one way or the other. Simple.

But Tanner didn't dare ignore the warning

sign. Whether it was real or imaginary, Therese couldn't afford any mistakes on his part.

The food was spicy hot but delicious, Carly thought as she patted her mouth with the bright red napkin, then sipped her wine. Even though the day was half gone, Carly lingered over the meal. Since everyone was preparing for their *siestas,* she'd decided to wait until late afternoon to hit the streets again. Her luck in finding someone who'd seen or maybe even knew Therese would be much better then.

Carly scanned the hotel's dining area, seeing other tourists enjoying their meals. The waiters were hopping, serving hot plates of food, filling glasses and taking orders. It might be futile, she thought, but she was going to stop the next one who came by and ask if he'd ever seen her sister. She rummaged through her purse and pulled out the stack of pictures she'd been showing, sure that Therese's blonde, waist-length hair wouldn't have gone unnoticed in this country.

A waiter, Carly guessed was in his late thirties, noticed her looking at him and rushed to see what she needed. She was charmed by his smile and curious about the scar that slashed through one of his thick black eyebrows.

"Was your meal not satisfactory, señorita?" he asked.

Carly grinned. "It was great, but that isn't why I was looking at you."

He arched his brow and smiled even more broadly, completely mistaking Carly's meaning. She laughed softly at his error, then handed him the stack of pictures.

"I was wondering if you'd ever seen this woman." She pointed at Therese. "She's my sister and has been missing for some time now. I just recently discovered that she was in this part of Mexico."

The waiter blinked, taking several moments to study the snapshots. He tilted his head and looked at them doubtfully, but he thumbed through the pictures a second time.

"It's very important that I find her as soon as possible. You see, she doesn't know that our father has died and she's needed at home."

"I feel I have seen her before, but I do not know where." Turning his eyes from one of the pictures, he glanced down at Carly. "I must think. May I keep this for awhile?"

"Keep it as long as you wish. I'm staying here," she said, taking the rest of the pictures from him. "My name is Carly Jameson. If you remember anything, please leave word for me at the desk." She jotted down her name and room number and handed it to the man. "Please, if you remember anything, I'll be deeply grateful."

"Give me time," he answered, nodding his good-bye. Carly watched him take up his position again near the entryway to the dining room, then sat back in her seat. Could she have been lucky enough to have asked the right person at the right time? she wondered, taking a sip of wine. *Don't get too hopeful because of the man's interest,* she told herself. She knew her disappointment would be much less if it came to nothing. Sighing, she took one last taste of the wine and stood up. As she did so, her leg sharply hit the edge of the table. Before she could grab the teetering wineglass, it toppled and the remaining wine sloshed all over the front of her dress.

"Great," she muttered, grabbing the napkin and blotting away at the bright red stain. Now she'd have to make a trip to her room and change. Digging money out of her purse to pay for her meal she placed it on the table and turned to go, but stopped in her tracks, puzzled. The waiter was no longer there. She glanced around the room, not seeing him anywhere, then shrugged. As busy as the restaurant was, he must have gone into the kitchen to help.

Without another thought Carly left the dining room, climbed the stairs, and let herself into her room. Then, tossing her purse on the bed, she stripped off the dress but before selecting another, she walked to the window and stared at the famed volcano again. This time she experienced a different feeling than she had when she'd first seen the enormous mountain—awe. Part of her desperately wanted the chance to travel up the graceful slope to the snow-capped peak, but another part of her shivered, as if frightened by what she might find if she dared. She spun away from the sight, but the peculiar feeling stayed with her as she readied herself to approach the people of the city.

Benito took off at a dead run. Tanner dropped the glasses in his lap and gripped the steering wheel, jerking himself straight up in the seat. Momentarily stunned, he watched in disbelief as a black sedan with dark-tinted windows sped down the street, bearing down on the group of men walking out of the brewery. When the first man was struck down, Tanner shoved his door open, then jumped back to the passenger's side; his car was the next target. He braced himself for the impact, but the vehicle merely sideswiped him in its pursuit of the other pedestrians.

The unmistakable thump of another body being hit rang in his ears. He leaped up, too late to save anyone, and watched as three more men were hit. Tanner shook his head at the gruesome sight, then gritted his teeth, outraged at the slaughter. Tires squealed as the driver slammed on the brakes; gears groaned as they were forced into reverse. In a matter of seconds the car was zeroing in on its next victim. A tall, lanky Mexican man ran helplessly down the street, his scream a testimony to his fear of the inevitable outcome. The driver toyed with him, gunning the engine, then slowing down, unmercifully prolonging the agony of his coming death. Finally tiring of the game, the driver struck, knocking the man high into the air. Tanner's face screwed up in pain as he watched the broken body slam onto the hood, then slide off to the side. A roaring sound filled his ears, but he was compelled to witness the execution of another group of men.

He swallowed against a hard lump in his throat, then felt his facial muscles tighten when the car made a last-ditch effort to maim and kill. But the sport was now hampered by a lack of targets, for the men who were left had scattered in all directions. The driver punched the accelerator, and the car swerved from side to side as it sped away, leaving twin black stripes in its wake.

Tanner was out of the car and among the dead and injured bodies before he even realized he'd left the car. *Rodrigo!* He had to find Rodrigo. He had to be alive. Tanner stopped, a cold, helpless feeling coming over him. He was lost without Benito's help.

"Rodrigo!" he called out, sweat popping out on his forehead. He cupped his hands around his mouth and called out again. Anger built to a peak in his mind. If Benito's cowardly disappearance cost Therese her life, Tanner would find the Mexican and personally revenge her death.

"Rodrigo!" he shouted, praying that by some miracle Rodrigo would appear.

"Señor Stewart."

Tanner swung around, his heart pounding in his chest.

"No," Benito yelled, throwing his arms up to protect himself.

But Tanner knocked him to the ground, totally losing control as he fell upon Benito, wrapping his hands around the man's throat.

Benito fought back, kicking, scratching, bucking his body in an attempt to throw Tanner off. Unaffected, Tanner tightened his grip, squeezing Benito's throat until the man's face darkened from lack of air.

Benito made a strangling sound, then ceased fighting, his arms limply falling away. Tanner suddenly came to his senses; what in the hell was he doing! He jerked his hands away, then slid off the nearly unconscious man. His anger disappeared almost as quickly as it had erupted. He stood and looked down at Benito as he struggled to sit up, coughing hard and holding his arm up against another attack from Tanner. Instead, Tanner gripped his hand and helped a surprised Benito to his feet.

"I'm sorry," Tanner said, words meant for Benito but his brusque tone directed at himself.

Benito massaged his aching throat. "It is all right," he said. "I . . ."

"Benito," Tanner interrupted, "we have to find Rodrigo before the police arrive."

Benito swallowed, then nodded. As they raced through the prone bodies, groans and cries reached Tanner's ears. He couldn't tell who had been hit and who had not, it had happened so fast. Benito bent and searched among all of the nearly dozen men who had fallen victim to the attack. Tanner was torn between relief and dread each time Benito shook his head and moved on. Surely one of them had to be Rodrigo. After countless moments Tanner spotted a man lying at the side of the street; he grabbed Benito and pointed, then sped toward the unconscious form, Benito close on his heels.

As they reached the body, Tanner anxiously asked, "Is it Rodrigo?"

Out of breath and leaning on Tanner's arm, Benito nodded, then raggedly whispered, "*Sí*."

Tanner knelt down and carefully tilted the man's head back. He checked for a pulse at Rodrigo's throat, but his own heartbeat interfered with his search. He shook his hand as he gained control of his emotions, then put his hand back on Rodrigo's throat. Tanner shut his eyes as relief washed over him. A steady pulse beat against his fingers. Rodrigo seemed not too severely injured.

Tanner carefully felt the unconscious man's body, but the only injury he discovered was a large lump already forming on Rodrigo's forehead.

"Rodrigo!" Tanner tapped Rodrigo's cheek gently. He seemed to want to awaken but couldn't. Not wanting the man to slip into unconsciousness, Tanner repeated the action, calling Rodrigo's name out sharply. He had to wake up!

"Benito, run and open the back of the car. I'll drag him there if I have to." As Benito ran for the car, Tanner anxiously continued working on the injured man. "Open your eyes, dammit!" he said between gritted teeth. Rodrigo's lids fluttered and Tanner's hopes soared. "Atta boy, come on, wake up!"

Slowly Rodrigo's eyes opened, but his stare was vacant. "Rodrigo, I'm Stewart. Come on man, keep your eyes open. We haven't got much time. Where's Therese? Damn! I mean Linda. Wake up!" Tanner smacked Rodrigo's cheek again, knowing it had to be stinging like hell by now. Still, he was losing Rodrigo.

"Rodrigo, you have to wake up," Tanner said, putting his arm behind Rodrigo's neck and sitting him up. "Where's Linda? Who has her?"

Rodrigo made a conscious effort to remain alert. He reached up and touched his forehead, wincing as his finger encountered the knot, then he shook his head as if trying to clear it.

"Where's Linda, Rodrigo? Who has her?" Tanner all but growled, fighting the urge to shake him.

Suddenly Rodrigo let loose a string of Spanish, speaking too rapidly for Tanner to grasp all he was saying.

"In English, Rodrigo. Speak in English."

"We must get out of here!" Rodrigo said, panic lacing his voice. "They will be back when they find out I did not die!"

"All right, all right. Come on." Tanner lifted Rodrigo to his feet and half dragged him across the street. Thankfully the sun was setting and darkness was falling. He needed all the help he could get. The fewer eyes that saw him the better. Already a crowd of people from the brewery had formed, most of them helping the injured. Tanner hoped they were all too stunned to remember seeing him.

The faint sound of sirens reached his ears and he moved more quickly. When they reached the back seat of the car, Benito lifted Rodrigo by the ankles and slid him in before racing around to the passenger's seat and climbing in himself.

With only moments to spare Tanner slid behind the wheel and started the engine, easing the car through the street just as the first patrol car passed by.

Seeing how rapidly night was falling, Carly walked back to the hotel, afraid to stay out on the street after dark. She was irritated. Not one person she'd stopped and asked had seen her sister. It was probably because she couldn't speak their language and they didn't understand what she was after, Carly thought, angry at herself. What she needed was an interpreter, she decided, walking briskly by the few vendors who were still out trying to make a peso. The lack of communication had definitely been a barrier.

"Señorita! Señorita!" Carly paused and turned to see who was calling out. Squinting her eyes, she saw the waiter from the hotel and her heart skipped a beat; he must have remembered something.

"Señorita, *por favor*, come with me?" he asked, smiling as he reached for her arm.

Carly pulled away from him. "Why?"

"*Por favor*, no questions. Come. It will not take long." He spoke calmly.

"Wait a minute," Carly said sharply. The smile she had so admired earlier now had no affect on her. "Have you seen my sister or not?"

"No. *Mi amigo* has seen her. Please, *por favor*, come with me. *Mi amigo* owns the cantina. Come."

Carly took a deep breath. She wasn't particularly thrilled about going into a cantina, but what choice did she have? She had to follow any lead; it was the only hope she had to find Therese. Hitching her purse strap high on her shoulders, she reluctantly followed the waiter down the street. As he turned between two buildings, however, Carly saw nothing but an alley and hesitated.

The waiter stopped, and Carly saw his exasperation. She ran her fingers down the front of her full, pale yellow skirt, wondering if this was such a good idea. Her memories of the Diamond Lounge were still too fresh to be ignored.

"Why can't your friend meet me out here?"

"He is very busy," the waiter said, walking back toward her. "He has to tend to the customers."

Carly knew he was right. Still . . . She bit her lip. She had braved it out at the Diamond Lounge, she could brave it out again. After all, she was the one looking for help, not the other way around. Nodding her head, she followed the waiter down the alley and through the small door of the cantina.

Carly wrinkled her nose, deciding that if she'd had her preference the seedy bar on Galveston Island would have won any day over this dark, sour-smelling place. A few candles and a lone lamp, attached to a rough-looking cedar wall, provided all the light in the small barroom.

"This way, *par favor*. He is back here." Carly admitted that if nothing else, at least her guide was well mannered. She thought she'd scream if she heard one more *por favor*! The waiter swung aside a long, dirty, brown curtain, revealing an arched doorway that led to the back of the bar, and gestured for Carly to enter. Not really wanting to, Carly walked through, feeling a shiver of apprehension race down her spine as the curtain dropped back into place.

Without warning the waiter shoved her forward. She gasped as her hands and knees hit the rough plank floor. In absolute shock she stared as a huge Mexican, weighing at least three hundred pounds, advanced on her. Knowing she was in terrible trouble she tried to scream, but her throat seemed paralyzed. She scrambled to her feet, backing away, nearly falling again as she bumped into a stack of crates. But she continued to retreat. She wasn't about to allow anything to stop her.

Except for a wall.

"Oh, damn," she cried, slapping the solid structure behind her. A smile lifted the oily mustache on the Mexican's upper lip and he stepped forward, reaching for her.

"No!" she screamed. Surprising even herself, she lunged out of his grasp and ran across the room. Spying an empty tequila bottle sitting on a dilapitated desk, Carly grabbed it without thinking and cracked it against the desk. The jagged edges of

251

glass boosted her courage and she swung it boldly at the enormous man, then whimpered when he threw his head back and laughed. Completely undaunted, he mumbled something Carly was sure she didn't want to know. Carly continued to edge backward, placing her hand on the desk to guide her blind retreat. Still laughing, the huge man narrowed the gap between them. Carly was sure she looked ridiculous wielding the broken bottle, but nothing was going to foil her attempt to escape.

Where was the waiter? she suddenly thought. Afraid that he might grab her from behind, Carly risked a quick glance over her shoulder. The curtain still fluttered from his departure.

Taking advantage of her momentary distraction, the huge man backhanded the bottle out of her grasp. Pain shot through her fingers and up her arm. She swallowed when thick drops of blood fell heavily from a deep gash on his arm. Her stomach turned when he held up the injured limb and laughed even harder than before. She covered her ears, wanting to block out the insane sound. But he advanced once more, and again she found herself retreating, praying she could beat him to the curtain and out of the cantina. She was so close to escape. If she could just . . .

Hands clamped on her from behind. Terrified, she screamed, but it never left her throat. A sharp pain bit into the back of her neck and she found herself falling helplessly, blacking out before she even hit the floor.

CHAPTER TWELVE

T anner drove slowly, not saying a word until he was reasonably sure the police weren't going to stop him. He glanced worriedly over his shoulder, wondering how badly injured Rodrigo was, and saw that he was conscious. Maybe the bump on his head looked worse than it was, Tanner thought and hoped he was right. There was no way he could take the injured man to a hospital. The people they were dealing with down here worked for one leader and, although the Mexicans were slow and easy-going for the most part, Tanner knew they wouldn't chance upsetting that leader by withholding any knowledge of having seen Rodrigo—or himself, for that matter. The big man's henchmen would be questioning people the moment he realized Rodrigo wasn't among the injured or dead.

Jarred by the car hitting a pothole in the street, Tanner turned his attention back to the road. He couldn't risk returning to the hotel room he'd stayed in the previous night, not with his own safety now in question. The occupants of the black car might very well have seen his face when they'd sideswiped his car.

"We need a place to go, Benito. Rodrigo needs protection now."

Benito scratched his head. "*Mi padre* lives near."

"In town?" Tanner asked, not liking the idea.

"No, he lives in the . . ."

A movement in the back seat drew Tanner's gaze to the rearview mirror.

"Benito's father lives in the country, Señor Stewart," Rodrigo said after he sat upright in the seat. "It would be the perfect place to wait this out." He closed his eyes and leaned his head back. Tanner's brows shot up. Now that he was out of immediate danger, Rodrigo was extremely calm.

"How's the head?"

Rodrigo smiled wanly. "It feels as if I am hit by a train."

"More like a demon-possessed car," Tanner said, not laughing when Benito crossed himself.

"I must have landed on the curb when I jump out of the way," Rodrigo said, grimacing as he felt the huge lump on his head.

"This could have been avoided if you'd met with me as planned." Tanner wanted to say more, but he wasn't sure how much Benito knew.

"I would have been dead."

Tanner frowned, irritated that he wasn't free to question the man. "Then why did you go to the brewery?"

"For money, to hide. I did not go there to work. After our conversation last night, some men came to visit. I narrowly escaped being caught by them."

Tanner frowned again. "If you were hiding, why did you leave the brewery just now when the shift changed?"

"I thought it would be the safest time. I didn't think . . . Do you really think that massacre was just to get me?"

Tanner could tell by the haunted look in Rodrigo's eyes that he knew the answer, but he needed to be told again.

"Yes," Tanner said. "Obviously these men don't care how many people they kill." Tanner sighed, then shook his head. "How far is it to your father's house, Benito?"

"It will take about twenty minutes, señor," Benito responded.

Tanner listened to Benito's directions, hoping the house would offer enough protection against the outside world. Having to keep a constant watch over his shoulder was the last thing he needed.

As he turned down a dirt road, rippled like waves from a recent rain, he wondered just how much help Rodrigo was going to be to him now, especially since everyone in the countryside was looking for him. Conseulo came to mind, this time devoid of any playful thoughts. He'd have to contact her, get her down here as soon as possible. He needed someone he could depend on, someone he could trust, someone who could move among the people without a problem. Damn, but he wished Hank was there.

"Damn!" Tanner barked, causing Rodrigo to lift his head. "Do you know that old man?" Tanner asked brusquely, staring at the Mexican villager who was flagging them down.

"*Sí,*" Benito said in a relieved voice. "*Él es mi padre.*"

"Why would he want to wave me down?"

Benito shrugged, scratching his ear. "You will have to ask him."

Tanner braked the car, then said, "You ask him. My Spanish isn't what it should be."

The old man leaned on Benito's open window, his face weathered and lined. He wanted to know what was going on; two men had been there looking for Rodrigo and the gringo who had taken Rodrigo away.

Tanner turned to face Rodrigo, then looked back at Benito. "Ask him how long it's been since the men came by."

Benito listened, then said to Tanner, "Not long, about fifteen minutes." In frustration, Tanner slapped the steering wheel.

"We cannot stay here," Rodrigo said. "We must hide. They will look everywhere for us."

Hearing the fear returning to Rodrigo's voice angered Tanner. "Where are we going to hide, Rodrigo? In the trees, perhaps?" He couldn't believe how his luck was running. It seemed to have gone from bad to worse since the first time he'd heard the name Carly Jameson. But she wasn't involved now, thank God. Otherwise his predicament would probably have been ten times worse than it was.

"Señor," Benito said calmly, *"mi padre* has a barn."

Tanner rubbed his brow. "Where?"

"It is close." Benito pointed toward a wall of trees. "It is through there."

"Benito, do you think anyone at the brewery recognized you?"

"¿Quién sabe?"

"Tell your father to get in. They may be back at any time."

Tanner drove through a narrow opening in the trees, surprised that the car was able to pass through the dense foliage. The car rocked back and forth as it rolled over the bumpy road. Branches slapped and scratched the windows, doors, and hood, making Tanner wonder how often a car traveled down the path. It couldn't have been an everyday occurrence.

Suddenly the car entered a clearing and Tanner

immediately saw an aged house but no barn.

Benito, seeing the puzzled expression on his face, said, "You must drive behind the house. There is another road to the barn."

Tanner didn't like any of it. He'd been through these scenes a hundred times. Hiding until the heat passed was nothing new, but dammit, he hadn't wanted this assignment and he resented being here now, especially with an informant who was still wet behind the ears and two other men who obviously didn't know what in hell was going on. If it weren't for the fact that Therese was in danger, he'd have told Omi to stick it where the sun never shined.

As the car passed to the rear of the house Tanner spotted the small road Benito had spoken of. Once again, with limbs and branches attacking his car, Tanner plunged through dense growth, whistling sharply under his breath as a ramshackle barn came into view. It couldn't have been used for years. Trees and brush had grown all around it, blocking all the sunlight. But it was a hiding place, Tanner thought, and, he had to admit, a pretty damn good one.

Tanner stopped and let the old man out. As soon as he opened the rickety barn door, Tanner put the car in gear, only to have to brake again as a flock of pigeons flew wildly through the opening.

"I can't believe this," he mumbled as the cloud of gray-and-white fowl filled the air. He shook his head, then drove into the fragile structure.

Exposed rafters hung precariously overhead; several had rotted through and fallen, leaving Tanner to wonder if it would be safer simply to remain in the car.

"What's your father's name?" Tanner asked Benito.

"Huerve."

"How long has it been since Huerve used this barn?" Tanner asked.

Benito obviously sensed Tanner's apprehension. "It has been several years. Do not worry, señor, the barn is still strong."

And pigs fly, Tanner thought, deciding to change the subject and get rid of Benito at the same time. "Does your father have anything in his house that will help Rodrigo's head?"

"I will see."

"Tell your father to stay here."

Benito reluctantly nodded. "*Por favor*, do not hurt him."

"He'll be fine," Tanner said, "just as long as you return."

Tanner watched as Benito left the car and spoke with his father. After a few moments Huerve settled himself on the ground and leaned against the barn wall. Benito studied him for a moment, then left.

Tanner turned in his seat. Staring directly into Rodrigo's black eyes, he said, "What happened to Linda?"

"Diego's men have her," Rodrigo said without blinking.

"Start at the beginning. Who's Diego?"

"Diego is the mouthpiece, as Linda called him, for the big man, La Pantera. I was supposed to meet Linda early at the cathedral two mornings ago."

"Why the church?"

"I am not sure. Maybe she thought it was the safest place," he said, shrugging. "She called me the night before to tell me La Pantera was about to make his move. We were supposed to meet at her apartment. But something happened. Linda sent a message for me to meet her in private. When I arrived at the church, Diego's men already had her. I watched them put her in a car and drive away."

"Did she give any reason in the note for the private meeting?"

"None. But she never has. I have always met her when she has sent for me."

Tanner squinted his eyes. "How did you meet Linda in the first place?"

A pained look came over Rodrigo's features. "My sister was brutally killed six months ago. She was involved with La Pantera. I was working on my own investigation and was newly employed by La Pantera when I met Linda."

"You know quite a bit then?"

"Yes. Once I realized how far their drug dealing went I knew I would need outside help to put an end to their corruption. It was then that Linda approached me. She was seeing La Pantera socially or at least that is what I thought. You see, she had me figured out almost from the beginning."

She would, Tanner thought with admiration. "Did anyone see you at the church?"

"No. I was once an altar boy, and I know the cathedral well. I used a back door."

"When did they see you?"

"No one saw me."

Tanner was outwardly composed but inside he was wound up tightly. "If no one saw you why were you running? Why did Diego want to kill you?"

"Diego knows everything. He discovered my involvement with Linda." Rodrigo gently touched his head. "Somehow he discovered Linda's plan."

"How?" Tanner asked, glaring at Rodrigo. "Could Benito have told him?"

Rodrigo shook his head. "No, I only told Benito today."

"Then did Diego know Linda's intent?"

"I wish to God I could tell you, but I do not know."

Tanner lifted his hat and resettled it on his head. "Do you have any idea where they've taken her?"

"I am almost certain Diego has taken her to a small house he has on Orizaba. And if I am right, it will be heavily guarded by many men and very difficult to get there without Diego knowing it."

Tanner sat back, rubbing his chin as he thought. "Before we do anything we have to find out if she's there. Do you know exactly where the house is?"

"Yes, but only one road leads to and away from it."

"Is the house always guarded?"

"Not always, only when something big is about to happen."

"Which is . . .?"

"Nothing now. A large shipment of marijuana was scheduled to leave by ship yesterday, but when word on Linda came . . . It is probably safely stored away. They would not have shipped it knowing the U.S. authorities were going to close in."

Tanner sat back, wrinkling his forehead as he made a hasty decision. "What kind of man is Benito?"

"I have never known a more honorable man."

"It is possible that Diego was driving that car at the brewery?"

"No; it was sent by La Pantera."

"Then Diego wouldn't know Benito."

"No."

"Hmm." Tanner's mind was racing. "Does the road end at Diego's house?"

"It continues up the mountain."

"Then there is only one thing we can do. We'll send Benito up there to see if the house is guarded.

If it is, we'll know exactly where to go from there." Tanner looked sharply at Rodrigo. "Benito does drive?"

"Very well."

"Good. Now the only problem we have is to find a car for him to use. This one," Tanner said, patting the dashboard, "isn't going to leave this barn."

Tanner sat on the dirt floor and, through the cracks in the barn, watched the sun slowly set. How much time could it take, Tanner wondered for the umpteenth time, to drive up that mountain and back? Over three hours had passed and Benito still hadn't returned. Tanner scratched his head, then leaned his shoulder against the wall. He glanced at Huerve, who was asleep on the ground, and felt certain that Benito would return; the man loved his father too much not to. But he'd been gone longer than he should have.

Any number of things might have detained Benito, Tanner decided, and again dwelled on how much he hated having to depend on these people. If only Hank were here, things would be much better. Together they'd have probably already zeroed in on Therese and . . .

Tanner grabbed a handful of dirt and hurled it through the air. Hank wasn't here and Benito and Rodrigo were, and he had to accept that. But before things went any further, he knew it was imperative that he reach a telephone. Consuelo wasn't that far away; she could be there within two hours. And Tanner knew he'd feel a lot easier once she was there to assist him.

"Where the hell is Benito?" he finally asked.

"He will be here soon," Rodrigo said. "His cousin may not have been at home with the car."

True, Tanner thought, but he didn't necessarily like the idea. He looked at Rodrigo. "How's the head?"

"It has felt better."

"The swelling seems to have gone down some."

Rodrigo felt the bump, then shrugged. "If the pain would lessen I would be a very happy man."

"If Benito would return, I would be a very happy man."

"He will, señor."

He'd better, Tanner thought. Once again he looked through the crack in the wood and saw how rapidly darkness was falling. They'd be stuck here for most of the night, he decided. There was no way he was going to try to find a phone until the early morning hours, when no one would suspect him of being out. There was also no way he was going to attempt to rescue Therese from Diego's house without Conseulo. If things went according to his tentative plan, he had the perfect course of action plotted to secure Therese's release.

He suddenly thought of Carly and what Therese's return would mean to her. He wondered if she'd ever know. . . . Dammit, he had to get Carly Jameson out of his head and keep her out. But that wasn't about to happen, not yet, anyway. Until this unexpected mission was completed, Tanner knew thoughts of Carly were never going to be far from his mind.

"Look, Señor Stewart, I see lights."

Tanner jumped to his feet and pulled out his gun, angry with himself for allowing thoughts of Carly to interfere with his concentration. He slapped a clip into the pistol and moved behind the barn door, preparing to take action if Benito had been foolish enough not to return alone.

Carly groaned, refusing to open her eyes against the pain that filled her skull. Her stomach churned from the intensity of the pain. Her arms ached, feeling as if they'd been twisted out of their sockets. She wanted to stretch her legs but found she was incapable of making such a simple move. She jerked her hands roughly, wondering why her body refused to comply with her commands. But all she succeeded in doing was alerting herself to the realization that her hands were bound behind her and that they hurt like hell.

Her eyes popped open and she blinked rapidly against the darkness. Fear, so intense it nearly took her breath away, consumed her. She cried out for help, panicking when nothing but muffled sobs reached her ears. She kicked her feet and jerked her hands, struggling to move her body, but her attempts were futile. She was tied from head to toe.

Her stomach suddenly roiled and she instantly became still, knowing she was on the brink of being violently ill. A sour taste filled her mouth and, with tears running down her face, she clamped her teeth down on the material stuffed in her mouth.

Oh, God, she silently prayed, please help me! It was all coming back to her—the cantina, the shabby back room, and the horrible man who'd been after her. Someone had hit her from behind. It must have been the waiter. But why would he lure her into such a situation? Chills suddenly rushed over her, momentarily robbing her of her control over her sick stomach. She bit down harder on the gag.

The surface beneath her felt rough and scratchy, yet it gave each time she moved. She had to be on someone's bed, she thought, cringing as she imagined what was going to happen to her.

She desperately tried to see something around her, but the area was so dark she doubted she could have seen her hand had she been able to put it in front of her face.

I can't just lie here, she thought frantically. Although the pain in her head was lessening, nausea still prevented her from moving. She breathed deeply through her nose, concentrating solely on overcoming the nausea long enough to permit her at least to roll over. Maybe she could make out something on the other side of her dark prison.

But she was kept from such an attempt as the sickness struck again. Tears ran down her temples and into her hair. She was going to be sick and nothing was going to prevent it. She closed her eyes as the first heave reached her throat.

At the sound of a car door slamming, Tanner tensed and, with elbow down, raised his pistol high against his shoulder. Huerve stared fearfully at Tanner, his eyes as wide as saucers. Tanner almost wished he could have assured the old man that his son was safe, but until he was certain of what awaited him, he was forced to remain silent. Tanner quickly looked at Rodrigo. He hadn't moved from his place in the corner of the barn, but Tanner could see that he was as apprehensive as Tanner was.

The old door creaked on rusty hinges as it slowly swung open. Tanner felt each solid beat of his heart, the rush of blood through his veins. When he saw Benito cautiously poke his head around the door, Tanner waved him in with the gun. Once Benito was standing next to his father, Tanner pushed the door shut and relaxed.

"Did you run into any trouble?"

"No," Benito said, then swallowed. "I made sure no one followed."

"Were there guards at the house?"

"Sí, mucho hombres."

Tanner looked at Rodrigo. "She has to be

there."

"I would say yes," Rodrigo said, slowing rising to his feet.

"Benito, how long will your cousin let you use his car?"

He shrugged.

"Will one more day matter?"

Again Benito shrugged.

Tanner said, "Do you think he'll come after it?"

This time Benito flipped his hands palms up.

The term "simpleminded" popped into Tanner's head, but he cast the notion away. Benito had served his purpose, and now that Tanner knew his plan would work he felt much too generous to chastise the man for his ignorance.

"Señor Stewart," Rodrigo said, a smile on his lips. "I am very hungry. Do you think Huerve can fix us something to eat?"

Tanner grinned back, then shrugged. "Ask Benito."

Carly screeched as loudly as she could, knowing she was about to strangle in her own vomit. Despite the pain in her stiff limbs she tried to roll over, knowing that whoever had kidnapped her was sure to hear the loud thump of her body hitting the floor. With a burst of energy she managed to roll a quarter of the way around, landing on her face and knees. Pushing again, she tumbled over and hit the floor. The jar was all her body needed to rebel violently.

A door crashed open; light spilled into the room. Guttural voices filled her ears. Someone grabbed her. She was helplessly choking as she was lifted from the floor and tossed about like a rag doll. They jerked her hair, almost ripping it from her scalp; then suddenly the gag fell away from her face and onto the floor. But they were too late, she thought dazedly, feeling herself blacking out. Someone pounded on her back, making her body finish the job it had begun. By the time it was over Carly felt as if everything in her system had poured out.

Finally the spasms ceased. Carly hung limply in the person's arms, unable to straighten her legs, since her feet were still tied to her hands. She groaned. It sounded pitiful even to her own ears. Although what she wanted most to do was cry, she refused to show any other sign of weakness. Being sick in front of her abductors was bad enough.

She lifted her head to see who the men were, but her hair fell over her eyes and face, obscuring her view. Someone else was touching her now; she felt him sawing at her bonds. Like a dead weight, her feet suddenly hit the floor. Her hands, however, remained tied.

She was shoved forward, and she gritted her teeth to keep from screaming. Her foot hit a wet spot on the floor and she slipped, landing on her knee, where the edge of her skirt became soaked in her own bile. She heaved again. Tears of humiliation streamed down her cheeks. Biting her lip, she controlled the spasm, refusing to disgrace herself again.

Jerked roughly to her feet, Carly kicked out against the abuse. She whipped her head back, tossing her hair out of her eyes, and fully expected to see the enormous man from the cantina or the waiter from the hotel. But she had never seen the man who stood before her now.

"Who are you?" she screamed at him.

With a flourish he said, "I am Diego, and don't you ever forget it."

"Why have you done this to me!"

He chucked softly. "Oh, señorita, if I had known what a mess you were going to make, perhaps I would have left you alone." He wrinkled his nose.

In her angry state, she ignored him and again demanded an answer. "What do you want with me?"

"I want you to take a bath. You are offending me. Jorge," he called to the man behind Carly, "take her outside and clean her up."

Carly lunged for the little creep, fully intending to scratch his eyes out. But she was stopped painfully when the man behind her—Jorge, she assumed—jerked the ropes on her wrists high behind her back.

Too enraged to care, Carly twisted around, striking out at whoever was within her reach. Catching Jorge unprepared, she kicked him solidly on the shin, winning her freedom as he dropped the rope and howled in pain.

"Tsk, tsk, Jorge. Are you going to allow this little woman to get the better of you?" Diego taunted.

Carly quickly looked at Jorge. "Are you going to allow this little bastard to run your life?" she asked.

"Jorge, take her, now." Diego crossed his arms over his chest, his brows coming together over his black eyes.

Carly inched back step by step. Jorge took a step toward her, his craggy features set in an intimidating frown. She knew it was futile, but she continued to move away from him. She would be damned if she'd make it easy for him to catch hold of her again.

"Why did you kidnap me?" she asked angrily, trying to buy time before Jorge grabbed her.

"You will find out soon enough, Señorita Jameson. But please, allow Jorge to escort you to the washroom. You need a good bath."

Carly wished she was close enough to fall on Diego. She would have taken immense pleasure in

273

rubbing her soiled body all over his immaculately clean suit. But her time was almost up; Jorge was only a few feet away and he was going to pounce on her any second.

Suddenly Carly realized that there might be neighbors. Maybe . . .

She stopped cold in her tracks; her mouth flew wide open. The loudest, most piercing scream she'd ever heard, let alone emitted, came tearing out of her throat. Jorge's eyes bulged, while Diego covered his ears. Even though Carly's throat felt as if it was on fire, she heaved another breath and screamed again. Suddenly, men came running into the room from all directions, mean, rough-looking men with wicked-looking rifles pointed at her.

A sob came from her throat. She clamped her mouth shut. With fear invading her soul, she lowered her chin and turned around, becoming the most docile hostage, she was sure, there had ever been.

CHAPTER THIRTEEN

Carly walked stiffly out of the house and into the dark yard, with Jorge following closely on her heels. Nothing but a small lamp lit the pale courtyard, making Carly especially cautious as she crossed the uneven ground. She had no idea where she was, only that it seemed to be miles from civilization.

Directly beneath the flickering light was a hand-cranked water pump, much like the ones she'd seen in old western movies. When Jorge nudged her in that direction, Carly almost laughed. If the little weasel inside expected her to get clean using that thing, he had another thing coming.

Jorge pulled her to a stop directly in front of the antiquated pump, but instead of using the pump he lifted a bucket of water and gestured to her to use it. She looked at him as if he were crazy. There was no telling how many men had washed in that very same water. Seeing her obvious reluctance, he lifted

275

the bucket almost to eye level, but Carly turned her face away. She heard Jorge sigh, then felt him move away. When he sat the bucket on the ground, Carly kicked it so fast he didn't have a chance to right it before it fell.

He turned angry black eyes on her.

"I want fresh water."

The nostrils of his wide, flat nose flared.

"And soap."

Thick lips thinned.

"And I can't wash with my hands tied . . ."

Jagged, clenched teeth appeared.

"So untie me." She tossed her head back as she made the insistent demand.

She found her herself roughly jerked to her knees, her surge of courage quickly subsiding. He was twice as big as she and could easily break her in two. Still, she tried to convince him she was unafraid, imperious, demanding.

"How can I wash with my hands tied?"

Jorge looked at her hands, then back at her face. Ignoring her, he lifted the bucket and poured what little water remained there into the pump, then suddenly began to lever the handle up and down. Carly watched, and within moments fresh water gushed into the bucket.

"Untie my hands, Jorge. I know you understand me, or you wouldn't have listened to that man inside."

He shook his head.

She frowned. "Come on, Jorge. What harm can it do?"

Again he shook his head.

"Why not?"

When he stared at her this time Carly could see his anger was gone. He acted as if he wanted to talk, but still he refrained.

"Look how much bigger you are than I am. What could I possibly do to get away from you?"

He sighed and Carly lowered her head, an expectant smile on her lips. His black eyes narrowed, but he relented and reached for her wrists. Carly felt him fumbling with the ropes; freed, her arms dropped to her sides, numb at first, then stinging as the pins-and-needles sensation rushed to her fingertips. She shook her hands, wincing as she saw the welts the ropes had caused.

"*Gracias,* Jorge," she whispered, then thrust her hands into the cool water, moaning as it eased the rope burns. She scooped up a handful of water and rinsed out her mouth, then splashed more on her face and the back of her neck. When she felt as clean as she possibly could without soap, she lifted her skirt and washed away the area she had soiled when she'd become ill. Blotting the front and back of her hands, she prepared to rise but stopped when she saw the soft look on Jorge's rough features. He reached for her and Carly flinched, but all he did was lift a lock of her hair. Carly tensed as he did so, but he merely rubbed it between his finger and thumb, then let it drop. Her hand automatically touched the hair he had held, but all she felt was a tangled mess, nothing that would evoke such an admiring look.

The sudden wish that she had a brush brought her small reprieve from reality to a crashing halt. She turned her head away sharply, biting her lip as she realized her purse was probably still at the cantina. Hatred for what these men had done to her welled inside. Why had she been kidnapped? If they thought she had money, well . . .

Jorge touched her shoulder and Carly jerked away, glaring at him. His mouth twisted angrily and he hauled her roughly to her feet. When he lifted the pieces of rope, she nearly cried.

"Please don't tie me up again."

He motioned to her to turn around, but Carly stepped back. "Please, Jorge."

He grabbed her shoulders and turned her around, obviously unaffected by the anguish in her voice.

Carly pivoted away, then reached for his massive forearms, squeezing them as tightly as she could. "My wrists are killing me. Please trust me, Jorge. I won't do anything that'll get you into trouble; just please don't tie my hands again."

In the dim light she watched indecision play across his almost ugly features. The grooves that bracketed each side of his thick lips deepened; his obsidian eyes lost their gleam in the moonless night.

Again the wide nostrils flared as he debated mentally, but for some reason Carly was no longer intimidated by him.

"I promise," she whispered softly. Jorge stared at her without acknowledging her plea, but some how Carly knew she had won. Smiling gratefully, she turned her back on him, not moving until she felt the pressure of his hand nudging her forward.

Carly's attention was caught by a movement on the flat roof of the house. Even though it was dark she made out the shadow of a man marching slowly back and forth, a rifle of some sort cradled in his arms. Alarmed, she wondered how many armed men there were guarding the house; then she realized her chances of escaping were almost nil. She turned anxious eyes to the side of the house and spotted another man, his rifle slung across his back, leaning against the corner of the building. She glanced quickly at the other side and saw his twin. How many more were there swallowed by the darkness, able to see her without her knowing it? She bit her lip, feeling more helpless than she'd ever felt in her life. Her father's death, Ellis's injuries, Therese's disappearance, all seemed insignificant. Carly Ann Jameson was in real trouble!

The back of her knees suddenly went weak; tremors shot up the backs of her thighs, and it became almost impossible for her to continue to walk. At the door Carly tripped on the stairs and would have fallen without Jorge's steadying hand.

He turned her slightly toward him, eyeing her suspiciously. But he must have seen the stark terror in her eyes, for he patted her arm once, then reached past her and opened the door. He held her upper arm as she stepped into the house, gently squeezing it when the screen door slammed and she jumped.

The room was not vacant, but Carly heard males voices coming from another part of the house. She stood still, waiting to see what Jorge intended to do. After a moment he pointed at a door directly in front of her, and Carly knew he was taking her to the voices.

Carly entered the room on leaden feet. Diego sat on a faded, somewhat worn couch, talking to another man who sat on a rickety old table that wobbled each time his foot swung through the air. But it was the sight of a woman seated next to him, her head lowered, her hands folded demurely in her lap, that surprised Carly. A dark curtain of blue-black hair hid her features, but Carly could see she wasn't much older than herself.

"Señorita," Diego greeted Carly, slanting a look at Jorge. "I see you have convinced Jorge to free you." He stood up and walked directly in front of Carly. "I am not surprised. You have a very angelic look about you. Very beautiful." His smile became self-satisfied, smug. Rising on the balls of his feet, he half turned from Carly. "There is someone I would like you to meet," he said, grabbing Carly by the hand and pulling her over to the woman. Then he reached down and wound his hand in the woman's thick black hair, viciously jerking her head up. Her eyes were tightly shut. The pinched look around her mouth was not caused by pain but by very obvious anger.

Carly's breath caught at the sight of the familiar features before her. A ringing sound filled her ears, and she wanted to shout to the woman not to open her eyes; Carly didn't think she could handle having her fears confirmed. But she was compelled to watch as the woman's lids opened, revealing large, brown eyes that held a warning in their depths.

It was Carly's turn to close her eyes. Her knees threatened to buckle; in fact, she knew she was swaying. *Control yourself,* she demanded of her senses. *For God's sake, control yourself!*

Carly slowly opened her eyes and hoped she was successful in keeping any emotion from showing on her face.

"Señorita Jameson," Diego began, and Carly could picture an axe falling, "I would like you to meet Linda Montoya, or, as you might know her, Therese Jameson."

Still Carly managed to stare blankly. "Pardon me?"

"No games, señorita. We have known who Linda is for several days now."

Carly didn't respond. With great effort she

avoided looking at Therese. There had to be a reason her sister now had black hair and brown eyes. There had to be a reason she was using an assumed name. There had to be a reason why this man was holding her and—Carly swallowed the lump in her throat—there had to be a reason why she, too, had been kidnapped.

Of course there was, Carly's mind snapped. It was because of the pictures she'd flashed around! It was because she had flung Therese's name all over the city. This situation was all her fault. If only she hadn't run away from Tanner, if she'd only given him a chance to explain. . . . Her throat suddenly felt tight. If only Tanner were here.

Diego gripped Carly's chin and tilted her face back. "There is little family resemblance between you two, but there is enough so that I can see the relationship. Too bad she had to come looking for you so soon," he said to Therese. "If she had waited a week more you would have been returned to her." He laughed softly, and Carly was stuck by how evil he looked. Then his hand slid from Carly's chin to her throat, where his thumb rested against her windpipe. "What a waste. You're far too pretty to die.

"Manuel," he said briskly, his hand, to her relief, falling away as he turned to the man on the table, "tonight I believe I will allow the two sisters to remain together, since it will be the last time they will see each other. You and Jorge will guard them." He flicked his wrist as if tired of the whole situation. "Take them away."

When Manuel shoved Carly out of his way and jerked Therese off the couch, Jorge stepped forward, and waited until Manuel moved. Then he reached for Carly, and even though his touch was not as gentle as it had been before, Carly didn't balk but walked beside him as he led her back to the room she had previously occupied.

The light was still on, giving Carly her first true glimpse of the furnishings, which weren't much— just a single bed. At least someone had cleaned the floor, she thought, glancing at the bare wood, scratched and worn from lack of care.

She and Therese were ushered to the bed and made to sit. Jorge handed Manuel the rope, but before Manuel could tie them Diego appeared in the doorway.

"I have had a change of heart, Manuel," he said, and Carly's heart fell, thinking he was going to separate them. "Do not tie them. The Blessed Virgin would never forgive me if I didn't let them have their freedom for the night. Besides, there is no place for them to run."

Therese shoved her fists down into the mattress and pushed herself to her feet. "Let her go, Diego!" she demanded, pointing at Carly. Carly reached for her sister, but Therese flung her hand away. "You have me; she doesn't even know why I'm here."

"And do you know why *she* is here?" Diego

asked, grinning as if he had a special surprise for Therese.

"No!" Carly said, coming to her feet.

"Shut up!" he shouted, shoving Carly roughly back to the bed. Therese stiffened—Diego's smile returned. "Your sister has traveled all this way to tell you that your father is dead." He laughed as Therese paled visibly.

"You sick son of a bitch," Therese whispered.

"But I tell you the truth. Señor Jameson has . . ." Diego made a slashing movement across his throat.

"You wouldn't know the truth if it bit you on the ass."

He shrugged, then threw back his head and laughed.

"I hope I live long enough to see you pay." Therese glared, not bothering to hide her hatred. Carly's stomach lurched at her sister's words.

Diego's laughter died and he moved toward Therese until he was within inches of her face. "*Querida,*" he said softly, mockingly. "You need no money. It is my fondest wish to have you too. All you must do is say the word." He paused, waiting for a response from her.

Carly could see it took every ounce of control Therese had to keep from attacking him. "I will get you, Diego. Somehow, someway."

The corner of his lip twitched. "No, *querida.* I'm afraid your days are definitely numbered.

Perhaps you should take advantage of my willing body now, while time allows."

For one desperate moment Carly thought he was going to drag her sister away with him and do things to her that Carly could hardly bear to imagine. But Diego merely threw his head back and laughed again. "Yes, your days are definitely numbered."

"As are yours," Therese bit out.

He lifted his brow, giving her a condescending look. Then he turned to the men. "Come, let us leave."

As the two men filed out, Diego stared hard into Therese's eyes. "Manuel will be at your door all night. Jorge will be at the window outside. Do not be foolish enough to try something stupid." He walked out, slamming the door loudly behind him.

Carly jumped from the bed. "Dear God, Therese, what have you gotten into?" Carly had pictured her reunion with her sister many times, but never had she seen them in such a dire situation.

"Is it true?" Therese asked quietly. "Is Father dead?"

Carly nodded, unable to speak.

"Sweet heaven!" Therese whispered, compressing her lips into a thin line.

Carly threw her arms around her sister, knowing Therese was desperately trying not to respond to the news. Therese, however, patted Carly on the back as if to console her, instead of the other way around.

Carly pulled back, staring deeply into the brown eyes that seemed so foreign to her sister.

"What happened?" Therese asked, her voice catching as she stepped back.

"Let's sit down," Carly suggested quietly. As soon as they were settled on the bed, Carly began to explain. "There was a car wreck. Father and Ellis were hit by an eighteen wheeler, and Father was killed instantly."

Therese clutched Carly's hands. "And Ellis?"

"He was severely injured. At first we didn't know if he would live. But he pulled out of it. Oh, Therese," Carly said despairingly, "he's paralyzed."

Tears welled in Therese's eyes, but she held them back. "When did this happen?" Her voice was so soft Carly barely heard her.

"Almost nine months ago."

"Nine months?"

Carly nodded. "It seems as if I've been trying to find you forever. I hired detectives, but they always came up empty. When no one could find a trace of you anywhere in Galveston, I was finally forced to search for you myself."

"I must have just left Galveston when it happened," Therese mumbled, her attention wandering.

Carly swallowed, allowing Therese time to come to grips with the news.

"We argued horribly the last time I was home,"

Therese added, as if Carly hadn't known of it.

"Therese." Carly reached for her sister's shoulders. "Why didn't you tell us what you were doing?"

"Tell you what?"

"That you were some sort of agent or investigator, or whatever it is you call yourself." Carly said.

"How did you find that out?" Therese asked tersely.

"You answer my question and then I'll answer yours."

Therese leaned over and cupped her palm beneath her eye; she blinked and Carly watched as first one brown contact lens fell out and then the other. "I guess I won't be needing these things anymore," Therese said, tossing them across the room.

"What kind of trouble are you in?" Carly asked impatiently, desperate for information.

Therese covered her eyes with her palms. "I can't tell you."

"Like hell you can't. I probably know more than you think I do."

"I doubt it," Therese replied sternly.

"I know you're some sort of investigator, Therese. I know that you've been living a double life for some time. And I also know that you're not the wild, willful person we always thought you were. Now, are you going to tell me what you're into or not!"

Therese frowned. "How did you find out?"

"Tanner Barnes."

"Tanner Barnes? He told you?" She was truly astonished.

Carly scratched the back of her head, then stood up and began to pace. "In a roundabout way. I took Ellis's yacht to Galveston. Tanner was docked next to me—some coincidence, huh? Anyway, to make a long story short, I did some investigating of my own. Tanner pretended to be my friend. Then I discovered he knew about you all along and I ducked out on him."

Therese ran her tongue over her front teeth. "And how did you discover that?"

"I eavesdropped on a conversation between him, Hank, and a man named Cornwall."

Therese laughed softly; it sounded completely out of place, considering the predicament they were in.

"It seems you were a little smarter than Tanner anticipated. I would have loved seeing you in action, Carly."

"I was horrible at it. You can't imagine all I went through."

Therese sobered. "Yes, I can. You're here, aren't you? How in the world did you end up with Diego?"

"I'm not really sure. I showed your picture to this waiter at the hotel I was staying in and he kept it. Then later he caught me on the street and told me he knew someone who knew where I could find you. So, like a fool, I followed him. He took me into his cantina, someone knocked me out, and when I came to I was here."

Therese shook her head. "He was obviously one of Diego's men."

"Why is Diego holding us?"

Therese didn't answer. Carly opened her mouth to ask more, but seeing the look on Therese's face, she said instead, "All right, I give up. For the moment anyway." Frowning at her sister, Carly added, "But this really isn't fair. Put yourself in my shoes and imagine how you'd feel."

"I'd be worse than you, that's for sure."

Carly sighed. She had to tell Therese more, yet she felt like a heel, breaking all the bad news to her at once. Still, it might be important; it could help Therese figure things out.

"What I haven't told you yet is that . . . Lisa Curtis was found dead in Galveston Bay."

"What? I can't believe that!"

Carly moved back to her sister's side. "We have to get out of here. Ellis . . . Father . . . Oh, damn! Father had a new will made after the last argument the two of you had. Therese, if all three of us aren't actively working in Jameson Steel in the next three months, then Jameson Steel will be taken away from us, as well as the house and everything that goes with it. We have to get home, for Ellis's sake if for nothing else. Therese, if he loses us after everything else that's happened, it'll kill him. He's not the same man he once was."

"I don't know what we can do." Therese was blunt.

"Well, we sure as hell can't sit here and patiently wait to be executed!"

"We can't do anything until they move us. If we tried to make a break for it now, we'd be mowed down in seconds. This house is guarded for miles around."

Carly turned away from Therese. It all seemed so futile, she thought. So damned unfair!

"Don't give up hope, Carly. I think my informant got away. If he did, we *might* have a chance."

"How did they discover you weren't who you said you were?" Carly asked, turning back to her sister.

"I wish I knew," Therese said in a tired voice. "Try to understand that I can't tell you anything. I never told any of you what I was really doing with my life because if you ever asked me where I was going or when I was coming back, I couldn't have told you. At least you've had these years of living without worrying. Now, if we manage to make it through this, you'll always wonder, Carly. You'll always live with a fear about me niggling in the back of your mind. I never wanted that for any of you."

"Father would have been so proud of you,"

Carly said, tears building in her eyes.

Therese turned away.

Several moments passed; then Carly asked, "Have you ever been in this much danger before?"

Therese paused before answering. "I've never been set up like this."

There was so much Carly wanted to ask, but the look in Therese's eyes killed her desire to push for answers.

"Let's change the subject," Therese continued, "Besides what you've told me, who else was involved with Tanner?"

"The only ones I know of are Hank and the man called Cornwall. He's the one who approached me in the Diamond Lounge."

"*You* went to the Diamond Lounge?" Therese asked.

"All by myself. At first Cornwall was friendly. Then, after I started asking questions about Lisa Curtis, he clammed up."

Therese smiled slightly. "Did he look well?"

"I suppose. Actually, he scared me spitless. You see, Hank was also at the lounge, and these three thugs hauled him outside and beat the pulp out of him. I followed Hank out, saw what was happening, and ran to get help. When I came back this Cornwall person was searching Hank's body. I thought he was robbing him, and Tiny . . ." Carly paused. "Tiny is another story. Tiny ran Cornwall off and helped me get Hank to a hospital."

"Hank was injured!"

"Pretty badly. But he's going to be all right. He just needs rest."

Therese pushed her hair off her shoulder and leaned back on her elbows. "I bet Tanner was fit to be tied."

"I guess he was. To tell you the truth, it all seems like a story someone told me. It's hard for me to believe I actually participated in the whole episode."

"What do you think about Tanner Barnes?"

Tanner Barnes. Now she remembered where she had heard the name before meeting him in Galveston. "Did you ever call him from the house, Therese?"

"Yes."

A funny sensation, very much like dread, coursed through her. "Were you lovers?"

Therese paused, looking first affronted, then sympathetic. Carly glanced away.

"It almost happened once, but . . . I see his good looks got to you too."

Carly ran her hand down her throat and swallowed. "Almost. I guess he has . . ."

"Animal magnetism?" Therese smiled. "I think he affects most women that way."

"Yeah." Carly grinned halfheartedly. "He must. Why didn't you become lovers—I mean . . . Did you love him?"

"No." Therese answered quickly, with conviction. "We were in such a stressful situation at the time that we both knew it—and avoided it. Relationships rarely last in this line of work."

Carly couldn't help the pang of jealousy that went through her. Was that why Tanner had stopped himself from making love to her that night? Because of the circumstances? It was too much for her to think about, so she changed the subject. "After we get out of this mess," she said with more confidence than she felt, "are you going to come home?"

Therese was silent.

"It's only for one year. Surely you would do it for Ellis."

"I'll have to work something out."

"For once in your life, can't you put your family first?"

"That's not fair!"

"What's not fair is that Ellis is permanently stuck in a wheelchair. My God, Jameson Steel will be all he has left."

"How can you say that?"

"You haven't seen him, Therese. Ellis is in bad shape, physically and emotionally. Besides, we haven't got time to wait for him to recover. Everything Dad worked for will be gone if we don't settle his will."

Therese sighed and closed her eyes.

"And Tina says . . ."

Therese's eyes popped open and she sat up.

"Tina?" she asked, and Carly detected the cautious note in her voice.

"His therapist."

"Who recommended her?"

"A doctor in Houston. Why?" When Therese didn't answer, Carly went on. "To tell you the truth, I don't really like her. She's bossy and pushy, and she thinks that the best thing for Ellis is just to let him come to grips with his condition on his own. And every time I try to get him to return to work, she has a fit." Carly saw the expression on Therese's face change. "What's the matter?"

"Nothing. We'll straighten things out somehow."

"Does that mean you're going to help save the company?"

Therese casually pressed her long hair over her shoulder and ran her fingers through the nearly waist-length tresses. "Right now it seems I'm going to do everything I can just to save our lives."

CHAPTER FOURTEEN

The lock wasn't hard to jimmy. Hell, Tanner thought, anyone with a minimum of strength could have pushed the door off its rusty hinges. But he didn't want to leave any trace of his presence at the small tourist shop; he just wanted to use their phone without the owner's knowledge. Twisting the knob, he opened the door and ushered Rodrigo in, but before he closed the door behind him, he glanced back at the car to make sure Benito hadn't left. Tanner smiled; Benito was sitting patiently in the back seat.

Leaving the door slightly ajar, Tanner followed Rodrigo to the rear of the building. "Are you sure there's a phone in here?" Tanner asked.

"Yes. I have used it before." Rodrigo paused near a small counter stacked with brightly colored *piñatas*. "It is in that corner."

Tanner nudged the wiry Mexican in that direction. "Remember," he told Rodrigo as he lifted the receiver, "once you get her on the phone, hand it to me." Rodrigo nodded and waited as Tanner dialed the number. Once the phone was ringing Tanner handed the receiver to Rodrigo. Then he glanced out the small window of the shop, noting that even though it was still dark outside, the sun would be rising soon. They couldn't waste much time. There was no telling when the owners of the shop would come to open for business.

"Señorita?" The sound of Rodrigo's voice abruptly brought Tanner's attention to the conversation. He listened as Rodrigo chatted idly, then smiled when Rodrigo dropped the name Tomas Stewart. Rodrigo's dark eyes glimmered in the predawn light as he handed Tanner the phone.

"Consuelo, it's been too long," Tanner said in a seductive murmur.

"Much, much too long," a feminine voice responded.

"I need you now, Consuelo. How soon can we meet?"

"As soon as you like." Tanner sensed that Consuelo was aware of the urgency behind his loverlike attitude.

"The Fortress of the Flowers is a wonderful place. How long will it be until I can surround you with orchids?"

There was a slight hesitation at Consuelo's end of the line. "One hour."

"I'll be waiting. Meet me in the dining room of

the local hotel. I promise you excitement such as you've never known."

"No one has ever been as exciting as you, *querido*. I will see you soon. *¡Adiós!*"

As Tanner handed Rodrigo the phone, he chewed on the inside of his lip, pondering all that had to be done. "Get an outside operator. I've got to call the States."

In a matter of moments Rodrigo was again handing Tanner the receiver. "This is Stewart."

"What the hell is going on?" Omi asked gruffly, his voice anxious.

"Linda is being held in the mountains by a man named Diego. What do you have on him?" Tanner felt he had to use Therese's alias in front of Rodrigo.

"Hell, hold on a minute." Omi ordered one of his secretaries to call up the name on the computer. While waiting for the information he continued to talk to Tanner. "Is she still alive?"

"As far as I know."

"What're your plans?"

"I've called Consuelo. She's on her way. From what Rodrigo has said, the house where they're holding Linda is heavily guarded. It's right in the middle of nowhere, extremely hard to get to without being spotted."

"Hmmm. I think I've got the picture. There's not much here on Diego. As you know, Therese has been out of touch with us for some time. Diego is mainly a stepping-stone on the way to the heart of the ring."

"The leader's name is La Pantera."

"Yeah, I know, but we haven't got anything more on him yet."

"You're kidding," Tanner said. "Linda's obviously known about him for awhile."

"She's known his name for some time, but the last time I spoke to her she still wasn't sure who he was. Rodrigo probably knows more than I do. Has he been any help?"

"More than I expected, especially once he knew I was here to help him."

"Good. Give me some time; I'll run through all the files and see what I can come up with on these two names."

"I haven't *got* time. In fact, things are going to be pretty rough for the next twenty-four hours, so don't expect to hear from me for awhile. Once I secure Linda's release I'll hear all the details firsthand."

"I have one more bit of news for you," Omi said.

"What's that?"

"Miss Jameson is now in Mexico. Orizaba, to be exact."

"How did she find out Linda was here?" Tanner didn't like the cold feeling that was creeping into his guts.

"Why don't you tell me?" Omi retorted.

"How in hell am I supposed to know?" Tanner replied tersely. "She *was* in Beaumont." Damn her! Hell, damn himself. He should have known better than to assume she'd stay in Beaumont. But he'd thought once Carly discovered Lisa Curtis was dead she'd stay home, out of trouble. He had believed she'd left without speaking to him because of all the unanswered questions she'd had about his coming to the hospital to see Hank. Stupidly he had taken too much for granted!

"Why didn't Tina contact you sooner than this?" Tanner all but barked.

"She didn't discover Miss Jameson's departure until yesterday morning. It seems Therese's sister slipped out before either Tina or the brother awoke. Try to avoid her if you see her. I've sent another man to watch her."

"Who?"

"Armand."

"Dammit! Hank isn't in any shape to make the trip, let alone take care of Carly."

"He wanted the assignment."

Tanner wished he could reach through the phone and strangle the man. "When did he leave?"

"Yesterday morning."

Tanner sighed. It would be useless to raise hell with Omi. Omi only saw things one way—if there was a job to be done, do it. Nothing else could stand in the way. Surely Hank would find Carly and convince her to follow his advice, explain to her all

299

the things Tanner had wanted to tell her himself.

"I'll contact you in twenty-four hours. Find something on this Diego character." Tanner deliberately made it sound like an order, knowing it would infuriate his superior.

"Just get Therese out of there. . . ."

Tanner hung up the phone, not waiting to hear Omi's dressing-down. "Let's go, Rodrigo."

Rodrigo moved ahead of him and Tanner followed. At the door Tanner grimaced. The sun was rising much earlier than he had anticipated.

"Tell me if the way is clear," he said to Rodrigo, who stepped out and checked the back street. Rodrigo merely nodded and gestured with his hand for Tanner to come. Without looking back, he made it to the car before Tanner did.

Tanner climbed in and started the engine. "We're going on to Fortin de las Flores," he said, mainly to Benito. "Your father will be all right until we return."

"*Sí,* he is a very smart man. He will not take any chances."

"Good. Now, which one of you wants to give me directions? There's going to be a little señorita there who needs my attention."

Thirty minutes later Tanner parked the car near the hotel at the Fortress of the Flowers. "Benito, stay in the car again. Pretend to be asleep or something until we return." He looked at

300

Rodrigo. "Do you have the note and map?"

"They are in my pocket."

"All right, you go into the lobby and watch. If you see anything that doesn't look right, signal me. I want to be able to see you at all times. I'll be in the dining room. When Consuelo enters, I'll point her out to you, although I doubt you'll have any trouble spotting her after the description I gave you. Make damned sure she has that note and map in her hand before she leaves; otherwise she'll never know where to meet us."

"Everything will work out. You will see."

"Go ahead and get out. I'll follow you in five minutes."

Tanner watched until Rodrigo disappeared into the stucco building; then he sighed heavily, admitting that his thoughts were bouncing between this assignment and Carly. He'd been preoccupied with her since he'd spoken to Omi. Tanner suddenly felt a strange, tightening sensation around his mouth. Why in hell had she come? he thought, angry at her. If she had learned anything about Therese's involvement in Mexico, then she also had to know what a risk it was to come here. Hell, anyone with half a brain would have stayed home. He almost hoped he'd never see her again, because he was sure he'd strangle her if he did. What he'd begun to admire as spunk and guts he now considered foolish and rash. She wouldn't last a minute if she ended up in Diego's hands. And the very idea of that happening scared the hell out of him.

Tanner stopped his mental tirade, finally admitting that his anger was actually desperate worry. Sick inside, he felt torn between finishing this assignment and going after Carly. But Therese's life was hanging by a thread. As far as Tanner knew, Carly was all right, and he also knew she would be in good hands—Hank's. That thought at least made it bearable for Tanner.

He glanced at his watch. It was time to move. He was going after Therese, no matter how hard his heart cried out for him to check on Carly. He shook his head, concentrating his attention on the matter at hand. Although he and Rodrigo were probably safe in Fortin de las Flores for the time being, Tanner was not one to take chances. This area of Mexico was like a small town—everybody knew everybody else and everything that happened. At most, Orizaba was only eight miles away from this village, and big news traveled swiftly, too swiftly in this instance.

Looking at the surrounding area, Tanner noticed that everything seemed sleepy and quiet. Still . . . Beneath his jacket he touched the cold metal of his gun. He stuck his hand down his boot and made sure his small .38 was safely tucked away. Then he turned to Benito.

"We shouldn't be gone long."

When Benito's only reaction was to blink his

eyes, Tanner shook his head, then swung out of the car and walked to the entrance. In the hallway he spotted Rodrigo sitting on a bench thumbing through a magazine. Without pausing, Tanner walked past him into the dining room and took a table, not waiting for the hostess to seat him.

A waiter appeared and Tanner ordered *huevos rancheros* and coffee. He realized he was starving and asked the waiter to add extra tortillas to his meal. The waiter brought his coffee, and just as Tanner took his first savory sip Consuelo walked in, causing him to spill coffee down his chin. He grabbed a napkin and held it to his face, wondering where the hell she'd found such . . . vulgar clothing.

She looked like the brassiest whore he'd ever seen. Her clothes were cheap, bright, and gaudy. A large gold earring dangled from one ear, while a huge orange disk ornamented the other. Her peasant blouse was bright lime green and cut so low it . . . Well, Tanner was sure if she lifted her arm even a little, the blouse would slip right down her ample bosom, giving everyone in the room an unimpeded view of the flesh beneath. A tight narrow skirt was slit open to her thigh and squeezed her rounded hips. He choked back a chuckle as he avoided looking her in the eye. But he had to hand it to her—she had it and she flaunted it. But orange hair? he thought, blinking at the blinding halo it made. She looked like a tropical bird, with the top of her hair cut short and standing up in spikes, clearly resembling a plume, and the rest of it hanging in wild curls down to her hips. Last time he'd seen her, her hair had been as black as coal. Now it was as red as the devil's . . .

Tanner coughed discreetly and turned away, letting her know he didn't want her to approach him at this time. Lord knew *everyone* would remember seeing him if she did.

The waiter brought his meal, and he wasted no time putting it away. He rolled a tortilla in his hand and dipped it in the spicy red sauce on top of the scrambled eggs, then bit off a huge chunk, munching heartily. Before he knew it, he was finished and feeling a little guilty because all Benito and Rodrigo had had was a bowl of beans each hours before. He signaled the waiter and ordered two breakfasts to go.

Consuelo did her best to keep everyone's attention on her as she sat down at a table. She was a pro. Tanner lowered his head and smiled. She made a production of crossing her legs, knowing that every eye, male and female, was riveted on her hip. Tossing back the length of flaming red hair, she tucked her fingers into the bodice of her blouse and adjusted her top, causing her upper body to jiggle for several seconds after she removed her fingers.

Just keep it up, sweetheart, he thought, as the waiter brought him the take-out meals. He planned to have her repeat her performance very soon.

Tanner paid for the meals and left with a smile on his face. In the car he waited for Consuelo to depart. It wasn't long before she sauntered out into the sunlight, swaying her hips as she left. Rodrigo slowly appeared in her wake, his eyes glued on Consuelo's voluptuous bottom. Tanner thought he was going to have to honk the horn to regain the man's attention. But Rodrigo finally shook his head as if to clear it, then turned and walked, almost trancelike, to the car.

"She has it," he said, and Tanner wondered briefly from the look in Rodrigo's eyes if he meant her body or the note.

He tossed the bag with the food into Rodrigo's hand. "Here. There's a meal for each of you. You're going to need your strength."

"Gracias," Rodrigo replied but merely clutched the food to his chest. Tanner frowned. Poor Benito would have to eat squashed food.

"Have you known her long?" Rodrigo asked breathlessly.

"For some time." Tanner found his reaction amusing.

Benito, not caring about Rodrigo's infatuation, reached over the seat and snatched his share of the food.

"I always believed that Linda was the most beautiful woman I had ever seen, but *ai, chihuahua!* That señorita is . . ."

"Yeah, she is," Tanner answered dryly. But the

feeling Consuelo usually aroused in him was noticeably absent. He suddenly found himself thinking of another body, not quite so full but altogether feminine. He refused to think about the face that matched that body.

He started the car. "You'll be seeing her again, Rodrigo. In about thirty minutes, if all goes right."

As Tanner drove up the narrow road, he thought about Omi's reaction to the bill he would undoubtedly receive for damages done to the rented car. Thankfully he had Benito's cousin's car to use today. At least it helped them keep a low profile. He was certain Diego's people were hunting for the rented car at that very moment.

"There is the path," Rodrigo said, pointing to a barely perceptible road, much like the one to Huerve's barn, that veered off through the trees.

"Were you raised here?" Tanner asked.

"No. Why do you ask?"

"It's just that you're very familiar with this area. You must have spent some time here." Giving the car some gas, Tanner plowed through the bushes and drove straight ahead.

"I played here as a child. My father had a woman here, and when he visited her he brought me along so my poor mother would not be suspicious. They always sent me off to play while they . . ."

"I see." Tanner grinned, understanding Rodrigo exactly.

The small circle of flat land Rodrigo had told him about came into view. Tanner stopped the car, then looked at his watch. It was eight-thirty in the morning. The whole day loomed before them, but he needed most of that time to formulate and organize his plan to rescue Therese from the house on the mountain and bring her back here to Fortin de las Flores. If things worked out, Tanner was going to contact Hank and get Carly and Therese out of the country together.

Tanner looked at Rodrigo. "I meant to ask how your head's feeling?"

"Better, *mucho* better."

"It looks awful," Tanner said, intentionally blunt.

Rodrigo whipped the rearview mirror around and stared in horror at the dark bruise covering his forehead and blackening his left eye. "Consuelo must have thought I looked terrible," he said, grimacing.

"Not Consuelo. She loves macho men." Tanner turned his face away and grinned.

"Señor, will we be finish before this afternoon?" Benito asked, finally breaking the silence he'd maintained since they'd left Orizaba.

"I don't think so, Benito. Why?"

He shrugged, then sighed. "No reason, señor."

Tanner was really beginning to feel badly for the squatty little man. He didn't want to drag Benito around with him, but dammit, he'd no choice. "Just think, Benito, in a few days this'll all be over and you can settle back and relax." Benito didn't seem too thrilled.

The faint sound of an engine reached Tanner's ears. He stared anxiously at the path, anticipating the sight of Consuelo's late-model Volkswagen. He wasn't disappointed. It cleared the brush and pulled up alongside his car. Tanner got out, with Rodrigo and Benito following, and met Consuelo as she opened the door and stepped out.

He whistled softly, bringing a gentle smile to her lips. She sauntered toward him, giving his body an appreciative going-over. Upon reaching him, she leaned her well-endowed form against him and gave him a long, lingering kiss.

"It has been too long, *hombre*. I am glad you have returned."

Tanner held back a sigh. Whatever he had felt for her—or her body—was gone. The kiss had proven that to him.

"It's good to see you too, Consuelo. I just wish the circumstances were different."

"What is the problem? Who is your friend?" She pointed toward a wide-eyed Rodrigo.

"This is Rodrigo. He worked with Linda Montoya."

"Who?" Consuelo asked, turning on her charm as she reached for Rodrigo's hand.

"I'll explain later," Tanner reponded, realizing she didn't know Therese as Linda. "And this is

Benito. He's sort of along for the ride."

"I see," Consuelo said, dropping Rodrigo's hand. "What has happened?"

"Linda"—Tanner smiled at Consuelo's obvious confusion—"was picked up two days ago by a man named Diego. Do you know of him?"

She paused a moment, then shook her head. "I do not think so." She flipped her hair saucily over her shoulder. "But I cannot truthfully say I remember every man I meet."

Or make, Tanner silently added. "He works for a very important man around here. La Pantera is the only name we know him by. His men are holding Linda, and, if possible, we have to get her out of there tonight—if she's still alive. Did you bring the chopper?"

"How do you think I made it here so quickly from Mexico City?" Consuelo asked, smiling.

"Where you're concerned," Tanner said, "one never knows. Now, this is what I've planned. . . ."

Carly stared at Therese. After hours of talking and worrying, the fear she felt had not lessened. There had to be a way out of this mess, Carly thought. The Jameson family couldn't survive another disaster.

She and Therese were still in the same room, and it was stiflingly hot. Carly stared at the shade drawn over the closed window and wondered how they were going to stand the heat throughout the rest of the afternoon.

"Do you think they'll feed us before we face the firing squad?" Carly asked.

"Not funny, Carly," Therese replied, her temper obviously short.

Carly ignored her. "Maybe that's how they plan to do us in, by starvation."

Therese favored her with a sharp glare. "They haven't decided what to do with us yet. Be glad everything's still quiet."

"Everything but my stomach. My God, Therese, it must be two o'clock at least."

"Maybe they're waiting until it gets dark."

Carly lowered her head. Nighttime, blackness, when evil things happened. She shook her head vigorously, refusing to believe she could possibly die. The thought seemed ludicrous; she was too young, she had too much living to do! God wouldn't be so cruel.

She stretched out on the rough blanket covering the bed and clutched a hard pillow to her breast. She decided to give Therese a reprieve and be quiet.

Therese, however, paced the room like a caged animal. Every few minutes she lifted the shade on the window and peered out. Carly knew that all she would see was a different guard. Jorge had been relieved earlier that morning.

"Damn them!" Therese finally exploded, slapping the shade down. "These bastards are going to succeed. All my work has been for nothing. Do you realize . . ." She stopped herself in midsentence. "No, you couldn't begin to understand."

Carly rolled over and sat up. "Maybe not," Carly said, her own temper flaring. "But I'm not an idiot, and I'm not the same naive little sister you used to know. Do you have any idea what it's been like for me these past nine months? Can you imagine what it was like making funeral arrangements for Father, praying to God with all my heart that I wouldn't have to repeat the same arrangements a week later for Ellis? Trying to find out where in hell you were—wondering if you were dead too! I may not be half as worldly as you, but I damn well don't deserve your condenscending remarks either."

Therese brushed her long black hair away from her face. Carly realized that Therese was walking a tightrope, that more than she could ever imagine depended on Therese's release. But she wasn't going to take the brunt of her sister's tension any longer.

"I'm sorry, Carly," Therese finally said. "I know it must have been hell on you. My God, he was my father too. I wish . . ." She bit her lip and turned away.

Carly felt a little ashamed of herself. "I'm sorry too. Let's quit bickering, all right?" Therese nodded.

"I can't get used to you as a brunette," Carly said, changing the subject. "How long do you think it'll take until you're a blond again?"

311

"Only my hairdresser knows for sure." Therese smiled, then walked over and placed her arm around Carly. "What a time I've had keeping the blond roots covered up." She bent her head and parted her hair so that Carly could see. "If I don't watch out I'm going to look like a skunk."

"At least you don't smell like one. I think I'd give anything for a bath."

"I would too." Therese fanned the air with an exaggerated motion of her hand.

Carly laughed, then reached for a lock of her sister's silky hair. "I've always envied you and Ellis your blonde hair."

"And I've always envied your thick curls."

Carly held up a lock of her hair. "Wanna trade?"

Carly lifted the shade and looked out into the night. Her shoulders slumped; she felt defeated. Being cooped up in the room all day with Therese had been wearing. They had been allowed to leave the room only for personal reasons and were forced to return before they'd had time to think of doing anything else. They'd eaten one meal several hours before, but it had hardly been filling.

Therese was leaning against the wall, staring vacantly at the ceiling. "There's no way out of here," she said, breaking the silence. "I've thought of a hundred different possibilities for escape, but none of them will work as long as I'm kept in this room."

Carly dropped the shade and copied Therese's pose. The ceiling was filthy. "How can we convince them to let us out of here?"

"I don't know. Think you can manage to barf again?" Therese asked, smiling weakly.

"Probably, if I knew for sure what I'd eaten for supper."

Therese wrinkled her nose. "It was mainly *frijoles*. Might have been a little horse meat in it, but not much."

"Yuck! Don't say any more."

Therese pushed herself away from the wall and crossed her arms in front of her. "This room is making me crazy. I need some fresh air."

"Want me to break the window?"

"Not unless you're prepared to hit the dirt when they start shooting."

"I don't have that much energy. I wonder if Jorge is back on guard duty."

"Didn't you see him out there when you looked?"

"It's so dark I couldn't see a thing. I wonder if anyone is out there?" Carly said hopefully, lifting the shade again and straining to see something.

"You can bet someone's out there," Therese said. "And whoever it is is probably getting a cheap thrill every time you look out."

Carly's eye brows shot up. "Do you suppose . . ."

"Don't even think that, Carly. We'd only end up getting hurt. They don't barter that way. If they wanted you, they'd take you."

"I hope I repulse them then."

"I doubt it. Diego's probably warned—"

The bedroom door flew open and slammed against the wall. The guard, Manuel, entered, pointing his rifle at the two women and ordering them outside. Carly reached for Therese, holding onto her as they were led back to the house and the room in which they'd been reunited the night before.

Diego sat, grinning sadistically as they entered. "So, the two sisters are now openly showing their relationship. That is good. Families should stick together in a crisis, which is what you are both about to face." He looked at the guard. "Manuel, take Señorita Linda to the car."

"Wait just a damned minute!" Carly said, taking a step toward the man. "Where do you plan to take her?"

Diego smiled. "Ah, little one, I wonder if La Pantera would be as anxious to meet you as he is to be reunited with your sister. Perhaps I should have told him you were here. But I didn't want to upset his special plans for Linda. He does not take to change very well, does he?" This he asked Therese.

"How should I know?"

"You will see how . . . disappointed he is in you soon enough. You should not have tried to trick

314

him."

Obviously undaunted, Therese stepped forward and grabbed Carly by the arm. "I want my sister to go with me."

Did he always have to smile? Carly thought as he answered Therese. "This is not possible. La Pantera has no use for her."

There had to be a way out of this, Carly thought. "He might change his mind if he sees me," she retorted boldly.

"Little jewel, you are mine. . . ." Again he gestured for Manuel. "Take Linda to the car," he said, then turned back to Carly. "Your fate is in your hands. You may spend your remaining hours with me, or eternity in a stinking hole in the mountain."

"No!" Therese shoved Manuel into Diego, knocking them both to the floor. She grabbed Carly by the arm and ran, but Manuel was too fast. He leapt to his feet, blocking the door. Without hesitating, Therese jumped and kicked him, catching him on the jaw. Again he fell to the floor, this time losing his grip on the rifle. Therese lunged for it, gripping it tightly in her hands. Carly stood dumbfounded. As Therese spun around, the cracking sound of a pistol exploded.

"No!" Carly screamed, watching in horror as Therese's body was thrown backward, the rifle slipping through her fingers. A red stain seeped through her blouse, coating her shoulder.

Carly turned on Diego, but the gun he held in his hand stopped her. He threw back his head and laughed. "You'd better cooperate, señorita, unless you want to end my anticipated pleasure with your body by provoking me into taking your life now."

Carly twisted to look at Therese, who was struggling to sit up. Regardless of the consequences, Carly rushed to her side. "Are you all right?" she asked, her voice strained.

Therese placed her hand over the wound. "I think so." It seemed to Carly that the blood was rushing from Therese's face, leaving it white, to run out through the wound.

Carly glared at Diego. "Don't just sit there, you moron. She needs help!"

"And I will see that she gets it," he replied casually. "La Pantera would have me killed if she did not make it to see him. As it is, he is going to be very angry with me." He shrugged nonchalantly. "Manuel, take her to the car."

Carly tried to hang on to her sister, but Manuel kicked her, then shoved her out of the way.

"Don't fight them, Carly," Therese begged.

"What am I supposed to do?" Carly screamed. "Just give up?"

With sad eyes, Therese stared at her as she was hauled out. She refrained from saying anything more.

As Therese disappeared through the door, hatred in its purest form coursed through Carly.

316

She lunged for Diego; the pistol he held could have been a toy for all the notice she gave it. She raked her nails down the side of his face, bits of flesh clinging to them. The pistol fell from his hand but before either of them could reach for it, Carly felt someone's fingers biting into her shoulder. The pain nearly paralyzed her.

"*¡Perra!*" Diego screamed, backhanding her. She blinked against the blackness that threatened to overcome her. She heard Diego chastise Jorge. But why? He hadn't done anything.

Suddenly the fingers gripped her shoulder again. Pain made her head swim. It was the same feeling she'd experienced at the cantina. She fought against the dizziness; she had to see where they were taking Therese. But pain won and she shut her eyes, unable to do anything but stand as she was, shaking.

CHAPTER FIFTEEN

"Get her out of my sight," Diego ordered, anger singeing every word.

Carly groaned as the pressure on her shoulder eased. She opened her eyes and discovered it was Jorge who had been hurting her, who still had the power to do so as long as he kept his hand on her. For some reason that upset her terribly, and she was sure it showed on her face.

He pulled her forward and Carly had no choice but to follow him. With hatred burning in her eyes, she glared at Diego, feeling a modicum of satisfaction as she watched him mop his cheek with a blood-soaked handkerchief. She silently prayed he'd die of poisoning from those scratches. No one had the right to put her through such anguish, fear, and pain.

"Let go of me, Jorge!" she whispered firmly.

He eased his grip but didn't release her. Carly winced at the sounds of a car door slamming and the unmistakable hum of an engine starting. *Oh, God, what am I going to do?* she cried mentally, knowing she might never see her sister again. Tears rose in her eyes as she blindly followed Jorge back into the room—her cell.

Jorge released her and shut the door. Taking her by the hand, he walked to the window, lifted the shade, and pointed to the window catch—it was unlocked. He held his fingers up to his lips, warming her not to speak. Tears again built in Carly's eyes. He was trying to show her that she had a chance to escape; he was giving her that chance. Seeing her tears, he placed his hand on her shoulder and gently massaged the area he had hurt.

"Why?" she whispered.

His features remained somber, but he lifted her hand, keeping his eyes glued to her face, and kissed her open palm. A sob caught in her throat.

"You were the one behind me at the cantina, weren't you?"

He blinked.

"Please talk to me," she begged, clutching desperately at his hands.

He shook his head.

"Please, Jorge."

He opened his mouth wide, then closed his eyes as if in pain. Carly's breath caught in her throat; her stomach felt as if it had dropped to her toes. His tongue had been cut out.

"Who did that to you? Diego?"

He turned away from her, but Carly grabbed his arm and held him still.

"Leave with me," she begged. He pried her fingers from his arm. "Don't you understand?" she insisted. "Together we could make it away from here." Jorge looked down at her, his black eyes dull. Carly shook her head sadly. "You won't come, will you?"

He blinked, then, almost regretfully, shook his head. Gently pushing her aside, he moved to leave.

Carly didn't turn to look at him as she whispered, *"Muchos gracias, Jorge."*

He left quickly, closing the door firmly behind him. Carly ran to the window and lifted the shade. Through the glass she saw red taillights disappear into the night. Therese was gone.

But Carly didn't give in to the immense pain that struck her; she made herself go on. She strained to see if anyone was guarding her window. If she could just make it far enough into the woods, she thought, she could hide for days. . . . But she didn't have days! Therese was injured; she needed medical attention now.

Controlling the impulse to jerk the window up and run, Carly calmed herself. She had to think rationally. She had only one shot at escape, one chance to make it safely back to the city for help.

She moved away from the window and sat down on the bed. The main thing was to reach Orizaba safely, she thought. She had to find help to

321

get Therese back. But she had no idea where they had taken her sister, nor how far away the city was.

It suddenly dawned on her that Jorge had probably intended her to leave immediately. If she moved now, while Diego was still in an uproar, she'd have more time and a better chance of success than if she waited until everything settled down. He'd never expect her to try to escape right beneath his nose.

The thought of dying while making a run for it was infinitely more appealing than the threat of rape.

Carly crept to the window but stopped just short of lifting the shade. The light was on. It would shine out the window, giving everyone around a clear view of her. Quietly, and with a calm that surprised even herself, she went to the light switch and turned it off, plunging the room into the same blackness she had awakened to the night before. She returned to the window and slid the shade up as far as it would go, biting her lip at the fluttering sound it made. She paused, waiting to see if the noise had aroused anyone. When several moments passed she heaved a sigh of relief and reached for the window. It was heavy, and she had to strain to lift it. It was an old window, the kind that had to be propped open, but there wasn't any slat to place beneath it. There was no screen either. She would just have to hold it open herself until she slid out.

Carly pushed it up as high as it would go, then

hoisted her skirt around her hips and lifted her leg through the opening. Switching hands on the window, she lifted her other leg and swung it out. Now she was sitting on the window ledge holding up the window with both hands. Keeping her balance, she leaned forward and lowered the window until it rested on her shoulders. Then, gripping the sill with her hands, she slid forward slowly.

As she inched out, the window moved downard, still supported by her body. But soon she was forced to stop. There was no way her feet were going to touch the ground without her jumping, and if she jumped the window would slam shut.

She couldn't let something this stupid be her downfall, she thought, taking a moment to decide what she had to do. She pushed the window up a few inches, then rolled onto her stomach, letting the window down again until it rested on her back. She began to slide out backward, wanting to cry each time the rough wood of the window frame scraped her back. Finally her head cleared the opening and, reaching up, she was able to ease the window down and jump, grunting softly as her feet landed solidly on the ground.

She bent over at the waist, catching her breath, but didn't allow herself the luxury of resting. She moved quickly to the back of the house, stopping at the corner where she flattened herself against the rough stucco wall. Please, don't let anyone be there, she thought as she cautiously peered around the corner. She took a deep breath; either her luck was running good or Jorge had taken care of it, for no one was guarding the rear of the house.

A light from one of the windows clearly illuminated a wall of trees some hundred yards away. If she could just make it to the trees, she knew she had a good chance of escaping. She clutched her skirt, wishing it were a darker color than yellow. Hoping no one happened to be looking out the window, she prepared herself for a mad dash across the tall grass.

Tanner reached the grove of trees behind Diego's house just in time to see a palely dressed figure, obviously a woman, climb out of the window. Damn, he thought, a smile pulling at his lips. Maybe his plan was going to work more smoothly than he'd expected. That *had* to be Therese. He watched as she reached the edge of the house, then hesitated as if undecided about what to do. Maybe she'd run right toward him, he thought, making his mission that much easier—if one could call anything about this mess easy—to accomplish. He moved back behind a tree and waited, keeping an eye on the woman as she hovered, getting ready to run.

He glanced at his watch. Consuelo would be arriving at any moment. According to the plan he had concocted, he had landed the chopper several miles up the mountain and hiked down to the house, leaving Rodrigo and Bonito waiting in the chopper. Consuelo was to pretend that her car had broken down a mile or so down the road, leaving the Volkswagen parked as she walked to the house for help. Once in the house, her seductive charms were to take over, causing a disturbance among the men and giving Tanner enough time to enter the house, find Therese, and get her out. Consuelo would then be on her own, while he and Therese raced back to the chopper and left.

Tanner remembered how Consuelo had smiled at him, telling him she had no doubt that she would be able to leave when the time was right. She'd told him bluntly that if Therese would only use her body the right way, she wouldn't be in the situation she was in. But, since Consuelo liked the *Anglo* girl and taking risks, she didn't mind helping Therese out.

From the looks of things, Tanner thought, still smiling, Therese wouldn't need Consuelo's help after all. Therese had always been a woman with principles and had stuck to them no matter what. And until now she had always managed to find a way out. She was going to be pretty damned surprised, however, when she finally sprinted into the trees and was grabbed by Tanner.

He tensed. He could hear Consuelo bitching as she walked up the road. The guards in the front of the house heard her too, and all prepared for action. Why wasn't someone guarding Therese's side of the house? he thought, then wondered what she'd done to whoever had been posted there.

Suddenly one of the men began to laugh. Tanner heard him tell the others that Consuelo was a whore who had come to service them.

The unmistakable sound of a palm striking a cheek rang out. Then Consuelo let loose a string of obscenities. The guards relaxed and, all of them moved from their posts to get a good look at the woman, who was still in the darkness. Tanner nearly laughed. He had no trouble understanding the foul Spanish she used to explain about her stupid car.

"No!" Tanner suddenly mouthed, seeing Therese's figure poised to run. *Don't! Not yet!* he wanted to shout. What was the matter with her? She should have realized something was about to come down.

"Son-of-a-bitch!" he bit out under his breath as she bolted. There was nothing he could do now but pray that she made it.

Carly heard the guards' voices and knew they were after her. The sound of their feet hitting the ground at a dead run forced her into action sooner than she wished. She leaped out from behind the house, running as fast as she could make her legs move. Carly sprinted halfway across the back of the house, then darted across the ground ahead of her, her mind set on reaching the trees.

She stretched her legs, covering a lot of ground

with each long stride. Her arms swung in rhythm, helping her maintain her footing. The closer she came to the trees the safer she felt. She was going to make it! In a matter of seconds she knew she'd be deep in the woods and able to hide herself. Yes, she nearly shouted, she was going to make it!

Even when she reached the trees she didn't stop. She ran as far as she could until the thick underbrush made her slow down. Finally out of breath, with a stitch in her side, she was forced to stop. Her chest heaved from her exertions, as she gulped in huge amounts of air. Not able to stand up without pain, she bent over at the waist.

She had made it. She had really made it!

From out of nowhere, a huge hand covered her mouth; its twin encircled her waist. Before she could react she was jerked upright and held against a rock-hard body. Her blood went cold; chills ran down her spine, and when her heart stopped beating she knew she was going to die of fear before whoever had her could do her any harm.

No, dammit! She had come too far to be stopped like this.

She kicked backward, her foot solidly connecting with the man's shin. She twisted and turned, clawed and scratched.

"Stop it!" the man growled in her ear.

Her heart leaped into her throat. It couldn't be, yet the rough voice was so familiar, she immediately ceased her struggle.

Tense all over, she flinched as his arm tightened on her waist.

"Dammit, Therese, do you want the entire camp to know where we are?"

Carly stopped moving and allowed him to turn her around.

When she saw the gleam in his dark eyes, she whispered venonmously, "Sorry Tanner, you have the wrong sister."

"Carly?" He grabbed her by the upper arms and shook her. "What the hell are you doing here?"

An almost hysterical giggle escaped her. "Would you believe I missed you so badly that I set this up so you could rescue me?"

"Stop it!" He shook her again. "How the hell . . ."

A gun blasted nearby, snapping his attention back to the house. Half dragging her behind him, he stomped to the edge of the trees.

Carly felt hollow; she trembled uncontrollably. Rubbing her arms, she tried not to imagine what was happening at the house. She wanted to laugh, she wanted to cry. She wanted to wrap herself around Tanner and be held, wanted to hold him. She wanted to slap him, rail at him. But above all, she wanted him to get her safely away. She wanted him to help her save Therese.

Her breath caught as another gun exploded, and she dug her nails into Tanner's arms. She wanted to run, desperately, wanted him to run with her. "We have to get out of here," she whispered frantically. "They've discovered I'm gone."

He glared at her as if she were dispicable. "We're not going anywhere until we get your sister out of there."

"If she was there I'd be the first to go after her. But she's gone. They took her away a little while ago."

Tanner gripped her arms again. "What do you mean, they took her away? Dammit, where did they take her?"

"I don't know! A man—person—someone called La Pantera sent for her."

A growl tore from his throat. Tightening his grip on her, he took off, dragging her after him. He walked fast, trampling down the tall bushes as he went and pulling Carly willy-nilly behind him. They must have traveled ten minutes at breakneck speed before he stopped.

His chest moved as rapidly as hers from the exertion. "We have to make it to the chopper. That's our only hope of getting away. No whining or crying if you get tired. Just keep up or I'll leave you behind."

"Go to hell!" she exclaimed, shoving him. "You just go to hell!"

"I probably will. But I don't want to go there tonight. Now move."

He shoved her roughly, keeping her close to him as he moved steadily ahead. Carly hated him intensely at that moment. If she hadn't wanted to make it to the chopper as badly as he did, she'd have dug in her heels and remained behind. But her freedom was the only hope she had of helping Therese. Swallowing her anger, she followed him for what seemed like hours.

A branch snagged her skirt, pulling her to a halt. Her abrupt stop caused Tanner to curse until he realized she was struggling to free her clothing. Carly felt him digging into his pocket, heard a strange click, then felt him sawing away at her skirt. As he worked to free her, she shook her head. This was a complete nightmare, but she was acutely awake, living each horror in minute detail.

The material fell around her ankles, and before she knew what Tanner was about, he had lifted it and stuffed it into his pocket. "We can't leave a trail," he explained; then he grabbed her arm—her sore, aching arm—again and once more plunged through the darkness.

In the distance she heard a noise very much like pebbles being hurled against a tin roof. Tanner stopped suddenly, holding his hand to her mouth.

When the noise came again it was more distinct, and Tanner stiffened; his anxiety was very apparent.

"Stay right here," he finally said.

"Where are you going?" she asked, desperately afraid of being left behind.

"You hear that noise?" She nodded. "That's

an Uzi, a small machine gun. I'm afraid our chopper is under fire."

"What are we going to do?" she whispered frantically.

"*We* aren't going to do a damned thing. *You* are going to stay put until I come back to get you."

Knowing this was no time to argue, she silently gave in.

"Find a place to hide and don't come out until you're positive it's me." He gripped her hand tightly.

"Tanner," she whispered, choking on her fear, "please be careful."

He cupped her head and pulled her tightly against him, kissing her hard on the mouth. "I'll be back as soon as everything is safe. Now go and hide." He pushed her away, pulled out his pistol, and left without looking back.

Damn! How had Diego's men found the chopper so fast? He'd been careful not to fly over the house. But someone, somewhere, must have seen or heard it and notified Diego.

Rodrigo and Benito were in big trouble. Tanner wasn't sure how good either of them was as a marksman, especially somber-faced Benito, but he was fairly certain neither of them had handled firearms very often. He had to reach them, had to be in time to help them. Neither of them deserved to be in such a rotten mess. As Tanner raced through

331

the gnarled bushes and trees, a distorted picture of Benito's face, screwed up in fear, flashed before his eyes. God, he said silently, please let me be in time.

Thanks to the pale light of the quarter moon, Tanner could see the blades of the chopper. He was within a hundred yards of the aircraft when he stopped. So far he'd heard only one gun, but that was all it would take to alert the rest of Diego's men that something was wrong.

The short blasts and the rain of bullets caused him to back away. The sniper was a fool! Didn't he know he could hit the fuel tank and blow it and himself away! Judging by the dull white flash that accompanied each shot, Tanner knew the gunman was unaware of his own danger.

Tanner spotted the sniper not twenty feet from the chopper, and he backed away, intending to circle in from behind. But time ran out; a low rumble was the only warning. Tanner hit the ground as the chopper exploded in a huge ball of red fire. Flaming pieces of metal flew everywhere, raining down all around him; his ears rang from the shock waves.

But for the moment Tanner didn't care. Rodrigo was gone. *Benito* was gone. Tanner rolled his face against the cool dirt beneath him. It was his fault for making them come with him.

Tanner grabbed a handful of dirt, then leaped to his feet and hurled it angrily into the night. Dammit, Diego wasn't going to win. Whatever it took, Tanner was going to make damned sure that Carly got away safely, and then he was coming back. He had a score to settle with the faceless Diego.

He glanced one last time at the burning skeleton of the chopper, then ran back to where he had left Carly.

"Carly!" he called out softly and waited for a response. But none came.

"Carly," he called again, turning his head as he heard a soft cry. "Carly?" Was she hurt? "Carly!" The crying grew louder. Tanner shoved shrubs and weeds out of his way, knowing she was somewhere beneath them. He found her huddled in a ball, her face resting on her knees.

"Are you hurt?" he asked, bending down to her.

She shook her head vigorously, then lifted her face to his. "We're not going to make it, are we?"

He took her in his arms, knowing it was impossible to comfort her, yet he needed the reassurance of holding her warm body for a moment. "We still have a chance. There's a car parked several miles away from here. If we hurry we just might make it yet." He pulled her to her feet and they took off again, heading back toward the house. But before they reached it, Tanner detoured, pulling Carly farther back into the dense foilage.

Carly's body stung from head to toe. She thought if another branch slapped her she'd scream. But then she heard the sudden yells of the Mexican guards close by, and her pain was quickly replaced by abject fear. The guards were firing their guns at anything that moved, and Carly knew that if she or Tanner were spotted, they wouldn't have the chance to surrender. Diego and his people wanted her—dead or alive. The same was true for Tanner, maybe even more so, since they probably knew he was somehow connected to Therese. A burst of adrenaline made Carly run even faster, so that Tanner was no longer actually pulling her along; although he was still ahead of her and still gripping her hand, she was now keeping pace with him.

When Tanner stopped unexpectedly, Carly ran into his back. He placed his hand briefly over her mouth, then released it. Carly knew she was not to make a sound. When Tanner took her by the hand again and crept slowly ahead, Carly made sure she stayed right behind him. She was so turned around she didn't have any idea where they were.

He crouched and tugged at her to do the same, causing her to lose her balance so that she fell into his lap. Tanner calmly slid her bottom onto the ground, then placed his hand on her shoulder.

"I have to leave you here for a few minutes," he whispered directly into her ear. But Carly wasn't about to let that happen. She shook her head, trying to turn around and face him, but he held her in place, painfully squeezing her shoulder. "I have to see if they've found the car."

In spite of his bone-crushing grip, Carly turned her head around, her face mere inches from his. "You may not have enough time to come back for me. Take me with you. I'll do exactly as you say; just don't leave me here."

He paused for a moment, then nodded. "Stay right behind me, and if I tell you to run, don't stop for any reason."

A stray moonbeam suddenly illuminated them and Tanner knocked Carly to the ground, falling on her with all his weight. Crushed beneath him, she felt safe; she wanted to wrap her arms around him and hold him tightly. It had to be the tension, the danger, the adreneline that were making her body suddenly respond to his. It couldn't be that she still felt attracted to him after all he'd put her through. The stream of light passed over them swiftly, plunging them into darkness again. Carly pressed her palms into Tanner's shoulders and shoved. For a brief moment he resisted, then, almost reluctantly she thought, he rolled away and sat up.

She, too, sat up and brushed herself off, glad that the darkness hid the blush that heated her cheeks.

"Let's go," he whispered tersely.

Carly scrambled to her feet, her legs feeling like rubber, but she followed closely, even though they slipped down small ravines and tripped over exposed tree roots. Her only desire was to make it to the car, not to have to run like a frightened animal anymore.

Again he stopped abruptly, and she felt him tense. Squinting her eyes, she searched the darkness, but all she saw were the silhouettes of trees.

Suddenly Tanner shoved her down, knocking the breath out of her as he landed painfully on her back. She couldn't breathe and she panicked.

"Stop it, Carly!" he ordered softly. "For God's sake, don't make a sound."

She became still instantly. Suffocating was a painless death, much less traumatic than a bullet hole through her head, she thought, her head swimming. Then miraculously she inhaled deeply, and her senses cleared. Tanner flattened against her even more, mashing her deeply into the ground, shoving out almost all the air she had managed to suck in. She closed her eyes tightly, suddenly understanding Tanner's motives as a beam of light shone several feet directly in front of her. The crunch of boots in the underbrush drew close, too close for comfort. They were going to be found, Carly thought frantically, they were going to be caught and killed. She didn't want to die!

She buried her face in the dirt, not wanting to see what was going to happen, who was going to execute them, when the first shot was going to come. But her sense of hearing suddenly seemed to become very acute, for every sound was magnified in her ears.

The guards were almost upon them she knew. Her breath caught in a silent sob, and Tanner again pressed against her in warning. Carly froze in her face-down position, but she was unable to prevent the shiver of fear that raced down her spine. When she became aware that someone was walking all around their bodies, she couldn't stand it any longer. She had to look. Her eyes popped open and she tensed from head to toe. A booted foot was now visible in the light beam, the boot of a large man. Tanner's light squeeze on her arm was the only reassurance she had not to move, that they hadn't been spotted.

Seconds, minutes, hours later—Carly didn't know how long they lay there—the guard finally moved on, walking away from them. Tanner eased his torso off her but kept the lower part of his body firmly in place. Carly, now able to breathe a little more easily with much of his weight removed, couldn't remember a time in her life she'd ever been so weak from fear, and she hated it. She hated knowing how easily one's life could be taken, hated the power one human being had over another.

Drawing on unexpected reserved energy, she lifted herself on her elbows. Tanner's breath coursed down the back of her neck, the soft warmth of it completely foreign to the circumstances they were in.

He finally rose to his knees and crawled off her. When Carly remained as she was, he rolled her over and sat her up, gently caressing her face before he enfolded her in his arms. Carly nestled against his chest, taking comfort in the steady heartbeat drumming against her ear.

"Carly," he said quietly, the sound of his voice an unexpected break in the silence. "I'm afraid we have a big problem." He spoke softly and slowly, to make sure she understood each word.

Sensing his alarm, she pulled away to face him. Again he ran his palm over her cheek, then brushed back her tangled hair.

Not wanting to hear the news he was about to impart, Carly grabbed Tanner's face and pulled his head down, surprising even herself when she kissed him deeply, passionately, with every ounce of emotion she possessed. For a moment Tanner resisted, but with a soft groan he relented and kissed her with a fervor that matched her own. She opened her mouth, accepted the total intimacy he gave, allowing him to block out all the evil she felt lurking about her. She leaned backward, drawing him down with her, wanting him to make her forget, however briefly, that she might die before the night was through. At first he moved with her, following her to the ground, then abruptly tore his mouth away.

"You've picked a helluva time to start something, sweetheart," he said hoarsely.

"Please, Tanner . . ."

His palm cupped the lower half of her face. "Carly, we have a problem much larger than this one." His eyes glittered in the darkness; Carly saw desire in their depths. But his words were beginning to sink in and she sagged against him, no longer trying to coerce him into making love to her.

"We didn't make it to the road in time," he said, keeping his voice low. "The car is gone."

She swallowed against the urge to cry. "How do you know?"

"The guards are all over the place. They may even have the car themselves, or they could be leaving it as a trap."

"What'll we do?" she asked in a weak voice.

Tanner sighed. "Walk. We're going to have to walk the rest of the night if we want to get away safely. It may take us days to make it off this damned volcano, but we'll do it! I promise you that."

Her chest tightened painfully and she closed her eyes. "What about Therese?"

"She's on her own."

"On her own," Carly repeated, a flash of anger siezing her. She sat up abruptly. "She's on her own against at least two dozen crazy men! That's really good odds, don't you think?" She grabbed Tanner by the forearms and tried to shake him, but he hardly budged. "Isn't there some way we can get off this mountain tonight?"

He in turn grabbed her by the arms. "Sure," he said sarcastically. "You could also win a one-way trip to the grave. Take your choice, sweetheart. But whatever you decide, don't think I'll go along with it. I've been around too long to let some pea-shooting sons of bitches take me out." He thrust her away and stood up. "You've got ten seconds to make up your mind."

Carly grasped a fistful of dirt. She wanted nothing more than to throw it in his face. But she didn't, because she knew he was right. No matter how badly she wanted to save her sister, it was impossible at this point.

She hesitated too long and Tanner took off, swallowed by the darkness. She scrambled to her feet and ran through the night, panicking when she realized he had truly left her. Suddenly an arm wrapped itself around her waist, and her knees buckled in fear. Spun around and lifted off her feet, Carly was just about to scream her head off when a voice tinged with humor said, "I thought you'd see it my way."

"Tanner," she whispered, weak with relief, "kiss my ass."

CHAPTER SIXTEEN

Carly was exhausted, Tanner thought, still pushing to cover as much ground as possible before the night was over. He looked at the sky, seeing the first pink rays of dawn breaking through the darkness, and shook his head in dread. The night had been their only advantage over their pursuers. Now they'd have to be more cautious than ever.

Stepping over a fallen tree, Tanner paused to help Carly maneuver it, then again set a steady pace.

He silently cursed fate.

He'd truly believed that he and Carly would make it to the car earlier that night. If Consuelo had known that he and Carly were coming she would have waited or returned somehow. The only thing Tanner could imagine was that Consuelo, knowing where the helicopter was supposed to be, had seen the ball of fire and assumed that he had died in the

343

explosion. He hoped she somehow eluded Diego's clutches and escaped in her car during all the excitement, since Tanner was almost certain it was gone. Unfortunately, now he was on his own with an unseasoned woman who, he granted, had held up beautifully so far but was apt to leap before she looked.

With the right training Carly would make a hell of an investigator, Tanner decided. Her instincts were good; she had a knack for being at the right place at the right time. She just wasn't trained to find the best way out of a tight situation.

Still, she had stamina. He wondered how many of the women he *had* worked with, including Therese and Consuelo, could have endured the strenuous hike they'd been forced to take. Hell, he was doing his best to ignore his own body's urgings to slow down and rest. But for the last five hours Carly had followed him up and down and over every obstacle without uttering a word.

He almost wished she had griped or collapsed, or even fainted. He didn't like the respect he was feeling for her, didn't like anything at all about the way he felt about her. Damn it, she was supposed to be out of his life already. When she left Galveston Island he'd thought it was ended. . . . But the emotions he had felt for her then had never left; in fact, they were mild compared to the way he felt now. One minute she was falling into his arms, the next she was shoving him away.

344

"Tanner?"

He stopped, turning at the sound of her voice.

"Tanner," she repeated as she leaned over at the waist and bent her knees, "I don't think I can go much farther without a rest." Her tangled, rust-colored hair fell over her face.

"We can't stop yet."

She lifted her head, peering at him through the strands of her hair. "I'm not asking for a nap, Heman. I just need a few minutes."

"If we stop now it'll be twice as hard to get going again."

She stood up straight, pushing her matted hair out of her face. "Then let's go," she replied dully, "before I fall on my face."

Tanner knew how she felt; even his steps were slower now. His calves ached from the unaccustomed strain of walking so far; Carly's legs had to be knotted with pain by now.

Again he stopped abruptly and again Carly walked into his back.

"Dammit, Tanner," she scolded, "if you don't quit stopping in front of me like that, I'm going to do my best to knock you down next time!"

He looked at her skeptically. "You'd better get a running start when you do."

She clenched her hands into fists. "Why can't you just hold up a hand or do *something* when you're going to stop? I feel as if I've run into a brick wall about ten times tonight."

"All right," he said, sighing, but conceding her point. "I'll try not to stop so quickly. There, are you satisfied?"

Her response was to look away from him. He could see that she was nearing the limits of her endurance. Her lips were compressed into a thin line, and her green eyes were bright with fatigue and a low, simmering temper.

"Why did we stop?" she asked, keeping her gaze locked on the horizon.

"Listen carefully," he said, "and maybe you can tell me."

He watched as she concentrated, then smiled when she smiled and said, "Do I hear running water?"

"I must have a Girl Scout on my hands."

"I believe I'd kill just for a drop."

"That won't be necessary." He pointed. "If we follow that small path we should find our water."

"If there's a path, there must be people nearby," Carly said apprehensively.

"Look closely, Carly. See the tracks? This path was made by deer."

"Deer? As in Bambi?"

"His cousins."

"That's good enough for me."

"Then what are we waiting for?"

Tanner led her down the path, as anxious for a cool drink as she was. The rush of water grew louder; he didn't realize he had so much energy left, but the sound drew him, making their steps lighter and quicker. Suddenly they entered a large clearing. He threw back his head and laughed. Carly kicked off her shoes and raced past him, plunging— clothes and all—into the small stream.

When her head broke the surface, she shouted, "This is heaven."

"That was dangerous," he called back, pulling off his gun harness and shirt. He tugged off his boots, then ran like a madman and fell face down in the water, losing his breath in its icy coldness.

He could hear Carly laughing as his head bobbed to the surface. "You could have warned me," he said, shaking the hair out of his eyes.

"Any fool should know that spring water is cold."

"I forgot."

"Betcha remembered fast enough, huh?"

He ignored her. "God, this feels good."

"Uh-huh," Carly agreed, scooping up a handful of water and drinking greedily. "It tastes even better."

He followed her example, but the water hit his empty stomach like lead. "Carly, don't drink too much," he said in a serious voice.

"Why? It's obviously fresh."

"I know that, but too much water on an empty stomach will make you sick."

"Couldn't I have just a little bit more?" she asked in mock despair.

"Wait awhile first."

"Tanner, really!"

"Don't drink anymore."

Carly slapped the water angrily, splashing him in the face. Turning, she stomped toward the shore.

Tanner wiped his eyes. "Where are you going?" he asked, staring at her retreating back.

"Away from you."

"What's that supposed to mean?" he asked, starting after her.

"Exactly what I said. Away from you!" Carly reached the shore; then, bunching up the tattered remains of her skirt, she squeezed it out in front of her.

Tanner was within several feet of her, with only his ankles still in the water. "You haven't always felt that way," he said calmly.

Carly spun around. "That was before I found out what a . . . a . . . That was before I discovered why you were so interested in me."

Tanner planted his hands on his hips. "And how did you discover that?"

Carly pressed her thumb against her chest, and Tanner had to tear his eyes away from the wet material clinging to her breasts and hugging her hips.

Carly, seeing his reaction, plucked her blouse away from her body. "I eavesdropped on you, just like you guys do to everybody else!"

"Spying, were you?"

"I never claimed to be anything other than what I was—a woman looking for her missing sister."

"You never told me that."

"I never lied to you either?"

"When did I lie to you?"

"Oh, come on, Tanner. Didn't you realize I'd put two and two together after you showed up at the hospital that night?"

Tanner sighed. "I was surprised you didn't corner me the minute you spotted me," he answered truthfully.

Carly's chest heaved. The wet top clung to her body, revealing that she wore the skimpiest of undergarments. "I didn't put it all together until later that night." She looked disgustedly at the ragged edges of her shorn skirt; then she spun around and walked away.

Tanner stepped out of the water and followed her. She sat down, staring off in the distance and ignored him.

"Why didn't you wait for an explanation from me? Why did you run back to Beaumont without a word?"

She glared at him. "How could I have trusted anything that came out of your mouth?"

He sat down beside her. "It seems to me that we both had our wires crossed."

"Tanner, I was going around in circles trying to find Lisa Curtis. Can you imagine what a shock it was to discover that she was dead? The woman had been my sister's roommate. Can you imagine what I thought when I first saw the Diamond Lounge? Do you have any idea of what went through my mind when I realized that my sister had actually worked in that rat hole?"

"Carly . . ."

"But you had all the answers. You knew where Therese was. You knew why I was looking for her, and yet you listened to me tell you I had a job to do and never batted an eye. You tried to manipulate me into staying with you instead of seeking help. And then, when I came running back from the Coast Guard base that morning, I overheard you telling your partners in crime everything I needed to know. Do I have to go on? I may have had my wires crossed, but you sure as hell didn't."

"I was doing my job," he answered bluntly.

"Your job stinks."

"It might, but it sure as hell saved your ass last night."

"If you had just been truthful with me in Galveston, I'd never have gotten into the trouble I was in."

"How the hell *did* you find our Therese was at Diego's house?"

"I didn't. I was knocked out and brought there."

"Carly, you have to tell me everything that Therese said to you—anything you can remember the men saying."

"She wouldn't tell me anything."

"Do you know where she was taken?"

"No. All I know is that someone called La Pantera wanted her brought to him. Tanner," Carly said, tears welling in her eyes, "she was shot in the shoulder."

"How bad was it?"

"I don't know. It bled everywhere, but she was able to walk."

Tanner managed to keep from expressing his anxiety. "The last thing you're going to want to do is keep walking, but we have to get off this mountain and back to Orizaba. Hank's probably called in—"

"Hank . . .?"

"He was sent to watch out for you, but obviously you were gone by the time he arrived."

"But he was hurt," Carly said anxiously.

Tanner smiled. "It was supposed to be an easy assignment for him. But he doesn't know you like I do."

"Very funny."

"But true. Anyway, he's in Orizaba. And if we want to save your sister we've got to get there as quickly and safely as possible."

"How long will it take us?" Carly asked.

"I don't know. We're not high enough to be above the snow line, but we're a far cry from the bottom too. The traveling is going to be rough, but

351

at least it's all downhill."

"How long?" she asked impatiently.

"Twenty-four to thirty-six hours." Tanner stood up. "Come on. We've got to cover as many miles as we can. Before long it'll be too hot to do anything."

"I don't care how hot it is. I just want to reach Orizaba and get my sister out of danger. I don't think I could stand it if anything were to happen to her."

"It won't," he said, gently taking her in his arms.

Carly leaned against his chest, the fight going out of her. His heartbeat accelerated. "I hope you're right," she whispered.

Tanner eased her back, looking deeply into her eyes. "I am right," he said. "Come on. We have to get going."

Carly took his outstretched hand and pulled herself up. She brushed leaves and dirt from her damp shirt, then bent down and lifted the heavy leather harness holding Tanner's gun. "I believe this is yours, sir," she said, marveling at the way her spirits had lifted.

"How right you are, dear. Shall we go?"

"But of course."

As the morning wore on the heat grew unbearable. Carly unbuttoned the bottom half of her shirt and tied it into a knot beneath her breasts; then she lifted the hem of her skirt and tucked it into her waistband. Tanner had removed his shirt earlier and tied the sleeves around his neck. The gun harness, looped around his shoulder, rubbed against his bare skin and Carly could see the painful-looking blister it had formed. Slick with perspiration, his skin was coated with leaves and twigs, making him look as grimy as she felt.

The pain had long ago left her legs to be replaced by a welcomed numbness. Her steps were automatic; each move she made was an exact duplicate of Tanner's. The air was so thin, talking became impossible. Each previous breath she sucked into her lungs was used just to sustain her through the journey; every time her mind screamed at her to stop, she made herself remember that Therese was injured, shot in the shoulder, that her life was in Carly's hands. If Carly didn't reach the city soon Therese would die.

Die! Die! Die! The word resounded in her mind, a chant that propelled her feet, pushed her body forward, sharpened her eyes.

She walked right into Tanner again; the force of the impact knocked her on her rump.

"Dammit, Carly, I help my hand up!" he said as he leaned down to help her up.

She wiped the sweat out of her burning eyes. "I wasn't looking," she said, refusing to take his hand.

He knelt beside her and brushed his hand

lightly across her head. "I'm sorry. Next time I'll turn around and catch you when you walk into me."

"I never realized a body could endure so much," she said, smiling weakly. "Did I hurt you?" Tanner shook his head. "Why did we stop?"

"I think I've found a place where we'll be safe until dark."

"Where?" She looked up eagerly.

"You have to stand up to see it."

With a groan Carly got to her feet. Following the direction of Tanner's pointing finger, she glanced through the trees, and there, no more than twenty feet away, was the poorest excuse for a hut she'd ever seen. Like gnarled fingers, vines had wrapped themselves all around it, giving the impression that they were the only thing holding the hut together.

"Do you think it's safe?" she asked skeptically.

"Safer than suffering a heat stroke or a bullet wound."

"Surely by now we've lost anyone who might be trailing us," she said.

"I wish I could tell you that was true, Carly. . . ."

"But?"

"They're not going to give up on us. We . . ." Tanner wiped his forearm across his brow. "Let's just say they stand to lose too much by letting us go free."

Carly didn't answer immediately. She understood the message; they were sitting ducks until they reached the safety of the city. "I'm all for taking a rest. Do you want to lead or follow?"

Tanner smiled and, as they had the first time Carly had ever seen him, his teeth glimmered in the sunlight. He was grimy and sweaty, and his hair was plastered to his head. A new growth of beard shadowed his face, making him look as intimidating as any of the men she'd seen on the waterfront in Galveston, yet that smile still did something to her. The lower half of her body quickened, and the desire to know him as intimately as a woman could know a man became strong, too strong.

She couldn't listen to her body. If she gave in to her desire now, she knew she'd only end up being more hurt than when she'd left him in Galveston.

The grin left Tanner's face. The expression in his eyes changed, narrowing into a look that told Carly he felt the same things she was feeling, and she was suddenly overwhelmed with sadness, for it could never be; there was no future for them.

She blinked and looked away. "Shall we go?" she asked quietly.

"Yes, but not that way." She frowned at him. "Let's walk a little farther, then we'll backtrack. It was only by accident that I saw the hut in the first place."

She was confused. Tanner smiled. "I was looking for a place to relieve myself. It just

355

happened to be the right time for me to go."

Carly giggled. "It must have been fate."

"Or a weak bladder."

"Whatever."

In no time at all Tanner had led her several hundred yards ahead; then, walking off to the side of their path, he backtracked to the hut, where he excused himself for a few moments. As soon as he returned he lifted a broken tree limb and began to pry a vine away from the window.

"Why don't we use the door?"

He looked at her as if she were a nitwit. "I don't want the front of the hut disturbed." He laced his fingers together palms up. "Face away from the window and step in my hands, and I'll boost you up."

Carly did as she was told, gasping as her rump hit the window ledge and the rotted wood crumbled beneath her weight.

"I wonder how old this place is," she said as she swung her legs around and into the hut.

Tanner patted her lightly on the back. "Be careful; the floor may not hold you."

"I beg your pardon?"

He grinned. "I mean the floor may be weak, and I'd hate to see you fall through."

Carly grinned back, thankful that the tension between them had been broken; then she carefully lowered herself to the dirty floor.

"So far so good," she said, sticking her head

out the window. "But it might not hold both of us. Why don't you just stay outside?" she added tongue in cheek.

"And why don't you just move out of the way?" he answered, reaching up and tweaking her hair.

Carly sighed dramatically. "If I must."

"You must," Tanner replied as he placed his palms on the rotted wood and pushed himself up. In a matter of moments he, too, was standing inside the hut, carefully checking each step he made across the filthy floor.

The hut was tiny, no more than fifteen feet long and eight feet wide. A rickety partition separated the room into two halves—one, Carly assumed, for cooking, the other for sleeping. No furniture had been left. A makeshift counter was leaning to one side, the weak boards that supported it were slowly pulling away from the wall.

Carly wrung her hands together. "It looks as if a good breeze would blow the roof off," she said, nodding toward the bare rafters overhead.

"I don't imagine it'll fall any time too soon," Tanner replied. "But be careful anyway." His features looked strained. "The last thing we need is an injury."

Squeezing her fingers until they hurt, Carly nodded, her brief period of teasing doused by reality.

"Why don't you lie down and rest for awhile?"

Tanner suggested.

Carly glanced down and shuddered at the thought of lying on the inch-thick dirt that coated the floor. Then she shook her head at her foolishness. Which was worse—being too tired to travel or adding a little more dirt to her already filthy person? Opting for the latter, she eased herself down.

"What about you?" she asked, lying on her side and pillowing her head on her arm.

"I have to close the window first. It's probably going to be like a furnace in here, but it can't be helped."

"It couldn't be any worse than that storeroom I sat in at the yacht basin."

Tanner smiled at her over his shoulder. "I was going to ask you about that."

She shrugged. "There isn't much to tell."

"Hmmm," Tanner grunted as he worked.

As she watched him, her eyelids grew heavy and she blinked, intending to wait until Tanner was ready to lie down before she fell asleep. But her lids grew increasingly heavy and difficult to hold open, and she closed them just for a moment. . . .

"Carly, would you help me for a minute?" Tanner asked. When she didn't answer he looked over his shoulder; then he smiled. She was fast asleep. He managed to secure the window without her help.

Thankfully the little room wasn't completely dark. The cracks in the roof admitted enough light so that he could see every corner of the interior. Several steps brought him right beside Carly's slumbering form and he knelt down. She may not like it, he thought, but he was going to sleep right beside her, just in case he had to awaken her quickly and soundlessly.

He stretched out beside her, grimacing as the dirt on the floor shifted beneath his weight. It definitely wasn't the same as sleeping on the packed earth outside.

Damn, but he was tired. He took several moments to work himself into a state of alertness even though he was going to be asleep. He concentrated on listening to the changing sounds of the outdoors, to the way the bushes rustled. Only when he was certain he'd awaken at the slightest difference in the sound pattern did he close his eyes and doze.

In her sleep, Carly saw the small clearing. She could hear the water running, calling her to come near. But she hesitated. It was the same spot she and Tanner had been at earlier that morning, yet it was different. How had she gotten back there? She didn't remember making the trip.

Tree branches hung like gnarled, arthritic fingers, moss dripping from their tips. But they hadn't looked that way before, she thought, wondering how they'd changed so quickly. The water suddenly roared angrily and sloshed over the bank, chanting to her to step to its edge. Why was she there? Where was Tanner? He must still be at the hut. She'd never catch up with him. He'd leave her!

"I'm scared, Tanner!" she called out.

Something was wrong—oh, so terribly wrong. The sound of water grew increasingly loud and she covered her ears, blocking out its insistent call.

"No!" she screamed, knowing it was impossible to understand the roar, yet realizing that she did. "I can't come nearer. Tanner said it wasn't safe. *Tanner!"* she screamed, desperately hoping he would come to help her. She was quickly being drained of her ability to resist.

Suddenly her feet moved of their own volition, bringing her closer and closer to the water's edge; they carried her calmly, so calmly it was a complete contradiction to her inner turmoil. Still, an unseen force compelled her forward, intent on making her see what was lurking there. Instinctively Carly covered her eyes, knowing as sure as she was breathing that she didn't want to see this mystery solved, didn't want to know what lay beneath the water's surface.

Even though she fought against it, the unseen force tore her hands away from her face, stripping her of all control, and her eyes flew open to focus unbelievingly on what floated. She opened her mouth to scream, but regardless of how hard she tried, no sound would come out. She thrashed her head back and forth, her hair whipping against her cheeks, in a frantic denial of what she saw.

Beneath the icy surface of the stream Therese and Tanner floated face up, features of each frozen in a horrible, wide-eyed expression, their skin the pale, waxy color of death.

"*Noooo!*" she cried, then gasped as Tanner suddenly came alive; his mouth moved, but his eyes were unblinking.

"*Carly,*" he called and his voice sounded like the roaring water. Angry, rolling clouds covered the sun; lightning flashed across the darkened sky.

"*Come.*" His waxlike hand broke through the surface and reached for her as he chanted, "*Come, come . . .*"

"*No!*" she screamed, sitting bolt upright.

"Carly!" Tanner barked, shaking her.

"Nooooo!" she screamed again, covering her face.

"It's all right, Carly," he said, prying her fingers away from her eyes.

"No! No!" She covered her ears. She had to fight it. Tanner's voice was a cross between the heinous chant of her dream and the frantic, pleading tone of a warm, normal, concerned, *live* man.

"Carly, please . . ." This time Tanner shook her hard, jarring her so that her eyes opened and she caught her breath.

The hut—she was in the hut. It was a dream, she had been dreaming! A hysterical sob bubbled forth.

Tanner pulled her into his arms and held her tightly, rubbing her back with his open palms. "Sweetheart, it was just a nightmare. You're safe."

Just a nightmare. If he only knew, she thought brokenly, hard sobs wracking her body.

"Shhh, Carly, you'll make yourself sick. Come on, babe, get hold of yourself."

Tanner didn't know what to do. It actually frightened him to see her in this condition. Until now she had been so strong, showed such endurance.

He pulled her into his lap. Placing his hands on either side of her face, he leaned her back and covered her mouth with his lips, kissing her deeply. She turned her head away, trying to break the contact, and as Tanner increased the pressure she clawed at his chest, kicking and thrashing. He suddenly realized she had focused her fear on him. He grasped her chin tightly, pushing her a few inches away from his face, and saw stark terror in the green eyes, the too-white face.

"It was just a dream." He enunciated each word carefully, then repeated, "It was just a dream."

"Tanner," she cried softly.

Relief coursed through him. She was all right.

He flicked the tears from her cheeks with his thumbs; then, unable to help himself, placed his lips over hers again.

This time she didn't fight him but leaned against him, returning the kiss, making him forget everything he'd told himself about becoming involved with her. With her warm, supple body fitting so perfectly against his, he could no longer control his own body's needs, no longer wanted to control his desire. With infinite care he pressed her to the floor and, never breaking the kiss, stretched out beside her. His hands went to the knot of her blouse, untying it with unbelievable ease. The few buttons there came undone, it seemed, at his slightest touch. He parted her blouse, then released the clasp on her bra. And at last, when she was free of all her clothing, he almost reverently placed his hand over her breast, caressing it as if it was the finest thing in the world he'd ever been given the privilege to touch.

Carly moaned into his mouth and arched herself against him, sending Tanner's blood surging through his veins. Had he ever felt this way before? Was he the one dreaming? . . .

Her hands danced over his bare chest and raised a thousand bumps over his body. It shouldn't be this way, he thought. Their lovemaking should have been slow, unhurried. But as she pulled him down, opening his mouth with her own, he knew he couldn't have proceeded more slowly if he'd wanted to.

He lifted her skirt and slid his hand beneath the waistband of her panties, then pulled them down the long length of her legs. In seconds he had unsnapped his pants and shoved them out of his way. His hungry mouth went to her breast; she was even softer than he'd imagined—fuller, sweeter.

The sudden touch of her fingers in his hair caused him to glance up and his eyes locked with hers. Silently she beckoned him to move closer, over her. At the slight pressure of her hand, Tanner covered her with his body, and as she parted her legs he thrust into her. The feeling was so exquisite it took his breath away. Shutting his eyes tightly, he rocked back and forth, losing himself within her. She met every movement he made. When she lifted her hips and cried out, his body shook with the release. The sensations rushing over him were unlike any he'd ever experienced—like none, he knew, he would ever experience again.

CHAPTER SEVENTEEN

Carly held Tanner's sweaty body close, reveling in the afterglow of their loving. She nuzzled his throat, then kissed him there, wishing with all her heart that he was in love with her, because she was, without a doubt, head over heels in love with him.

It no longer mattered that she'd decided not to become involved with a man until her family was once again settled. Even the deception through which she'd met Tanner seemed unimportant now. The fact was she wanted Tanner, not only for today but for always.

He moved against her and she caught her breath, but instead of prolonging the intimacy he eased away from her and rolled to his side, pulling her snugly up against him.

"You have dirty cheeks," he said quietly, stroking her hair away from her face.

She grinned. "I'm sure you're right."

"I meant your face."

Carly stared, mesmerized by the warmth in his dark blue eyes. Suddenly feeling vulnerable, she wondered if he could see how much she loved him, if the truth was written on her face. His eyes were bright, almost feverish, yet she refused to read anything in his gaze, denying the hope that perhaps he loved her too. For the moment he was hers and that was enough.

Minutes ticked by as they lay there silent, lost in their separate thoughts. Finally Tanner lifted his head and smiled, reaching for her again. His slightly abrasive whiskers just grazed her face as he kissed her, causing her to smile against his smooth lips.

He pulled back. "What's so funny?"

"Nothing. Everything." At his puzzled look, she said, "I know, I know. Here we are on top of a volcano, surrounded by men who want to kill us, and I'm smiling."

"You forgot to mention our exhaustion."

"Forgive me."

"So why are you smiling?"

"I'm glad we made love, Tanner."

His lips brushed hers. "I'd be a fool to deny how relieved I am to hear you say that."

Carly frowned at him. "I wanted you. Why would I . . .?"

"Because of the dream."

"Nightmare," she corrected.

366

He paused for a moment, then said, "Do you want to talk about it?"

"No. I just want to forget it." She buried her face against his throat. The strong thumping of his heart made her feel safe, but the total quiet allowed fear to raise its ugly head again. The nightmare was still fresh in her mind; the picture of Therese's lifeless body floating just beneath the surface of the water flashed in her mind, causing Carly to tense involuntarily.

"Tanner, what are Therese's chances?" she asked, lifting her head to see his expression.

"In all honesty, I don't know." He sat up, bracing himself on his arm as he leaned toward her. "Carly, I'd like to believe that she'll be all right as long as she doesn't break and tell them anything. But I don't know what they want from her. There has to be a reason they've kept her alive this long, and Therese will use that to her benefit."

"But she's injured!" Carly sat up too, pulling the sides of her blouse together. "What if she becomes too weak to help herself? What if she becomes delirious with fever?"

"She'll do whatever it takes to survive."

"That's not what I wanted to hear."

"The situation is bad," he said bluntly. "What can I tell you that you don't already know?"

"Plenty, I'm sure." She jerked her skirt over her legs, then plucked at a dirty spot on the cloth, knowing she was piling too much on Tanner and unable to help it. She desperately had to cling to the hope that Therese would be all right.

Tanner grasped her hands. "I can't lie to you—I won't lie to you. But right now our worst problem is just to get off this damned mountain alive."

"Then let's go," Carly said sharply. "We're wasting time as it is."

"We can't. The heat would kill us. Once it's cooler we'll cover twice as much territory."

Carly pressed her palms over her eyes. Tired, she was so tired. "How much longer until we reach the city?"

"I'm hoping we'll be there by morning."

"I'm sorry I'm so cross," she said, fighting the tears building in her eyes. "Please bear with me."

"I thought I already had," Tanner said, laughing softly when her hands dropped and her eyes flew open. "Want me to *bare* with you again?"

She swatted him and he grabbed her, pulling her against him. "Please let me bare with you again." His voice was deep and sultry and, needing him, Carly wrapped her arms around his neck, surrendering completely as he pushed her gently on her back. . . .

"I want you to try to sleep awhile," Tanner said, long moments after the loving ended.

"I can't. Every time I think about Therese my stomach ties in knots." Carly pushed away from him and rose to her feet. "And I've taken about all I can stand of wallowing in this dirt."

"I thought it was rather enjoyable myself," Tanner said from where he lay behind her.

Carly felt a blush steal into her cheeks and was glad he couldn't see her face. "It was . . ." she replied softly, ". . . very enjoyable." She squelched the desire to ask if their lovemaking had meant anything more to him than simple enjoyment. It was too soon to bring it up, they faced too many problems at the moment to be able to discuss their personal situation.

Maybe, she admitted, she wanted to put off facing the fact that Tanner would more than likely wish her well and continue living the kind of life he obviously craved—danger, intrigue, challenge. What kind of challenge would she be to him? None, absolutely none. Until her father's death her life had moved at a snail's pace. Even everything that faced her at Jameson Steel probably seemed like child's play to a man like Tanner.

She heard Tanner move behind her and turned just in time to see him zip his pants. He lifted her lacy panties from the floor, held them up to eye level, and then, with a lopsided grin on his face, tossed them to her.

"I would love it if you never put these on again, but just in case there's trouble . . . I don't want anyone . . ." He stepped forward and placed his lips over hers, pulling her against his bare chest as he kissed her deeply. She could scarcely breathe as his fingers skimmed up her sides to cup her breasts, and when he flicked his thumbs gently over their tips, she felt desire rage again.

Finally, without haste, Tanner broke the contact of their mouths. "We're never going to leave if we don't stop this."

Carly nodded, unable to speak, and reluctantly stepped back, watching as Tanner lifted his shirt and put it on.

"I'm going to check outside. Will you be okay for a few minutes?" he asked as he slipped the gun harness over his shoulder and buckled it around his chest.

"I suppose," she said with a sigh.

"Just stay inside until I come back." He planted a quick kiss on her forehead, then went to the window and eased himself out.

As Tanner's feet hit the dirt, he swore silently under his breath, wishing he'd never touched Carly. But he had done more than just touch her. He had loved her heatedly, quickly, and then slowly, completely, and still his body cried out for more.

"Damn!" he muttered as he placed the sheet of wood back over the window. Carly Jameson had plainly and simply gotten under his skin. Without even trying, she'd aroused feelings in him he hadn't been aware he possessed. And it scared the hell out of him—*she* scared the hell out of him. When he was with her there was no happy medium; he was either angry with her or aroused by her—never indifferent. When he was away from her she never completely left his mind. He didn't know what name to put to his feelings, all he knew was that they were stronger than anything he'd ever had before.

So what are you going to do about it, Barnes! he berated himself as he took off down the path. He wasn't the marrying kind. Hell, he'd never even lived with a woman—well, for no more than a week or two, anyway. Living meant always being on the go, searching every horizon for something new. He'd never before been tied to anything, with the exception of his work, and soon even that was going to be history.

But leaving Carly when the time came . . . she'd be hurt for sure. And being totally candid, he admitted that he'd suffer too. He'd seen the raw emotion in her eyes after they'd made love and wondered if his expression had matched hers. Lord knew, inside he felt . . .

He cut off that thought. Maybe he wouldn't have to leave her once this was over. Traveling around the world was an opportunity few really ever got. He pictured her with him, warm and golden on the yacht, the wind whipping her hair around her face. Then Tanner frowned, his hopes diving. Carly would never leave her family in the dire straits they were in to go off with a man who could give her no promises.

He rubbed his brow. Why did he have to fall for a woman like her! He could see Therese sailing off to God knew where, but not Carly.

A twig snapped, abruptly bringing Tanner's attention back to the present. He crouched down, the fine hairs on the back of his neck rising. Fool! he berated himself. Whoever was out there would never have gotten this close if Tanner hadn't been dreaming!

Adrenaline pumped through Tanner's veins; his hand automatically reached for his pistol. Gripping the cold steel tightly he inched forward, then stopped, the rustle of the underbrush betraying his position. Regardless of how much he hated to do it, he'd have to wait and let his enemy appear first.

The sounds grew louder; they were coming directly toward him. Tanner concentrated on the noise, decided that there was only one pursuer, and slid the gun back into the harness. With as little movement as possible he pulled the switchblade out of his pocket. He would do better with the knife; using a gun would be like broadcasting his whereabouts to the entire mountainside.

Suddenly the unmistakable *whoosh* of a helicopter reached his ears and Tanner dove down. Though the rough ground bit into his face, he didn't move a muscle. He lay there, vulnerable to attack as the chopper drowned out any sound the intruder might make.

372

Carly, please don't come out to see what's happening. His stomach lurched; he felt physical pain at the thought of Carly falling back into the Mexicans' hands. Fate had granted him the chance to get her safely away once—would she be that kind again?

He and Carly were in bad shape, worse than he'd imagined, if the big man had sent out the chopper. One way or the other La Pantera wanted them dead. Tanner rolled onto his side and peered up. The trees were so thickly entwined with one another he could barely see the sky. But he saw enough to know that the chopper was hovering over the area. He had to get Carly out of this mess, make her endure the obstacle course they would be forced to run. He gritted his teeth—nothing was going to keep him from securing her safety. Nothing!

For long minutes he lay there listening to the twirling blades, his senses finely tuned to pick up any signs of a sudden attack. The enemy was out there—maybe even momentarily stopped just as he was—but Tanner knew he wasn't about to give up.

Almost as suddenly as it had appeared, the helicopter moved on. Tanner tensed, listening for a break in the silence that had once again descended. There was none. Fear for Carly made him do what he normally would never have done on his own—he moved. For all he knew Carly could be in the tracker's hands at this moment.

He reached the hut with no trouble, then he

used his switchblade to pry the board off the window. He poked his head in; from the darkest corner of the hut he heard Carly gasp, and his heart leaped into his throat. Before he was able to tell if she was being held, she raced from the shadows, hardly containing herself as he climbed in the window.

As soon as his feet hit the floor she threw her arms around his neck. "I was so scared," she said, her voice weak with fear. "I just knew they'd found you."

"You heard the chopper?" he asked, holding her close and kissing the top of her head.

"Yes."

He held her away from him: "Carly, someone was out there about two hundred yards away. We have to leave now, before others arrive."

"Did he see you?"

"I don't think so, but I can't be sure." He drew out the snub-nosed .38 he'd hidden in his boot the day before and pressed it into her hand. "Have you ever shot a pistol?"

"Not in a long time."

He pointed at the small button in front of the trigger. "The gun won't fire unless you release this safety. In case something happens to me, shoot anything that moves and keep running. Don't stop for anything."

"But, Tanner . . ." Her voice trembled.

"I mean it, Carly. One of us has to get away."

She nodded, then tucked the gun into the waistband of her skirt.

"You ready?" he asked.

"As ready as I'll ever be."

Tanner climbed out the window, then helped Carly down and pulled her along as he forged a new path through the high brush.

As Tanner expected, the chopper returned. He shook his head angrily, knowing that even though he and Carly were well camouflaged from the chopper by the thick branches overhead, they still presented an open target for the man who'd been tracking them for the better part of ten minutes. It hadn't taken Tanner long to detect the third set of footsteps moving through the brush. What he hadn't been able to understand was why the man was simply following them, why he hadn't tried to subdue them; worse, why he hadn't shot them and been done with it.

Without speaking, Tanner ushered Carly in front of him, gently nudging her to take the lead. He knew she was puzzled, but she did as he indicated. Feeling sick at heart, Tanner knew what he had to do. They couldn't continue with the man on their heels, never knowing when or if he was going to shoot.

Once the chopper again moved on, Tanner gripped Carly's upper arms and whispered, "When I give you the word, take off like a rabbit—don't slow down or stop."

She opened her mouth, but Tanner silenced her. "No questions. Just do as I say." Squeezing her arms, he shoved her. "Now!"

Like a shot, Carly bolted through the bushes and disappeared. Then Tanner darted off to the side, lying in wait for the man trailing them.

The pursuer's footsteps were heavy, and Tanner knew by the clumsy approach the man was no professional; still . . . one lucky shot was all it took. Easing behind a large tree, Tanner poised to attack. Only a few seconds had passed when suddenly something crashed to the ground and there was the explosion of a gunshot. The man must have fallen down, and his gun had gone off accidentally.

Tanner leaned against the tree, his heart thumping wildly as he listened, hoping the bullet had taken out his foe. Then he cursed silently. The man was moving, but he didn't advance; instead, he crashed through the brush away from Tanner. Still keeping his back to the tree, Tanner edged around the trunk and peered cautiously at the place where the man must have fallen, an area where the grass was flattened to the ground. But there was no sign of blood, no sign of injury.

Tanner clenched his fist, knowing he faced a severe problem. The tracker's mishap had made him more alert. Tanner and his adversary now had to play a waiting game, each delaying to see if the other had been found out. Valuable time ticked away while Carly ran further and farther away. Immediately Tanner felt fear; he'd never intended Carly to be alone for very long. He'd believed he could take care of the pursuer within a matter of minutes and catch up to her. Now each minute was crucial because he had to succeed, then find Carly before she became lost in the tangle of the tropical forest.

Tanner relaxed for a moment as he realized the Mexican was moving forward, passing him along another route. Smiling, Tanner decided his original plan would still work, only this time he'd have to sneak up from behind.

Like a cat, Tanner moved silently, tracking the man easily. He purposely lingered a good distance behind, waiting for the right moment to strike. Still gripping his knife, Tanner spotted the Mexican dressed in green fatigues as he stepped over a fallen log. So far he was still making his own trail; he hadn't picked up Carly's tracks. An uncharacteristic lump filled Tanner's throat at what he was about to do; then he made his mind go blank and cold. He had a job to do, and if he failed . . .

Advancing, Tanner was about to strike when a shot rang out, followed by a scream, then another shot.

Carly! As if propelled by a magical force, the knife flew from Tanner's fingertips, planting itself firmly in the Mexican's back. Mad with fear, Tanner never looked back as he ran ahead, veering off to his left to pick up Carly's trail. The chopper suddenly reappeared from nowhere, it seemed, swooping down close to the ground as it spotted him. Heedless of the danger Tanner ran, ducking beneath the trees when he could, ignoring the shots that rained down around him when he couldn't. Carly was in trouble; he was her only hope.

"Tanner!"

He heart her shout, but the chopper was upon him and he lunged toward a cluster of trees, rolling quickly out of sight. Panting heavily, he looked for Carly, knowing she was nearby but carefully sheltered from his sight by the foliage. If only he knew how many men had her, what their weapons were . . .

The noise of the chopper completely drowned any other sound, making it impossible for him to shout to her. He looked up, a curse leaving his lips as he saw a rope ladder being tossed from the open door of the chopper. Within seconds three men were climbing down, all heavily armed. Tanner clenched his teeth, knowing the minute he fired the first shot the men holding Carly would have him. Still, there was no other option.

He readied his gun but just as he took aim a shot rang out and one man fell. Tanner, not believing what happened, looking quickly in the direction he'd thought Carly was being held. Another shot went off, this time only nicking one of the men. Not one to look a gift horse in the mouth,

Tanner fired his pistol, quickly taking care of the two remaining commandos.

The chopper was low enough to the ground for Tanner to see that no one but the pilot remained on board, and within seconds the aircraft soared away. Aware that the chopper would soon return with reinforcements, Tanner knew he had to work fast to get Carly. Yet even though two shots had been fired at the commandos, Tanner had no way of knowing what was happening some twenty feet away, who the third party was.

Not even a bird chirped as Tanner stood there. Nothing would muffle the sound of his movements, he thought anxiously. He quickly scanned the area, hoping someone would stir, something would give him an inkling as to where they were holding Carly.

Damn! Nothing—no help anywhere. All at once a faint sound reached his ears. At first Tanner thought his mind was playing tricks on him but no, he did hear weeping—a woman weeping. Carly! His heart swelled with pain. He knew how frightened she must be, what a horrible experience it was to be held by someone intent on killing. Moving back, he circled around, keeping close to the trees as he traveled. Her crying became clearer, drawing him closer and closer, until he was so near he could see her, alone, huddled pitifully on the ground.

No one was near her. In fact, Tanner quickly realized that no one had been with her through the whole episode. What the hell had happened!

He rushed forward, but Carly was so lost in her misery that she didn't stir. The minute he touched her she jerked up startled, startling Tanner too. She was covered with blood.

Before he could even determine if she was hurt she threw herself at him, holding him painfully tight, trying unsuccessfully to explain what had happened. Finally realizing he didn't understand, Carly pointed jerkily off to her side and Tanner saw exactly what had made her shoot and scream the first time, why she was covered with blood. A huge snake, at least ten feet long, lay on the ground, minus half its head.

He held her tightly, soothing her with soft words, rubbing her back as she trembled, until finally nothing but an occasional hiccup escaped.

"Are you all right? Did it bite you?" he asked, one he was sure she could answer.

"I'm fine. I had a stitch in my side and I stopped running for a moment, and it fell out of the tree on top of me. *Oh, Tanner, it was horrible!*"

"Don't think about it, Carly."

She pulled away and looked into his eyes. "Then that chopper came bearing down on you and I saw you roll to the ground—I thought you'd been hit. And those men . . ." Tears again welled in her eyes, and her chin quivered. ". . . I didn't know what else to do."

He eased her a little farther away so he could look at her fully. "*You* shot that man?"

She sniffed. "It was just luck."

"Where's the pistol?"

She looked stunned, and Tanner knew she thought he was being callous, but he couldn't allow her to dwell on her awful experience. They were in more danger than ever, now that Diego's men knew their location. Miles and miles lay ahead, with trouble riding their shoulders all the way.

She pointed toward the ground and Tanner, seeing the pistol lying several feet away, picked it up and stuffed it back into his boot. Then he extended his hand to Carly and pulled her up.

"We have to go. They'll be back any time."

Tanner pressed a button on his watch and looked at its illuminated face. Midnight. Was that all? It felt it should have been at least five o'clock in the morning. They'd done well though, covering a lot of territory in spite of the chopper that had continued to soar overhead until darkness had fallen. Perhaps they'd even reach Orizaba earlier than he'd originally thought. He sure as hell hoped so. The sooner he got Carly out of this country, the better. His guts were still tied in knots over the near-fatal encounter they'd had.

He swung his hand behind him and touched Carly's midsection; understanding his signal, she stopped.

"We'll rest here for a few minutes. Don't get too comfortable."

"I don't think I'll ever be comfortable again," she grumbled beneath her breath, carefully lowering herself to the ground.

Tanner smiled in the darkness and sat beside her. "Just keep telling yourself that you only have a few more hours to endure. Before night falls again you'll have had a steaming hot bath and a good, solid meal."

"A cold shower and a bologna sandwich sounds like heaven."

He chuckled. "I have to agree."

"Tanner"—she clutched at his hands—"where will we go once we reach the city?"

"I'll find us a small room somewhere until I can contact Hank. Do you have any money?" he asked, knowing he was low on cash.

"None."

"Well, we've made good progress. I think we'll make it to the city long before dawn."

"Great." Her reply lacked enthusiasm. "I can't wait to get out of this dark jungle."

Again Tanner laughed, relieved that she was becoming disgruntled. At least she was talking now. For hours she'd followed him blindly, obviously in a daze. He reached for her face, reveling in the freedom he now had to touch her whenever he wished, and pulled her forward for a kiss. Even as tired as he was his body responded. As her soft, sweet lips parted he felt a twinge of guilt. Carly would expect more than physical closeness in a

382

relationship. What was he going to do? The more he was with her the more he wanted to remain with her.

She pressed against his chest, breaking the lingering kiss.

"We should get under way," she said breathlessly. "I'm certain if we stay here any longer I'll end up collapsing from complete physical exhaustion."

Tanner kissed her again. "You're a glutton for punishment," he said as he stood up.

"Depends on the punishment."

He laughed. "You're so right."

Regardless of how optimistic Tanner was about reaching the city soon, Carly was beginning to believe they'd walked in circles all night. The brief rest periods did nothing to ease the pain searing her calves and thighs. Her muscles screamed for her to stop.

Damn Tanner, she thought. He continued to walk as if he were out on a stroll, never seeming to tire. He had to be bionic, she decided. His legs were mechanical limbs installed by the government. He didn't feel any pain or exhaustion because he was incapable of it. But she'd keep walking, she told herself, as she took a deep breath, just to show him what a *real* woman was made of.

If she didn't keel over first.

Tanner stopped suddenly and Carly plowed

into his back. Without thinking she swung a fist at him, connecting with his shoulder.

"Ouch! What the hell's the matter with you!" he barked, spinning around.

She could *see* his blazing blue eyes! It was still nighttime, yet she could see his eyes. Hesitantly, as if afraid to have her hopes come true, she looked over his shoulder and saw a dim street light.

She squealed, throwing her arms around him. "We made it. We really made it!"

Tanner wrapped his arms around her and swung her feet off the ground. "It took you long enough to realize it."

"I haven't been looking. It's been taking too much energy just to keep my head up. Oh, Tanner, I can't believe it."

"Well, you'd better. I didn't put us through this for nothing."

She looked into his eyes. "I was beginning to have my doubts. But not anymore. From now on I'll always believe anything you tell me. I promise."

He put her down, his face mere inches from hers. Carly pulled his head down, kissing him with every ounce of feeling she had.

This time Tanner ended it. "Carly," he said, breathing heavily. "If you don't stop, I'm going to take you right here on the ground."

"I wouldn't care," she replied, trying to capture his lips for another kiss.

"Carly, we have to find a place to stay—now,

while it's still dark."

She groaned against his chin. He was right, but it felt so good to be held in his arms, to kiss his lips, to have him love her. She released a pent-up breath. "All right. But once I finally settle down, don't count on *anything* from me for some time."

"I wouldn't dare." His smile contradicted his words.

Falling into step behind him, Carly followed him down a small rocky path and onto level ground. Even though a light shone from the lightpost, there were no buildings in sight. Carly made a sour face—of course they wouldn't be lucky enough to find a hotel this far out.

CHAPTER EIGHTEEN

A pigsty! Tanner had rented them a pigsty, Carly thought, wrinkling her nose at the musty odor in the room. But it was just a temporary waiting place, she mentally added, trying to convince herself they wouldn't be there long—only until Tanner contacted Hank and made plans for them to be picked up. Still . . .

It was so filthy! Carly sniffed at the sight of a chair with only three and a half legs, a bed—if you could call it that—with a thin mattress lying directly on the slats, and nothing else but a grimy floor and walls. Maybe she'd be lucky and Tanner would have them out of there before she fell to the floor unconscious from exhaustion. Looking at the yellow bed sheet that Carly felt sure had been white at one time, she knew that only by collapsing was she going to rest her body on anything in this room.

"God, you're a sight!" Tanner said.

She looked down at the tattered remnants of what had once been her favorite skirt and blouse. Dried blood and dirt had stiffened the material more than starch ever could. "I sure am," she said quietly, not wanting to imagine what the rest of her looked like.

"A good sight," Tanner added, tipping up her chin. "Will you be all right while I'm gone?"

She wanted to say no. "Sure."

"I shouldn't be long, but if you're too hungry to wait I could see if the owner of this fine establishment would send you something to eat."

"I can wait a little while longer."

"Don't drink the water."

"I wouldn't dare."

"Too bad there isn't a shower."

"But there is a sink."

Tanner took her in his arms and smiled down at her. "It could be worse, you know. We could still be climbing down the mountain."

"Or in the hands of . . ."

"Speaking of which, don't leave this room for any reason. Don't answer the door, don't open a window. . . ."

She sighed and leaned her body against his. "I get the message."

He kissed the top of her head. "I'll be back before you know it."

"I hope you." Her voice sounded weepy even

to her own ears.

"Lock the door behind me," he said against her lips. "I'll let myself in with the key when I get back." He kissed her quickly, then left.

After locking the door Carly took several steps back into the room, then stopped. How was she going to pass the time? How was she going to keep herself from sitting, especially when her body screamed at her to rest? She knew she was filthy, but her dirt was good, clean soil—this place reeked of infestation. Carly went to the sink and turned on the faucet, which proceeded to spit rusty, odorous water into the porcelain basin. Even though she grimaced in distaste, she still thrust her hands beneath the water and rinsed her face and neck. But that was all she could force herself to do.

She turned just in time to see a huge black roach, moving faster than Carly dreamed an insect could, charge at her across the floor. Dancing from foot to foot, she got nowhere fast trying to escape it. Finally, she hopped up on the sink, which promptly groaned under her weight and began to pull away from the wall. Knowing it was about to fall, Carly quickly glanced back at the roach. Now the horrible bug had sprouted wings, and before Carly could blink, the wings twitched and the roach left the floor. Just as quickly, Carly lunged for the bed, jolting herself silly when the slats failed to hold and she and the mattress collapsed and fell through the frame to the floor. But she didn't care about the bed—she didn't care about anything else but the roach that soared overhead, intent on attacking. She ducked each time it bounced off a wall, then hunkered down to stay out of its path. Finally, it gave up; it landed on the grimy windowsill, folded its wings, and climbed through a crack in the ledge.

She shuddered, then rubbed her arms, thanking God that the ugly little beast hadn't attacked her. She looked down at the wreck she'd made of the bed, then carefully stepped out of it, the thought that she might have picked up any live organism on her person literally making her sick.

For long moments she stood, swaying from exhaustion. There was no way she was going to sit on what was left of the bed, she decided. But the more she stared at it the better that three-legged chair began to look. If she sat only on the edge she could at least rest a little.

She dragged the chair into a corner, then propped its bad leg against the wall, carefully easing most of her weight onto the stable side. But she quickly realized it was impossible to be comfortable that way. Maybe she'd move back just a little farther, she thought, giving in to the urge, and before long she was firmly planted in the chair, her head cocked back as she slumbered deeply.

"You're *where*?" Hank said, the shock of

hearing Tanner's voice making him sit abruptly down on the bed. He gripped the phone more tightly. "We all thought you were dead."

"I assure you I'm alive and—if not well—the next best thing to it," Tanner said. "If you think you're surprised, you should have heard Omi."

"He told you where I was?" Hank swallowed painfully. The welcome realization that Tanner was alive was affecting him deeply, but he forced himself to push it aside.

"Yeah. How are the ribs?"

"Who cares! All hell has broken loose in the past twenty-four hours. I guess you know by now that Carly Jameson is missing." He didn't want to tell Tanner that he knew she'd been abducted.

"She's with me."

"What?" Hank tried to keep the astonishment out of his voice.

"It's a long story. I'm at a pay phone, but I left Carly at an old boardinghouse. Just come and get us. We'll talk then." Tanner told Hank the location. "I don't want the Mexican couple we're renting from to know we've left, so we'll meet you down the street."

"I'll be there in a few minutes," Hank said, then hung up. But he didn't move immediately; in fact, he wasn't certain he could. Tanner was alive and Carly was with him. Exquisite relief that was almost pain filled his heart, nearly overwhelming him, and he closed his eyes, simply listening to his heartbeat. Then he laughed softly, berating himself for believing that Tanner was gone.

He gained control over his emotions, then turned to look at the slumbering Consuelo. She'd been through a lot too, he realized. She must have been dead tired to have slept through the ringing of the phone. Somehow, Hank thought, a grin on his face, he knew it wouldn't bother Tanner in the least to know she was in his bed. Little sister was probably in Tanner's at this very moment.

He nudged Consuelo and she peeked at him through one eye.

"You're never going to believe this, but . . ."

Tanner quietly inserted the key in the door and twisted it, pushing the door open. His eyes widened at the sight that greeted him. What the hell had happened? he thought, seeing the wrecked bed and the sagging sink. Instantly alarmed, he scanned the room, quickly spotting Carly in her three-legged chair, spread out in a less-than-ladylike sprawl.

He sighed, then chuckled in relief. From the way her head tilted back he knew she was going to have a hell of a crick in her neck. He walked over to her and knelt on the floor.

"Carly," he said, patting her knee.

She moaned.

He ran his hand up her leg, squeezing the soft

flesh of her inner thigh, nearly moaning himself at how good she felt. He could see she was having trouble awakening and he smiled as he slid his palm even higher up her leg. "Carly . . . wake up."

"I'm trying to," she muttered, grasping his hand before it went any farther. She wasn't *that* far gone, he decided.

He turned his palm up in hers. "Try a little harder. Hank will be here in a moment. We've got to go."

"What?" she said, groaning as she lifted her head.

Tanner gently massaged the back of her neck. "I said we have to go." When her warm breath caressed his throat he had to use all his willpower not to kiss her.

She leaned forward, resting her head against Tanner's. "Just give me a second. I never should have fallen asleep." She sounded groggy.

Tanner briskly rubbed her shoulders, helping her to awaken and trying to make the stirrings in his body go away: he wanted her.

"Carly, we've got to go now. Come on, get up." He stood and pulled her to her feet, then took her by the hand and led her out of the room and through the back entrance of the house.

Dawn was just breaking, and Tanner kept to the shadows. He scanned the area for Hank; when he saw that the street was empty, he pulled Carly along and moved away from the house.

"How far do we have to go?" Carly asked, dragging her feet without realizing it.

Tanner slowed his steps. "I'm not sure."

About that time he saw the headlights of an approaching car. He gripped Carly's hand and pulled her behind him as the vehicle slowed down, then stopped before it reached them.

"Is it Hank?" she asked.

"It sure as hell better be," Tanner answered, his heartbeat accelerating. When the lights blinked off and on one time, Tanner relaxed and drew Carly alongside him.

"That's him," he whispered against her face. "Let's get out of here."

Tanner walked slowly, physically incapable of moving any faster. Poor Carly was barely able to put one foot in front of the other. "Come on, sweetheart, just a few steps further," he coaxed, knowing if he weren't so tired himself he would have carried her. But as it was, he wasn't much better off than she.

Before Tanner could open the door, Hank rolled down his window and said, "Man, you look like hell."

"We've been through hell," Carly mumbled in Tanner's defense.

Tanner smiled and opened the car door. Carly climbed in, barely moving over enough for him to fit in. But he didn't care; she felt good beside him and he wanted her to stay there.

"Consuelo's waiting in my room," Hank said quietly.

"It's a miracle she got away."

"She was pretty shaken up when she first returned. Want to tell me your version?"

Tanner rubbed his cheek against the top of Carly's head. "Let me get a hot shower and a cup of coffee first. There isn't much we can do until the sun's up." He didn't tell Hank that he was too damned tired to talk. But he ruefully admitted to himself that he was definitely getting older. The time when he'd have been able to go on like this for days was over. Besides, he didn't want to fill Hank in with Carly listening. Once he and Hank were alone, Tanner planned to tell him every detail.

"What about Therese?"

Tanner sighed and slumped in the overstuffed chair. Before he answered, he glanced around the room, thankful for Hank's luxurious accommodations.

"She was taken to La Pantera before I arrived. Carly said Diego shot her in the shoulder, but she doesn't know how badly Therese was injured."

"Damn," Hank muttered, pouring Tanner and himself another cup of coffee. "Someone was waiting for Carly."

"Diego," Tanner said flatly.

"How the hell could he have known she was coming to Mexico?"

"That's exactly what I intend to find out." Tanner sipped the coffee, savoring its strong bitter taste. "What were you told when you went to find Carly?"

"No one knew anything, other than she hadn't returned. Her suitcase was all I found when I broke into her room."

"You didn't take it?"

"There didn't seem to be anything of value in it, just her clothes and cosmetics." Hank smiled. "They seem to think she's going to turn up eventually."

"Let them."

"I knew she was in trouble somewhere. I can't believe all that's happened."

"Believe it. As an eyewitness I can testify to the entire story." As exhausted as he was, Tanner managed to sit up. "I can't begin to tell you how I felt when I discovered I had Carly instead of Therese in my hands that night."

Hank smiled a half grin. "I can well imagine."

"No, you can't. I wanted to strangle her." Tanner stared seriously at Hank. "I wanted to strangle her because I'd never in my life felt such fear. I was actually scared that I wouldn't be able to get her safely out of the way."

"We have to do some fast work, Tanner," Hank said, changing the subject. "We have to discover where Pantera is staying and how he ties into all of this."

"Consuelo filled you in?"

Hank nodded. "Rodrigo must have been on the up and up. His story tallies very closely with what Carly has told you."

Tanner's tone was somber. "He was. There was this other man too, Benito. I never should have made him come along."

"From what I've heard, I'd have done the same thing. Don't be so hard on yourself," Hank said, but Tanner just stared off into space. "What about Carly? Did she hear anything about La Pantera from Diego or one of the guards? Did Therese mention anything to her?"

"Just what I've told you," Tanner said. "La Pantera sent for Therese just before we arrived. When Diego was preparing to ship her out, there was a struggle and Therese was shot. Carly must've been dragged away at that point. Anyway, when I arrived I saw a woman climbing out the window and I just assumed it was Therese."

Hank chewed on his inner lip. "We've got to get started, but there's no way we can as long as Carly's still here."

"She'll never leave."

"Do you want her to?"

397

"Of course I do, but there's no way she'll listen to me. And frankly, I'd rather have her here with us, where I can keep an eye on her, than send her away knowing she'll only try to return."

"She can be persuaded to leave, Tanner. It just depends on how badly you want her to go."

Tanner looked at Hank. How badly did he want her to go? he asked himself, knowing the answer. He didn't want her out of his sight, but he was even more afraid to allow her to stay. He smelled danger, knew it was going to get pretty damned nasty before they managed to rescue Therese. Yes, he desperately wanted her to leave, but only because he knew she'd be out of harm's way.

"What've you got planned?"

"You're not going to like it."

Tanner leaned back and lit a cigarette, then narrowed his eyes as he exhaled a thin stream of smoke. "There's not much I do like anymore."

Carly felt ten pounds lighter once all the dirt and grime had been washed away. It was remarkable how a shower could revive a person, she thought, blotting a towel over her body. As she bent down to dry her legs she saw the ugly blisters on her feet, then noticed the bruises covering her shins. Now that it was all over, she wondered how she had managed to finish the journey.

She clutched the towel to her nude body. She'd made it because of Tanner. She'd told herself through all that had happened that she had suffered her ordeal to save Therese, and so she had, but it was the strength of Tanner's determination that had kept Carly going even when she felt the trip was impossible. And now that they were safely back, she had complete faith that Tanner would rescue Therese. It was just a matter of time.

Carly wrapped the towel saronglike around her, then sat on the edge of the bathtub. She was still extremely tired, but felt great relief knowing Tanner and Hank were in control. She was sure things were going to work out, at least where Therese was concerned.

She took a deep breath and began to feel jittery. Now that she and Tanner had made it back she was nervous about facing him. Then she smiled —she was being ridiculous. He had to have seen what a wonderful thing they had together. The pain she had experienced when she discovered he had been deceiving her had diminished. She now understood why he'd gone to so much trouble in Galveston to keep her in the dark. Had she only realized it then, she might have stayed in Beaumont and allowed him to finish his job. But trust between them hadn't yet been established then. Too many bad things had happened so soon before she met Tanner for her to have placed her faith in anyone.

Now that she'd seen him in action, knew how thoroughly trained he was, she felt secure. He would save Therese someway. Carly swallowed against the sudden lump that formed in her throat. Therese just couldn't end up the same way as Lisa Curtis.

Consuelo thrust her heavy breasts against Tanner's chest and wrapped her arms around his neck. "*Querido*, it has been much too long."

He heard the bathroom door open and, like an actor accepting his cue, squeezed Consuelo's body tightly. "That's the understatement of the year," he said huskily against her pouting lips. "You're almost more woman than I know how to handle."

Consuelo's laugh was deep and breathless. "No, *querido*, you are too much of a man for any one woman to handle, and I have the sense to realize this."

"Thank God. I've never liked a clinging vine." He parted her lips with his tongue and kissed her deeply, hating himself, feeling self-disgust at doing this to Carly. It took all his control to go through with this charade, to keep himself from shoving Consuelo and the cloying smell of her perfume away. His mind screamed at him to stop, to turn to Carly and explain. But he knew she'd never return home if he did. The next few hours meant life or death for Therese, and he had to devote every ounce of energy and brains he had left to make sure she lived.

He flattened his palm against Consuelo's meaty buttocks and pulled her against his groin. Swallowing, he ground himself vulgarly against her, wondering how long Carly was going to stand in the doorway before she was repulsed enough to flee.

It wasn't long before his thought was answered. A painful cry, the slam of a door, and she was gone. Then, without a word, he released Consuelo and left the room. He didn't even look at Hank as he let himself out on the balcony, where he remained waiting for Carly to come out and demand to leave.

"I think you should go for awhile," Tanner heard Hank say to Consuelo.

"*Sí*. I do not think I want to face the *niña bonita* after this."

Tanner swallowed. "Beautiful baby." Carly was beautiful, but she was a woman, completely. He rubbed his eyes, looking out toward the city. Sick at heart, he wondered if she'd ever understand. . . .

The outer door closed and he knew Consuelo had gone. Then, a few moments later, he heard Hank dialing the phone.

"Joaquin? Have the plane ready to go to the States. I'll meet you at the airstrip in an hour."

Good; Hank would have Carly airbound

before midmorning. She'd be out of the way, even if she did hate him for the rest of her life.

He listened as Hank knocked on the bathroom door. For a moment he almost hoped the plan had failed, that Carly would refuse to leave, regardless of what a bastard she thought he was. But then he made himself remember that it was for her own safety that he was doing this to get her out of the country. The man holding Therese wanted Carly too, even though she was of minor importance to his plans.

Hank rapped against the door again, and Tanner found himself moving toward the doorway to listen. Why he moved he wasn't certain; it just seemed important that he hear everything she had to say.

"Carly," Hank finally called through the door, worried that she might be able to hear him. He felt like a total heel because of his part in the deception; he could only imagine how badly Tanner must feel.

"Carly?"

"Just a minute." Her reply was faint, muffled.

Hank decided to give her a few more moments to pull herself together. After all she'd been through, this scene had to be the last straw.

"Hank?" At the sound of her voice he moved toward the door again.

"Yes?"

"I don't have any clothes."

He closed his eyes and smiled. "Just a minute."

Turning around, he stopped. What was she going to wear? He scanned the room, looking for something of Consuelo's, then realized Carly would probably never consent to wear anything of hers. Sighing softly, he stepped around the bed and went to the closet, pulling down a plain brown shirt and pair of white slacks. His clothing would swallow her, but at least she'd wear them with no objection.

He went back to the door and knocked softly. Carly barely cracked the door open to pull in the clothing. Within moments she was dressed and standing before him with her head high and proud, though her eyes were red, and he knew that she would be all right—eventually, anyway.

She bit her lower lip, and he knew she was waiting for him to speak. But he suddenly wondered what, exactly, he should say.

"I'm sorry." And he was. Even from the beginning, when this ridiculous charade had begun in Galveston, he had never wanted to see her hurt.

"Why?" she asked bitterly. "You had nothing to do with . . ." She flung her head out as if uncertain of how to word the rest of her sentence; then she turned away. "Are they still here?" she asked, her voice breaking slightly.

"No, they've gone." He stepped toward her, intending to comfort her, but she must have sensed his intention because she walked away, moving to the opposite side of the room. He could see her shaking as she lifted her hand to her mouth and began chewing nervously on a nail.

"Carly, I know you probably don't want to talk about this right now, but I have to know what you intend to do."

"Why? So you can run and tell Tanner Barnes that his 'clinging vine' is gone?"

"No, I just think you have to make a decision —no, not a decision, exactly. I think you should return to Beaumont."

"*Beaumont*? That's the last place I intend to go."

"Forget what just happened for a moment and try to see things clearly. Your sister is in a terrible situation. You can't help her and you know that. Do you want to stick around and complicate everything for her?"

"I won't complicate anything. All I want to do is see that she's rescued from those . . ."

"Exactly. But you aren't capable of rescuing her. Tanner and I are." Hank walked up to her and took her hand, pulling her down to sit beside him on the bed.

"Carly, there are men all over this city looking for you. They'll know you're here the minute you set foot outside this room. Then they'll either kill you and hold onto your sister, or they'll kill you both because they'll know the heat's on and that's far hotter than they can possibly handle. Killing you will be the easiest way out of the situation for them."

"Killing." A sob escaped her. "Did Tanner tell you I killed a man?"

"No," Hank said softly. There was a lot, he thought, that Tanner hadn't told him. As tears began to run down her pale cheeks, Hank's stomach muscles clenched. She looked worn down, tired, the faint bruises beneath her eyes attesting to her exhaustion. He knew too that he was responsible for a great deal of her pain. Still, the most important thing was to get her out of the country now, as soon as possible, so that he and Tanner could get on with their work.

"Regardless of what's happened, Carly, you have to know by now that Tanner is the best in his field, and that if anyone can get Therese out, it's Tanner."

"I know you're right, Hank." She was crying openly now, and he pulled her against his chest, comforting her as much as he was able. "It's just that I . . ." She stopped, her voice breaking, and she nodded her head against him, agreeing to do as he asked. Squeezing her tightly for a moment, he held her until she partially regained her self-control, then he let her go and stood up.

"Yes, I . . . Home sounds likes heaven right

now."

He nodded, then left her alone, closing the door behind him as he entered the sitting room. He walked to the balcony and stared at Tanner, who looked worse than Carly. "She's ready to leave," he said quietly.

Tanner nodded, then thrust his his hands deeply into his front pockets and turned away.

"I won't be gone long," he said to Tanner's back; then he stepped inside and went to get Carly.

CHAPTER NINETEEN

Carly sat numbly alone in one of six passenger seats and watched through a small window as Hank climbed back behind the wheel of his car. She never took her eyes off him as the plane began to move. It barely registered in her mind that the airstrip was little more than a clearing in the dense foliage, or that the plane seemed to be a relic of World War II. All she could concentrate on was that she was going home and she'd never have to see Tanner Barnes again. Period. Never.

But her heart was breaking. Tears rolled down her cheeks, blurring her vision until all she saw was a smear of green that quickly changed to the peaceful light blue of the sky. The plane was airborne, she was on her way, yet she couldn't stop the tears.

This is ridiculous! she told her herself, gripping the armrest of the seat as the plane ascended.

Most of her emotions were caused by her exhaustion, but knowing that and dealing with it were two different things. She roughly wiped the moisture from her face, then leaned back and closed her eyes; she just needed to rest. Sleep was the best healer. But the unease in her mind wouldn't allow her to relax enough to doze off. In fact, she was quickly reaching the point where her thoughts were nothing but a jumbled mess.

Every direction she turned held a problem, a painful problem. Therese, Ellis, Jameson Steel, and . . . Tanner. How could she have been so wrong about him? The picture of him taking up with Consuelo where he'd left off was vivid in her mind. She should have known that there had been something between him and that overblown floozy the minute they'd walked into Hank's room this morning. Consuelo had all but devoured him on the spot; in fact, she couldn't keep her hands off him. But Tanner hadn't been receptive to Consuelo then.

Maybe that was why Consuelo had been so agreeable to Hank's suggestion that she show Carly to the shower. It sure gave Consuelo the perfect opportunity to be with Tanner!

And dammit, Carly thought defensively, she hadn't been a clinging vine—if anything she'd been pretty strong, considering all they'd been forced to do. God! She hung her head and ran her hands wearily over her face. She'd even killed a man and . . .

I can't deal with this anymore, she thought. All the tragedy, the betrayals, the secrecy. And still the danger hovered. The mere idea that Therese might be killed was enough to send Carly into shock. She truly believed she couldn't handle it if something happened to her sister.

The sudden overwhelming urge to see Ellis was so intense Carly had to bite her lip to keep from crying out. If only he was strong again, he'd be able to handle this; he would reassure her that Therese was going to be fine, would soothe away the hurt Tanner had caused. But if he'd been strong and in charge already, Carly knew she would never have found herself in this situation in the first place. Ellis would have taken care of the problems long before they'd ballooned to the critical point they'd now reached.

She felt like such a failure.

Opening her eyes, she plucked at the huge brown shirt she wore. What was Ellis going to think when she walked into their home looking like this? Never in a million years would he believe what she had been through. She barely believed it herself.

Again she settled back and tried to rest. The last few days had been hell. It was amazing that she was still conscious.

But even as exhausted and disillusioned as she was, the minute she closed her eyes Tanner's face popped into her mind. She swallowed against the pain tightening her throat. She should have known that nothing had changed for him just because they'd made love. But was it naivete, stupidity, or simply wishful thinking that had made her believe things could have been special between them? Just because she had fallen head over heels in love with the man didn't mean he necessarily had to return those same emotions. But it would have been so fine if he had.

Tanner was finally forced to leave the balcony by the presence of people filling the streets on their way to work. Sluggishly he walked into the small sitting room of Hank's suite and sank into a chair.

The least she could have done was thrown a fit —hell, even thrown something at him! If it had been him, he would have torn Carly out of the arms of whoever was holding her and then killed the bastard for even touching her.

But Carly didn't work that way. With as much dignity as she could muster under the circumstances, she'd quickly closed the door and waited until Hank came to get her. God, Tanner felt like a louse. The ploy he'd used in Galveston was child's play compared to the rotten trick he'd pulled on her this morning. And the feelings she'd aroused in him in Galveston were weak compared to the emotion he felt for her now, after all they'd been through and shared. He sighed. He never knew falling in love could be so damned painful. And yes, dammit, he was in love with her.

The trouble was, it was too late. Carly would never forgive him for this.

Tanner scratched his bristly face and almost laughed at how ironic things had become. What he'd wanted to do as soon as this assignment was over still beckoned him, but not as strongly; in fact, his enthusiasm for that life had waned considerably. But he'd still get to do them, because Carly was gone forever out of his life.

No more time for recriminations; Tanner thought, pushing himself out of the chair. This was probably the only time he'd have to clean up before Hank returned, the only chance he'd have to prepare himself for the day's events—mainly tracking down Diego and beating the living hell out him: only, of course, Tanner added to himself, after Diego answered all the questions Tanner planned to ask.

Walking into the bedroom, Tanner stopped for a moment, his thoughts swinging erratically back to Carly. If nothing else, he thought, he'd make Diego pay for the anguish he'd put her through—anguish that Diego had inadvertently caused Tanner too.

Carly's nerves were frazzled. The plane had been in the air barely fifteen minutes, and for the last ten of those minutes the turbulence had been terrible. She rolled into a ball and rested her cheek against the seat. *Sleep, Carly,* she told herself, wanting to escape.

The fierce bouncing of the plane, however, quickly told her that this wasn't mere turbulence. She lifted her head. What was going on? The plane sounded as if it was falling apart. Or—Carly cocked her head and listened—was that the engine cutting in and out?

She straightened her legs, planting both feet firmly on the floor. Good heavens, it *was* the engine! Bounced roughly again, Carly jumped to her feet and raced to the cockpit. The swarthy pilot had a death grip on the wheel, and his knuckles were white from the effort he was exerting to control the plane.

"What is it?" Carly asked, scrambling into the copilot's seat.

He waved her away with his head. "Get back in your seat!"

Carly grabbed his shoulder. "What's the matter?"

Frantic, the pilot motioned her away again.

"Lady, for God's sake get into your seat and buckle up!"

"Look, mister—ooof . . ." The plane lurched, throwing Carly against the control panel. The man grabbed her by the arm and jerked her to her feet, screaming at her in Spanish. When he shoved her behind him, Carly did as she was told. In seconds she was back in her seat and buckled in.

"Dear God, we're going to crash! I know we are." Her head was suddenly thrown back against the seat as the plane went into a dive. When it leveled out again, she clenched the armrests, her nails breaking from the pressure she exerted. Then the plane dipped to one side, and Carly's heart leaped into her throat until, after several moments of extreme terror, it became apparent that they were turning back. The pilot was headed toward the field from which they'd taken off. Still Carly didn't relax; she prayed as she had never prayed before in her life.

Tanner turned anxiously at the sound of the door opening. When Consuelo, not Hank, walked in he nodded a brief greeting, then turned away again, not wanting to talk.

Consuelo walked up behind him and placed her hand on his shoulder, and even though he tensed at her touch, he remained silent, almost hating her for her part in the successful plan to make Carly leave.

"You shouldn't punish me, *querido,*" she said softly, coming around to stand before him. "I was only doing my job."

"Punishing you?"

"*Sí.*" She sat down and crossed her legs. "It was best that she went away. Surely you see this?"

"I'd have never gone through with the plan if I didn't." Why didn't she just drop the subject!

"Tanner . . ."

"We have a lot to do before Hank comes back. Let's get to work."

"Certainly, but not until I say what I came to say."

He glared at her. "And what could that possibly be?"

"I knew there was something different the minute I saw you in Fortin de las Flores. But I did not know what it was until this morning. I am sorry the *señorita bonita* has caused you so much pain."

She didn't cause me any pain. I did that all on my own." He shrugged. "Win a few, lose a few."

"*Sí,* win a few, lose a few."

Tanner narrowed his eyes. "What's that suppose to mean?"

"That you are not the only loser here. I, too, knew that I had lost the minute you touched me this

414

morning."

With disgust coating every word, Tanner said, "You never had me to lose."

"I care very deeply for you." She flinched at his abrasive laugh.

"Sure, as long as you're with me."

"That is not true."

"And I'm sure Hank would agree with me."

Consuelo's face lit up and Tanner felt sick. "I also happen to care very deeply about him. That is not impossible."

"No, you're right. It isn't impossible to care for two people at the same time." But caring is not the same as truly loving. But if he said that it would only prolong this ridiculous conversation. Besides, he'd barely had time to come to grips with what he felt before it had all been over. And he really hadn't had the time to dissect his feelings—not that he would.

The doorknob rattled and Tanner, relieved at the interruption, turned as Hank opened the door and walked in.

"Was she all right?" Tanner stood.

"Fine. She should be in Beaumont before afternoon." Hank walked further into the room. "All right, we have work to do, so let's get to it."

Once all three were seated, Hank said, "First of all, Tanner, you and Consuelo are going to have to keep a low profile, maybe even move to Fortin de las Flores until things come to a head."

"No way," Tanner said immediately.

"Then you're asking for trouble. Consuelo isn't someone who's easily forgotten, especially after the number of men who saw her at Diego's. Any one of them could be in town today."

"That is no problem, Hank." Consuelo lifted her bright red hair and let it fall back to her shoulders. "I can have this color changed by noon."

"No one actually saw me up close," Tanner said.

"I don't know about this." Hank looked from one to the other.

"I do. You're still sore from your go-round in Galveston, and you're going to need me to do the legwork." Tanner paused for a moment. "We don't have time to waste waiting for another man to get here." Tanner leaned back in his chair. When Hank didn't respond, he continued. "Now, Carly said she met Diego's informant at the hotel restaurant, and I plan to be there at noon to see if he happens to show up."

"You don't even know what he looks like," Hank said.

"It doesn't matter. All Consuelo has to do is ask about Diego and one of his men will approach her."

"No." Tanner's chin lifted at Hank's abrupt response. "I'll go with Consuelo."

"What?" Tanner asked.

"You'll wait in the car."

"In the car?" He felt like Benito.

"Yeah. We'll have to get Diego away from town before we can make him do anything."

Tanner smiled widely. "Fine; you just get him to the car. I know just the place to take him."

Carly shut her eyes, helpless to do anything but grip the chair with all her might as the plane descended. This was it; they had to make it. If the engine held they had a chance. But the plane was so tiny . . . Carly felt every bump of the emergency landing; every noise was a litany of possible danger. The rumble and roar of the faulty engine nearly overpowered her ability to think and fed the fear invading her soul.

The engine coughed and Carly gritted her teeth; every joint in her body throbbed from the fear-induced stiffness.

God couldn't be so cruel . . .

A wheel screeched in protest as it touched the ground, and just as quickly it ricocheted away.

"Please . . ." Carly begged.

Again the wheel scraped earth and this time bounced roughly as if the earth was rejecting it. Still the plane battled tenaciously to land and finally, after what seemed an eternity, all the wheels hit the ground and the plane rolled forward, shortly coming to a stop.

For long moments Carly sat unable to move, her head spinning, her heart hammering in her chest. Then, weak with relief, she let her head fall back against the seat.

"*Madre de Dios,*" she heard the pilot mutter and opened her eyes to seem him slumping against the door. "Are you all right?" he asked.

Carly managed to nod. "Are you?"

"*Sí.*"

Silence reigned. Neither seemed capable of any further speech. As if stricken with a fever, Carly began to tremble uncontrollably; her teeth chattered and she ached all over. The pilot pushed himself away from the door and moved to the back of the plane; before she knew it he was back, draping a blanket over her quivering form.

"You'll be all right in a minute," he said as his composure quickly returned. "I must see to the engine repairs. Please stay where you are."

As if she could move, Carly thought sardonically and closed her tired eyes. It would take more than a minute for her to recuperate.

Hank, looking over his newspaper, frowned at

Consuelo, who was seated at a separate table. What was she doing? he wondered as she flipped her now blue-black hair away from her face and stood up. She wasn't supposed to approach him.

Hank averted his gaze as she brushed by him; then, spotting the small piece of paper she dropped on the table, he understood what she'd been up to.

Moving casually, Hank laid the newspaper aside, and unfolded the note against the table. He wanted to smile—oh, how he wanted to smile as he lifted his head. Tanner was going to flip! Standing in the doorway, dressed in dark slacks and a pale green shirt, was a man Consuelo swore in her note was actually Diego, not his informant.

Dislike instantly filled Hank. He easily pictured the dark-complected man as one who enjoyed tormenting others. Well, not anymore; Diego was about to meet the two men who were going to end his sordid career forever.

Now to get him outside. Hank crumbled the note and stuffed it in his pocket. Then he pushed his chair back, stood up, and, with a friendly smile pasted across his face, approached Diego.

"How's it going?"

"*¿Perdón?*"

"I'm sorry. I just assumed you spoke English."

"*Sí,* I do. How may I help you?"

"I'm looking for a good friend of mine, and I

was told by a very reliable source that you could help me."

The man grinned widely. "Who is she, señor?"

"Therese Jameson."

There was just a hint of surprise on Diego's face, Hank noted as he pressed the barrel of his small derringer into Diego's ribs.

"You *do* know her." Hank smiled. "I thought so."

"Who are you?" Diego asked under his breath.

"One of your ardent admirers. Another is waiting outside." Hank pressed the barrel deep into Diego's side. "Let's go quietly."

Dicgo laughed softly. "What can a one-armed man do to me, heh? You will not have me long."

Hank grinned down at him and cocked the hammer. For once Consuelo rose from her seat without a flourish and walked easily by them as she left the building and went outside. By the time Hank and his hostage followed she was already standing at the car, holding the back door open. Hank shoved Diego in, then climbed in after him. Consuelo closed the door behind them, smiling as she opened the front door and crawled in beside Tanner, the driver.

"Shall we go?" she asked Hank over her shoulder.

"By all means."

Nothing more was said until they reached the outer limits of the city.

"I hope this old man will allow us to stay with him," Consuelo said to Tanner.

"His name is Huerve," Tanner said. "And once he knows about Benito's death and who's responsible, there won't be any problem."

"How did you discover all these out-of-the way places?" Hank asked, frowning slightly at Tanner's reflection in the rearview mirror.

"Through Rodrigo, the man Diego inadvertently had killed."

Tanner was glad a seat separated him from Diego. He could cheerfully have strangled the man, not only because of Rodrigo and Benito, but especially because he had intended to take Carly's life as well. Tanner clenched his teeth and gave his attention to the road. He had to curb these feelings, at least until the son of a bitch spilled his guts about Therese. Then, and only then, could Tanner make him pay.

Diego laughed. "You mean Rodrigo is dead? But that is wonderful."

You're going to think wonderful! Tanner thought, refusing to rise to the bait.

"*If* I killed him," Diego continued, "I would like to know how and when."

"The night Carly Jameson escaped from your

house on the mountain," Consuelo answered, "Rodrigo and another man were in the helicopter that exploded."

She turned in the seat, facing Diego. "You do not recognize this face, señor?" Tanner grinned in spite of himself. Consuelo couldn't stand to be ignored for too long.

"I am afraid not," Diego replied.

"¡*Estúpido*! It was *I* who came marching up to your house."

"Forgive me, señorita, But I was not looking at your face."

Consuelo flounced around, rigidly facing the front of the car.

"Would someone please tell me what happened to the *hermana bonita*?" Diego asked. "I had assumed she was still lost in the tangle of the tropical forest, perhaps even swallowed by a giant snake, or eaten by a . . ."

"Panther," Tanner neatly interjected.

". . . which bothered me greatly"—Diego pointedly ignored the bait—"since I wanted to bed her myself."

At that moment Consuelo spun around and made an indecent gesture with her hand. "Bed that, *hijo de puta*!"

Rage boiled inside Tanner. He had to restrain himself from braking the car and beating Diego to a pulp. Taking a deep breath, he suddenly realized how relieved he was that Carly was safely on her way home, even is she was going to hate him until the day she died, which, he hoped, would be a long, long time in the future, now that she was out of Mexico.

The sound of metal clanking against metal awakened Carly and she tossed off the blanket, wondering how long she'd been asleep. It had to have been awhile; the heat in the cabin was nearly unbearable. She took a deep breath and listened, finally realizing that the noise she heard was the pilot working on the faulty engine.

He was repairing it so he could fly again.

By no means was *she* going to be on it when it took off the second time.

Carly stood up and tucked in the long tail of Hank's shirt before she approached the pilot/mechanic. He'd just have to understand that, though she had nothing against him, her heart couldn't stand a repeat of the near disaster of their first flight. Somehow, regardless of how much she hated the idea of seeing Tanner again, Carly had to convince the pilot to take her back to Hank.

She took a step and stopped. No wonder it was so hot—the door was shut. Carly gripped the handle, but it didn't budge; it was firmly stuck.

423

"Hey, come open the door!" she shouted. The clanking stopped, but the door didn't open.

"Señorita, you must stay inside until I am finished," came a muffled reply.

Carly slapped the door. "You let me out of here right now!"

"It is not safe for you to be seen. The plane is almost ready; we will be taking off soon. *Por favor,* it will not be long."

"I am not a prisoner," Carly yelled. "I want out of here, now!"

"I am sorry. I have my orders."

She heard him move away. "Wait! Don't leave. It's hot in here. Can't you at least crack the door open so I can get some air?"

There was a long pause, then Carly heard him move back. "It will only be a little while longer."

"Mister, I'm not feeling well. I . . ." Carly dropped to the floor, then quietly and quickly rose back to her feet.

"¿Señorita?" she heard him call. *¡Señorita!*"

Carly didn't move a muscle; in fact, she held her breath. The door grated as he opened it. When she saw his face, she lunged, knocking him backward as she darted out of the plane and across the green field. If he caught her, he was going to have a hell of a time bringing her down. There was no way she was getting back on that plane.

"Señorita, nooooooo!" she heard him yell, but she ignored him as she raced for a stand of trees. She ran headlong through them, unaffected by the branches that slapped at her but not by the roots that protruded from the ground. Her toe caught and Carly fell hard on her face, the breath completely knocked out of her body. And it hurt like hell. It took so long for her to catch her breath she thought she was going to die; finally, with her head swimming dizzily, her muscles relaxed and sucked in deep breaths of air, filling her lungs.

"Oh God," she managed to whisper, wrapping her arms around her middle. She rolled onto her back, then opened her eyes, fully expecting to see the pilot standing over her. But there were only the trees—green, green trees.

She rose to her feet, looking back in the direction from which she had come. Her mouth fell open as she stood panic-stricken. The pilot hadn't come after her because he couldn't. A dark, ominous-looking car was parked directly in front of the plane. It must have arrived right after she'd bolted. Her heart pounded fiercely as two men, both dressed in dark suits, climbed out of the car. One of them jerked the pilot forward and Carly winced as the man slugged him in the stomach. The other boarded the plane, and Carly was certain he was searching for her. Now she had no choice but to get back to Hank somehow; she knew if the men found her, her life wouldn't be worth a plugged nickle.

Slowly she eased away, her eyes glued on the scene at the plane. *Please,* she prayed, *let me make it. Just let me make it this time.*

"Hank," Tanner said as he drove down the familiar washboard road. "I may need you to translate what I want to say to Huerve."

"Still avoiding the use of my language, I see," Hank replied.

"It's easier that way."

"I did not think you were telling the truth when you said you spoke no Spanish," Diego said, shaking his head at Hank.

"It wouldn't have mattered if I spoke in Japanese; the pistol in your ribs is multilingual."

Diego laughed, and Tanner gritted his teeth. The man acted as if he were on a pleasure cruise instead of being held by two men who were quite capable of killing him. But then again, Tanner added to his thought, Diego knew they wouldn't kill him. The information he held guaranteed his survival.

"Damn, are you sure there's a house out here?" Hank asked, as the car rolled through the thick growth of trees.

"Yeah, I'm sure. Actually, this isn't so bad. Wait until we pass the house to get to the barn."

"I think we'll need a bulldozer."

"This isn't anything compared to what Carly . . ." He sighed at his own mention of her name, then made himself finish what he'd begun to say. "This isn't anything compared to what Carly and I went through to get off that damned mountain."

"It's a wonder either of you made it back, especially as quickly as you did."

"Carly was determined. She loves her sister very much." Tanner suddenly stopped the car and spun around in his seat. "Speaking of which, Diego, how badly was Therese hurt?"

Diego smiled crookedly but didn't answer.

Tanner snatched him by the collar and jerked him half over the seat; Tanner's face was red with anger. Silence filled the car. No one said a word as they waited for Tanner's next move. Diego finally shrugged and tried to wedge a finger between Tanner's fist and his throat. "All right, señor, she was just grazed. Once the bleeding stopped she was fine."

"*Was* fine?" Tanner asked, shaking him.

"Is . . . fine," Diego finally managed to say.

"She'd better be," Tanner said, then thrust Diego back into his seat. "She'd better be," he repeated as he threw the car into gear and plowed through the trees.

He reached the small house and stopped.

"I think it would be better if I stay in the car and Consuelo goes with you," Hank said as Tanner moved to leave.

Tanner nodded and got out, waiting in front of the car for Consuelo to join him. Feeling somewhat guilty because of his earlier behavior, he placed his hand on the small of her back and led her to the front door.

He knocked, waited several moments, and knocked again. Where could Huerve be this time of morning?

"It doesn't seem that he is at home, *querido,*" Consuelo said, shrugging lightly.

Tanner frowned, then opened the door and stepped in, calling Huerve's name as he walked through the tiny house. He returned to the door and looked at Consuelo. "He isn't here. Come on."

Once they were again seated in the car, Tanner said to Hank, "He's gone somewhere. Let's get settled in the barn, then I'll come back."

When Hank agreed, Tanner started the engine, wishing the ordeal of telling Huerve the bad news was already over.

CHAPTER TWENTY

Tanner sat off to the side, slapping a length of rope in his hand as he listened to Hank reason with Diego.

"If you'd just come clean, Diego . . ."

"Why?" Diego asked. "Once it is discovered that I have been held by you"—he shrugged—"I am a dead man."

"Then what do you stand to lose by telling us everything you can about Therese? Surely you'd rather meet your Maker knowing you had some redeeming quality."

Diego's wicked grin was back. "I only wish I could tell you," he said. "But if I did, the *bonita* Therese would never suffer, and she must suffer."

"For what?" Hank asked, pacing back and forth. Tanner could tell that Hank was quickly getting fed up with the man.

"I asked you why Therese has to suffer," Hank repeated.

When Diego simply shrugged again, as he had been doing for the last few hours, Tanner knew that drastic measures would have to be taken to make Diego talk.

"We know that La Pantera has Therese. All we want to know is where," Hank said, towering over Diego, who was sitting on the barn floor.

"You're spinning your wheels, Hank," Tanner broke in. "Until you apply force he isn't going to tell you anything."

"You know how I hate violence," Hank responded.

"Then let *me* handle him," Tanner said, again slapping the rope against his palm. "I'll make damned short work of it."

"Sure," Hank said, "and then I'll have our superior on my neck for not handling you as I promised."

"Who the hell's going to know?" Tanner's voice rose. "If we waste much more time on him, Therese'll be history. Then they'll come down on you for sure."

Hank rubbed his chin, then turned his back on Diego.

Tanner gestured with the rope in Diego's direction. "Who's going to care what happens to him?"

Hank shook his head slightly, and Tanner knew he was having trouble keeping a straight face. Hank had fallen right in with Tanner's plan. Tanner was the heavy, Hank was the nice guy—a ruse they'd used many times before; usually just the threat of turning Tanner loose on the victim was enough to start him talking, only this time Tanner was obviously ready to act on his threat.

"Man, he has a point," Hank said, turning back to Diego. "I can't think of anyone who'd really care if something happened to you, a simple errand boy." Sighing, Hank bent closer to the Mexican, and Tanner was amazed at how sure of himself Diego remained.

"I wonder," Hank said, "is the price of your life worth that of Therese's suffering?"

"Ahh, but I know you will not kill me," Diego replied smugly. "I am too valuable to you, *no*?"

"Maybe, but then again, if you can't give us the information we need . . ." Hank, doing his best to looked pained, stared at Tanner and said almost regretfully, "He's all yours."

A line of perspiration popped out on Diego's brow, yet outwardly he maintained his composure. Tanner advanced but stopped abruptly as the barn door swung open and Consuelo walked in.

"What is it?" he asked.

"Your friend has returned," she said.

Tanner knew she meant Huerve. She'd been watching the house for him since they'd first arrived.

He glared down at Diego. "You've been given a reprieve, amigo. Use it wisely"—he dropped the rope at Diego's feet—" 'cause I'll be back real soon."

Taking Consuelo with him, Tanner left the barn and followed the narrow path to Huerve's house. As they walked, Tanner tried to think of the least painful way he could break the news about Benito to Huerve. He clenched his fists, knowing that no matter how he approached it the old man was going to be devastated by the loss of his son. Then Tanner worried that Huerve would ask them to leave, forcing him into possibly having to subdue the old man; the thought sickened Tanner. Huerve *had* to realize how important it was that they stay there.

As he and Consuelo reached the corner of the house, Tanner took a deep breath and went to the window. His gut clenched as he watched Huerve's feeble hands struggling just to hang his hat on a peg near the door.

"Mi padre, he is old. I am all he has left." Benito's words came back to Tanner. Guilt and grief struck him, but he refused to succumb to remorse. He had to stand firm. Nudging Consuelo forward, he went to the door and knocked.

Huerve's wrinkled face broke into a grin at the sight of Tanner. But his grin vanished as quickly as it appeared; his leathery skin suddenly paled and Tanner was sure the old man could tell from his expression that something was terribly wrong. Tanner turned to Consuelo to make sure she repeated his words verbatim in Spanish, but before they could leave his mouth, Huerve asked clearly in English, "Where is Benito?"

Taken aback, Tanner looked from Huerve to Consuelo and then back to Huerve.

Consuelo smiled at Tanner's expression. "I think you were mistaken. He speaks your language very well."

"What happened to my son?" Huerve ignored them, the dread he felt was clearly etched on his face.

"Go back to Hank," Tanner told Consuelo. "I'll handle this alone."

Consuelo patted the older man on the shoulder, then turned and left.

Forming the right words with great difficulty, Tanner stood silently for several moments. "This might be easier if we sit down, señor."

Huerve stepped back, granting Tanner's request. Once they were seated in straight-backed chairs, Huerve said, "My Benito is dead."

"Yes," Tanner answered quietly. "I'm sorry. He was a good man."

The loose, wrinkled skin on Huerve's throat bobbed as he swallowed; a look of pure anguish crossed his face. Tanner closed his eyes, unable to witness the man's pain. The time had gone when he'd been able to handle these scenes without becoming emotionally involved. A change had definitely occurred in the last few weeks.

433

"I need your help, Huerve."

"Why, señor?" Huerve's faded brown eyes watered. "I am a tired old man."

Tanner mentally flinched at the man's sorrow. "There is nothing I can do to bring your son back, but I can bring Diego, the man who was responsible for his and Rodrigo's death, to justice."

The mention of this was enough to transform Huerve's defeated look. He sat up straighter. "What is it you wish?"

"Just the use of your barn." Huerve looked confused. "I'm holding Diego in your barn."

"Mi casa es su casa," Huerve responded, and Tanner interpreted Huerve's phrase to mean more than the usual hospitality it offered. In fact, Tanner thought as he shook the old man's hand, barn or house, Huerve was prepared to aid them anyway he could.

Trepidation filled Carly as she walked down the familiar—oh, so familiar—street where Diego's man had first convinced her that he had information about Therese. Now fear of being rediscovered ran through her; she was being sought by higher forces. If she'd had anywhere else to go she would have, yet this was the only place she remembered how to find. When Hank had driven her to the tiny airstrip early that morning, she'd been so out of it that she hadn't paid any attention to the route he'd taken. And now she had no idea of how to find

434

Hank and no idea of the name of the hotel he was staying at, nor could she remember his last name.

She had to find a phone. It was time to contact Ellis. He was the only one who could help her get out of Mexico now. It no longer mattered that she'd been doing things on her own, asserting her independence, as it had when she'd first taken the reins at Jameson Steel. In fact, as deep in trouble as she was, she'd now welcome help. But not just anyone's. From now on she was only relying on someone she knew, loved, and trusted—namely, Ellis.

Carly walked slowly, trying to blend in with the few people who were still out on the street. She knew siesta time was rapidly approaching, a time when she would be forced to hide until the local people returned to work; it would be precious time lost if she didn't reach a phone soon. The trouble was she didn't have so much as a peso to her name. Still, if she reached the hotel where she'd stayed when she first arrived in Mexico, she could lock herself inside the walls of her room and make her calls. If Diego or one of his men didn't spot her first . . .

Her knees suddenly felt weak. She was so tired of all the craziness she'd lived through the past few days. It still wasn't over, but at least the knowledge that Hank and Tanner were doing all they could—at this very moment, she imagined—to rescue Therese from the maniac holding her made it bearable.

435

As weary as she was, Carly knew she still had several long blocks to travel before she reached the hotel. But there were fewer and fewer people in the street as each second passed. What were several more hours of waiting compared with her safety? She reasoned as she slipped into a shadowed doorway. She admitted she was procrastinating, that she was afraid, but she didn't know what she'd walk into once she entered the hotel.

Slipping through the barn doorway, Tanner stopped short at the sight of the pistol in Hank's hand. "Whoa, buddy, it's just me."

"One can never be sure," Hank replied, depositing his gun in his harness. Consuelo moved closer, wanting to hear everything that was said.

"How'd he take it?" Hank asked.

"Like the man he is," Tanner said, then leveled his eyes at Diego. "He was also full of information." Tanner's smile was chilling. "It just so happens he knows the exact location of La Pantera's house."

Hank smiled widely. Consuelo snuggled up to Tanner's side. "You are the luckiest man I have ever known."

Diego's face screwed up in anger; he attempted to stand up, but Tanner placed a foot in his midsection and shoved him back down.

"Hijo de puta!"

"Did he call me a bad name?" Tanner asked in

mock ignorance.

Hank nodded. "I believe he did."

"Tsk, tsk, Diego, you shouldn't be so angry. Hank here gave you ample opportunity to tell us what you knew, and you chose not to. Now you're pretty much on your own." Tanner paused for effect. "As soon as we're finished I guess you can return to La Pantera and his men, or what's left of them, anyway."

"Please, you cannot. I know things the old man does not. I will give you the information, but . . ."—Diego looked at Hank—". . . I will need protection in your country."

Consuelo tossed her head back. "I think you should leave him here to face his friends. That is what the snake deserves."

Tanner opened his mouth to respond, but Hank interrupted. "I don't know, Consuelo—he may be more useful than we think. It just depends on how much he can still help us."

"Hank," Tanner said as if disappointed in his friend, "would you really want someone like him roaming free in our homeland?"

Both men turned their eyes on Diego, then looked back at each other.

"I will give you the times and places of the drug shipments. I can guarantee they are correct," Diego said desperately.

Tanner shook his head. "I need more."

"I will give you records, names, connections,

everything I have."

"Where are they?" Hank's tone hardened.

Diego took a deep breath. "La Pantera didn't know I was stealing his information. I had planned eventually to become the power, to take it all away from him."

"You're not telling us a damned thing we need to know," Tanner said. "Where are the records?"

"I own a small apartment near the hotel where I intercepted the younger Miss Jameson. They are in a safe there."

"How did you know Carly Jameson was coming to Mexico?"

"From a contact La Pantera has in the States."

Tanner moved closer. "I need a name, Diego."

"Christina is the only name I know."

"I can't buy that," Hank said.

But Tanner frowned. Like Hank, he didn't want to accept it, yet the name Christina was awfully close to Tina. How else would anyone know what he hadn't even guessed—that Carly was on her way to Mexico? And the leak . . .

"It is true! La Pantera depends on her every call."

"I want *La Pantera's* real name," Tanner said.

"Gabriel de los Santos."

"What about the shipment of drugs that was due to go out several days ago? Has a new date been set?"

"Yes." Diego laughed scornfully. "The fool trusted me with all the information."

"What about the shipment date?" Tanner asked softly.

"Tomorrow it leaves for the coast of Florida."

"But it was scheduled for Galveston?"

"Of course."

"If La Pantera delegated responsibilities to you, why hasn't he terminated Therese?" Hank asked, frowning.

Diego sighed. "It is such a long story."

"We're all ears," Tanner said sarcastically.

"He had seen her many times in the city and had tried many times to convince her to be his woman, his mistress. She played upon his senses; each time she denied him it made him want her all the more. You see, Therese will be very safe until he breaks her spirit; then, of course, he will kill her. He is a very cruel man."

"And he knows who she is and why she's here?"

"He is no fool."

"You're lying," Tanner said.

"I am not."

"Then tell us something we can check. Where's the house they've taken her to?" Tanner asked.

"The old man has already told you."

"I want to hear it from you."

439

"It is several miles out of town. . . ."

Thirty minutes later, Tanner and Hank left the barn. As soon as they were a good distance away, Tanner began to chuckle under his breath.

"What's so funny?" Hank asked.

"It's Diego. The minute he thought Huerve knew anything about La Pantera, he spilled his guts."

Hank's frown caused Tanner to laugh again. "Huerve didn't know enough to fill a thimble."

Both men laughed, then Hank became serious. "You know, freeing Therese will only be the tip of the iceberg. Our job won't be finished until we bust this entire operation."

"Yes, but having Diego in our hands will make it much easier."

Tanner entered Diego's apartment and locked the door behind him, smiling at how simple his work could be at times. All he had to do was get the record book and run. But first he had to call Omi. The hunch—no, the near certainty—that Tina King was a major part of the leak had to be confirmed one way or the other.

The apartment was small and sparsely furnished, telling Tanner that its main use had been for secreting goods—Diego's goods, the records. Still, there were a few comforts: a settee, a lamp; and—Tanner smiled as his eyes lit on a table in the corner of the room—a telephone.

He wasted no time moving to it. With less trouble than he'd imagined it would take, the phone was soon ringing the States.

"Omi," Tanner said, recognizing the voice that answered.

"Barnes? What's happening down there?"

"We have Diego, and we know where La Pantera is. We'll be moving in on him within the next twenty-four hours."

"Everyone all right?"

Tanner lifted a brow. "Is that concern I hear in your voice?"

"Hell, no, I just needed something to say."

"I've never known you to be at a loss for words."

"Get on with it, Barnes."

Tanner smiled, then said, "I want Tina King pulled from the Jameson house at once. I think she's a part of the leak that put Therese where she is now—in deep trouble."

"How so?"

"Diego told us that there's someone in the states named Christina on whom La Pantera relies. This person informed La Pantera that Carly was on her way to Mexico. Whoever it was knew the exact

441

time Carly left her home. It had to be Tina." When Omi didn't respond, Tanner continued. "Look, I know you like her, but who else could have squealed?"

"I'll pull her immediately."

"Good, because Carly should be arriving in Texas sometime this afternoon, and I don't want anyone knowing she's home."

"You got her out of there, huh?"

"Yeah, thanks to Hank." Tanner gritted his teeth at Omi's soft chuckle. "I'll contact you as soon as everything goes down." He hung up before Omi could make one of his usual snide remarks.

Tanner stepped into the tiny hallway and spotted the rug Diego had said would be there. He shoved it out of the way with his toe, then smiled. So far Diego had told the truth; there was a safe built into the floor. Tanner knelt and quickly rolled the numbers of the combination, then pulled the handle and the safe door opened; a black loose-leaf binder was the only item inside. Tanner lifted it, quickly flipped through the pages, then whistled softly; the record book held more information than he'd hoped. The amount of money exchanged was phenomenal. He quickly stuffed the book into the inner pocket of his jacket, then closed the safe and tossed the rug down over it. He'd have time to study all the facts in the book later.

Just as he was preparing to leave, the unmistakable sound of footsteps reached his ears. He scanned the apartment for a place to hide, then cursed under his breath. The footsteps stopped in front of the door—the only exit.

Three rooms to choose from, two seconds to decide. Tanner felt trapped as he glanced from corner to corner. A key grated in the lock, and the doorknob rattled. Tanner slipped into the nearest room, a bathroom, and climbed into the shower stall just as the door scraped open. He literally held his breath to avoid discovery.

The male voices were low and spoke in Spanish, to his frustration. As Tanner tried to make out what they were saying, he pictured himself choking Diego purple. Diego had lied; he'd told Tanner that no one knew about the apartment or the book! Just one more dirty trick to tack onto the long list the slimy bastard had committed.

Not only were the men looking for the records, but they, too, wanted Diego. Dammit, Tanner thought as he clenched his hands into fists, maybe Diego *had* told the truth. His plan to take control of the operation must have been discovered during the course of this major shake-up. A grin split Tanner's face; from what Tanner was able to understand so far, Diego was in hot water all around. One way or the other he was going to pay a price for all he'd done.

Tanner tensed, sensing a movement toward the bathroom; it was confirmed by the sound of a voice that was too close for comfort. He shrank back against the wall of the shower stall, thankful its door was too dark to see through. His eyebrows shot up as he listened to one man tell the others that Diego was a dead man, that he never should have skipped out the night Carly had escaped.

Tanner frowned. Why the hell, then, had Diego gone back to the hotel?

Come on, Tanner thought, say something about Therese. He desperately had to know if she was still alive. But the men suddenly quit talking and Tanner tensed even more. They were tearing the apartment to pieces. And they weren't going to leave without searching the bathroom.

She should have been used to the heat by now, but she wasn't. Thankfully, the hottest part of the day was almost over. People were returning to work, and Carly knew it was time to leave the doorway. In fact, she was well aware of how lucky she'd been that no one had come or gone through the door since she'd first taken up her post over an hour before.

With a groan she rose to her feet, eased out onto the sidewalk, and walked hesitantly toward the hotel. The more she thought about it, the worse her plan seemed. It was almost as if she knew she was heading right back into Diego's clutches, yet she continued on the hazardous path.

If only she had an alternative, she thought, wrapping her arms around her waist. But she had nowhere else to go; she had to make an attempt to get out of Mexico. Her only hope was that if she saw Diego, she could avoid him, and if she avoided him . . .

For some reason, at that moment her gaze was drawn upward, along the side of a tall building. She gasped and stumbled several steps before she stopped. Her mouth fell open—she shook her head unbelievingly. It couldn't be, yet . . . there was Tanner Barnes on the outer ledge of a second-floor window! Her heart leaped into her throat. They were rescuing Therese right before her very eyes!

Carly quickly scanned the street, looking for a sign of Hank, Consuelo, anyone who looked even remotely out of place. Seeing no one, she immediately zoomed in on Tanner's precarious perch again.

He spotted her and lost his footing; her arms went out in a futile attempt to help him. But he didn't fall; he hung dangling from the ledge. She wanted to cry out—in fact, she must have, for suddenly several people crowded around her, all looking up.

Tanner scraped his booted foot against the

brick, catching his heel on the ledge. Thank God, she thought, he was all right . . .

A man suddenly stuck his head out of the window and pulled a gun.

"No!" Carly screamed, alerting Tanner. He looked up, then let go immediately and dropped to the ground, landing hard on his feet. The man fired; the bullets splintered the concrete inches away. Carly was jostled by people running for cover, but she was paralyzed, fear freezing her in place. Tanner ducked, then lunged toward her, but bullets danced between them, cutting them off, and Tanner was forced to run away. Then three men ran out of the building, all clutching guns, all after Tanner. When he cast a pained look back at her as he disappeared around the corner, the three men hard on his heels, Carly knew there was no way he could come back for her.

Suddenly the enormity of the danger he was in hit her, and she took off after them. She had to make sure he got away. A frantic sob tore from her throat. No matter what, she couldn't—*wouldn't* let them kill Tanner.

CHAPTER TWENTY-ONE

Tanner leaped into the car and twisted the key, fighting the urge to smash the dashboard when the engine whined sluggishly.

Come on, car, come on! he begged, furiously pumping the accelerator. Through the rearview mirror Tanner saw the three men turn the corner, and he ducked as a spray of bullets mowed a path before them. His heart pounded fiercely. They hadn't spotted Carly—he could make it around the block and pick her up. He twisted the key again, they shouted triumphantly as the engine caught. Tires screeched and the exhaust threw off black smoke, nearly blocking his view as he shoved the car into gear and swerved into the street.

"*No!*" He saw Carly chasing after the men— she should have run the other way!

Without thinking, Tanner jerked the wheel and recklessly spun the car around. There was no way he'd let them have her, not as long as he had a . . .

"Son-of-a-bitch!" he shouted. They had already recognized and grabbed her. One of the men held a gun to her head while the other two stood in front of her, pistols aimed and ready to fire as soon as Tanner crossed their paths. Tanner shook his head and floored the accelerator. If he stopped now they'd kill her and him too. There was nothing he could do but hope he made it past them, no way he could get her now.

The car raced by. Bullets flew and glass shattered all over Tanner's body. But it didn't slow him down; in fact, he never took his eyes off the road. He had to make it back to Hank; they had to move in now.

Carly had no idea where she was being taken and she didn't ask. Terrified, she sat in the back seat of the car between two fierce-looking men. The third, and meanest-looking of all, drove.

Yet, even in her fear, she was ecstatic that Tanner had gotten away. He was still free and able to come to her rescue—if these were indeed that Pantera man's goons, and if indeed they were taking her to him and Therese.

It was eerie. These guys had just been in a major shoot-out with Tanner, yet they seemed totally unaffected by what had happened. Not one had said a word, had not so much as grunted, since they'd shoved her in the car. They hadn't attempted to chase down Tanner. What was even stranger was they didn't look at each other, and, thank God, they seemed completely oblivious of her presence.

She tried not to hope, but she couldn't help it. If these were La Pantera's employees, maybe, just maybe, she'd be lucky enough to be taken to Therese. Then, at least, Tanner and Hank stood a chance of finding them.

But fear reared its ugly head along with the scene of the pilot being beaten. She was positive that the men sitting beside her now were the same two men who'd attacked the pilot; just as she somehow knew they had come after her—there was no other logical reason for their sudden appearance at the tiny airstrip.

But how had they known she was on that plane and that the plane had returned?

Nervously, she clasped her hands together. Then her eyes caught sight of a huge, sprawling hacienda set in the center of a sloping valley, and she gasped. Guards were scattered everywhere, some holding shotguns and pistols and others with wicked-looking machine guns. They made Diego's small crew look like Boy Scouts. Her stomach knotted; a sense of doom settled on her. If Tanner managed to get her out of this place he would truly be a superman—if they didn't kill her as soon as she stepped out of the car, and if Tanner even knew where she was.

Oh, God, she suddenly prayed, *please let this be Pantera's house. And please don't let Diego be here.*

Two enormous wrought-iron gates automatically opened; the driver never slowed as he maneuvered the car through the opening in the tall, imposing brick wall that encompassed the house. Finally, he pulled the car to the side of what seemed to be the garage, then braked with a heavy foot, bouncing Carly forward. With wide eyes she stared at the least menacing of the men, wanting to ask him what was going to happen, but his stony stare caused her to swallow the question and turn away. She'd know soon enough.

All three men climbed out, but Carly didn't move until the stony-faced one reached for her; then she quickly scooted away from him and out of the other door.

On shaky legs she was led through a side entrance into the cool, dark interior of the house. It took a moment for her eyes to adjust, but when she finally focused she gasped. Before her was one of the handsomest men she'd ever seen. Tall and lean, he stood there smiling as he negligently leaned on a cue stick. Tobacco brown hair waved away from a high forehead; his skin was clear and light, and his eyes were the greenest she'd ever seen. His features hinted of some Mexican heritage; his nose was long and straight, his cheekbones high and proud. And he was grinning from ear to ear.

Carly's emotions seesawed between fear and a sense of ease. He looked friendly, almost happy to see her, yet . . .

With a slight nod he turned away from her and placed the stick on a pool table Carly hadn't realized was there.

"Is this your sister?" he addressed a darkened corner.

Carly's heart leaped, even though she couldn't see into the darkness, she knew Therese was there.

"You know that she is," came her sister's familiar voice.

Thank God, Carly mentally cried.

"You're not thinking straight," Hank said.

"Dammit," Tanner argued, "they'll kill her. They have no reason to keep her alive." The muscles in his neck were corded from his anger.

Hank lifted a piece of glass from the hood of the car and flung it into the trees. "So we're supposed to rush in like the Green Berets and take her?" he asked, then shook his head vehemently. "This isn't the movies, and you're sure as hell no Rambo."

"Damn you."

"Tanner," Hank said, his voice calmer, "if Therese has any influence on La Pantera, as Diego suggested, there's no way she'll let him do anything to Carly."

"We'll exchange the book for her."

"No."

For the first time in Tanner's life he wanted to

flatten Hank.

"We can't bargain with them," Hank reasoned, then paused before adding, "but we can use the book."

Knowing he was being irrational, Tanner sighed in frustration. "How?"

"We'll set up a dummy exchange. While they're coming for the book, we'll hit the house."

"And if it doesn't work?" was Tanner's immediate response, but his mind caught Hank's train of thought.

"It has to." Hank stepped forward and placed his hand on Tanner's shoulder. "We're out of options."

Tanner lowered his head. "How the hell did she manage to get off that plane?"

"Only Carly knows, and we have a lot of work to do before we can hear her explanation."

"Aren't you going to greet her?" the green-eyed man asked, but before the woman Carly knew was Therese could respond Carly rushed forward.

"Not so fast, *chiquita*," the man said, grabbing her by the upper arm. His green eyes pierced her like shards of glass. Carly's unease erupted into fear and she attempted to twist away. Something was wrong; there had to be a reason Therese hadn't come forward.

His fingers gripped Carly's arm painfully, causing her to cry out, then freeze in place to prevent the agony from shooting up her shoulder.

"Get up, Therese, and come here or I will hurt her even more."

Carly bit her lip, forcing her attention away from the pain and to the darkened corner. Therese stepped out of the shadow; the whole right side of her face was bruised and swollen.

"You *monster,*" Carly whispered heatedly, then cried as he tightened his grip.

"I'm here, Gabriel." Therese's tone was unlike any Carly had ever heard from her before.

Immediately he released Carly's arm. But, horrified at the sight of her sister's face, Carly hardly noticed it.

Therese stared back but didn't speak, and Carly followed her example.

"Have dinner served," the man named Gabriel said over his shoulder to the men behind her. Silently they filed out of the room, and it dawned on her that they knew they were not to speak—no one spoke unless this monster decreed it so.

Acting as if Carly weren't even in the room, Gabriel moved next to Therese and, so gently it sickened Carly, caressed her bruised cheek.

"I'll bet you are starving, *querida.* I have a feast planned."

Therese lifted her head slightly. Although she appeared calm, Carly could see hatred shining in her bright blue eyes.

"Yes, Gabriel, I am . . . *starving.*" Carly didn't

miss the slight emphasis on Therese's last word. "And I imagine my sister is as well."

He suddenly jerked his head toward Carly and blinked. He *had* forgotten about her.

"Yes, of course she is." He crooked his arm and offered it to Carly. She started to back away, but the quick negative jerk of Therese's head made her warily place her arm through his. Then, again smiling as if all was right with the world, he offered Therese his other arm, which she took without hesitation. The urge to bawl like a baby nearly overwhelmed Carly, but she fought against it and allowed him to lead her to the feast.

A million questions rushed into her mind as Carly sat at the formally set table, questions she desperately wanted to ask, but fear squashed them. This man Gabriel was insane, dangerously so; just the look in his eyes petrified her. She could only imagine the hell Therese had been through.

Carly swallowed, trying not to stare, yet her eyes continued to dart toward Therese; Therese, however, didn't acknowledge Carly's presence. In fact, Therese did nothing but stare off into space, her bruised face carefully turned away from Gabriel's eyes, which he scarcely took off her.

Again, as if she'd been forgotten by the two, Carly felt that third-person experience. The scene was unreal, bizarre; it was as if she had wandered into the Twilight Zone.

The food grew cold in the dishes; not one

portion of the meal was touched. Carly sensed that something was about to occur, something that her presence had brought about, and she forced herself not to bolt. Whatever Gabriel had planned, she had to take, for she truly believed Therese could not.

"Therese, you must eat," Carly jumped when Gabriel spoke.

Without looking at him Therese answered. "Anita is not here to serve."

He shook his head as if clearing his mind; then he stood up, glancing around the room before he stalked through a different doorway than the one they'd used to enter.

"Are you all right?" Carly immediately asked.

"Shhh. Don't talk—don't do anything but sit and be quiet!"

"Therese . . ."

"I mean it. He's unpredictable and violent, as you can see," Therese said, gesturing toward her cheek.

"But . . ."

"Pretend you're invisible if you have to; just don't draw any attention toward yourself."

Carly's insides tied into knots. "All right, I won't, but Tanner . . ."

"Shut up!" The words were soft, but the meaning was loud.

What in the name of God were they going to do? Carly thought, her nerves all in pieces. If only she knew whether Gabriel was La Pantera. If only she was certain Tanner would find them.

"Damn them all to eternal hell!" Gabriel shouted. Carly's heart nearly jumped out of her chest as he stormed into the room and snatched Therese out of the chair by the hair of her head.

"What have you done with her?" he demanded, jerking her head back and glaring down into her face. Carly leaped to her feet.

"*Who*?" Therese managed to ask. When Gabriel drew his hand back to strike her, Carly grabbed a knife from the immaculately set table.

"Anita! She is gone."

"I . . ." He cracked her across the face, giving her no chance to defend herself.

Before Carly could race around the table the sound of rapid footsteps stopped her, robbing her of the pleasure of plunging the knife into Gabriel's black heart. She slid it beneath her blouse just as the men ran into the room.

"Where is Anita?" Gabriel demanded, ignoring everyone else.

"I'd tell you if I knew," Therese answered.

"Bitch, don't force my hand."

"I . . ."

"Señor, señor." A short, chubby Mexican woman came bustling into the dining room, wiping her hands on an apron. "Please, it is not her fault. I was late."

Gabriel shoved Therese away from him, then stormed toward the woman. "Where have you

456

been?"

"Señor, *tú hermano . . .*"

"My brother? He is here?"

"*Sí.*"

Gabriel threw back his head and laughed uproariously. "That is wonderful. Please show him in."

"I don't like it," Tanner said.

"What, my clothes?" In mock distress, Hank glanced down at his blue chambray shirt and faded jeans.

"You know what I mean."

"You're becoming a real pain," Hank said, all joking aside.

"I still don't like it," Tanner said.

"I don't either, so why don't you knock it off?"

"I should be the one to go."

"You'd stick out like a sore thumb, gringo." Hank put a straw hat on his head, then drew the chin strap tight.

"At least I'm not busted up."

"The ribs have healed quite nicely, thank you."

"We'll see, once you start riding Huerve's bike." Tanner paced the small confines of Huerve's bedroom, then sat heavily on the bed. "You should be back in an hour . . ."

"Do you realize what Omi's going to do when he learns he has to issue two checks to repair those cars?"

"An hour and a half at the most," Tanner said, ignoring Hank's comment and studying his watch.

"You're beginning to sound like my mother."

"If you're any later it'll be dark."

"See?"

Tanner sighed. "Make sure the car you steal is full of gas."

"I'll try."

"I know you will."

Oh my God! Carly thought. It couldn't be! She closed her eyes, pain filling her heart. Even though she was ignorant of the inner workings of Therese and Tanner's professions, Carly understood what it meant when the man she knew as Cornwall walked into the room.

He stopped and leaned negligently against the door frame, his smile smug. Carly tore her gaze away from him and focused on her sister. She could see all her own feelings written on Therese's face. Traitor, murderer, liar! But the one emotion Carly saw that she didn't feel was hurt—intense hurt, the kind of pain only a lover could inflict.

Gabriel raced forward, heartily grasping his brother. "You have finally come. I had almost given up on you."

Cornwall stared at Therese but answered his brother. "You worry too much." He brushed by Gabriel and walked to the end of the table. When his gaze suddenly turned from Therese to herself, Carly saw the golden hair, the tawny eyes, and she knew he was La Pantera.

"I tried to keep you out of this," he told her.

"I'm surprised you didn't handle me the way you must have handled Lisa Curtis."

He smiled. "I didn't recognize you as a threat then."

"She's still no threat," Therese said, breaking into the conversation.

Cornwall glared at Therese. "She is now."

"Nice," Tanner said, admiring the black station wagon Hank had borrowed from town. He glanced in the back. "You even managed to save Huerve's bike, I see."

"I thought you'd approve." Hank smiled.

"Did you run into any trouble?"

"Drove away clean."

Tanner passed around the hood of the car and came to stand next to Hank. "Man, I'm sorry for getting so bent out of shape earlier."

"You love her, don't you?" The smile vanished from Hank's face.

Tanner nodded. "I think I'll go crazy if we don't get her and Therese out of there soon."

"Well we can't have you going insane, you know."

Tanner smiled weakly. "I've studied the map Diego sketched. It's going to be hard getting into the house, but once we do I think we'll be all right. Did you get a chance to contact Joaquin?"

"He's dead," Hank said somberly. "I don't know how Carly managed to get away."

Tanner's guts clenched. "If she hadn't seen me she'd still be free."

"The phone in my room must have been tapped. La Pantera was lying in wait for us. Whoever the leak is has sure done his job."

"If it's Tina we'll be all right."

"Yeah, but something tells me that was too obvious."

"I know what you mean," Tanner said, then sighed. "Who's going to pilot us out of here tonight?"

"Marcos is on his way from Mexico City."

"Another chopper?"

"A better pilot too."

"You feeling up to contacting La Pantera now?"

"Just as soon as it gets a little darker."

Carly sat in the *sala*, as Gabriel had called it, swearing to herself that no matter what Cornwall asked her, she wouldn't answer. There was no way, even though she had no idea what Tanner's plans were, that she'd risk inadvertently giving away some small clue.

Cornwall stood in the corner, his arms behind him as he pierced her with a look that closely resembled Gabriel's. "Where has Tanner taken the book?"

"I don't know what you're talking about."

"I advise you not to play games, Ms. Jameson," he said. "You were there when he took it. Where was he going?"

"I told you I don't know. It was only by accident that I was there when everything happened."

Cornwall sighed heavily. "Unlike my brother, I hate to inflict pain . . ."

"Please forgive me if I find that hard to believe," Carly said, "but Lisa Curtis didn't die of natural causes."

Cornwall shrugged. "She didn't suffer either."

A tremor of fear raced down Carly's spine. "Where's my sister?"

"Therese is fine." He advanced, stopping several feet in front of her. "Now, I want you to think very hard before answering me. Think about your sister and your brother Ellis. Remember why you came to Mexico in the first place. Then imagine what will happen if you don't tell me everything you know."

Fear brought Carly to her feet before Cornwall. She clutched his hands. "I don't know anything. I swear." She squeezed his fingers, hating herself for even touching him, but she had to convince him that she was ignorant of everything.

"As soon as I arrived in Mexico a man named

Diego kidnapped me. I escaped his house and ran through the jungle for two nights . . ."

"Where did you get a gun?"

"What?"

"You shot several of my men when they spotted you from the air."

"I stole it before I escaped."

He grabbed her by the upper arms and she sucked in her breath. "Liar!" he said, shaking her. "Tanner Barnes was with you. In fact, he shot my men."

Carly pressed her hands against his chest. "All right, all right, I'll tell you," she said, cringing away from him. She stared helplessly into his gold eyes and he released her.

She stepped away from Cornwall and turned her back to him. "Yes, Tanner was there," she said quietly, hating herself for giving in. "And together we made it out of the jungle and back to the city. Just as soon as he could, he had me on a plane headed for home. But he plane had engine trouble and was forced to turn back. Stupid me decided that I wasn't going home and I ran, just missing the men you obviously sent after me." She turned back to him, hatred welling inside her. "I swear to you I just happened to be on that street, going back to the hotel room I'd originally rented, when Tanner and your three men decided to have a shoot-out. I no more know where he is than you do."

Cornwall almost looked friendly as he raked

his hand through his hair. "Why do I believe you?"

"Because it's the truth."

"All right. Tell me who's with him."

"I don't know what you mean."

"He has others helping him. Who are they?"

"I never met any of them."

"Carly, you know Hank."

She closed her eyes. She had to be careful, extremely cautious of every word she said. "If Hank was there, I didn't see him," she lied.

"He was there."

"How do you know?" Carly asked, peering up at him.

"How do you think we knew you were on that plane?" When Carly shrugged, he asked, "Who do you think damaged the plane engine, forcing it to return?" Still she didn't answer. "Hank's phone was wired."

Of course, Carly thought. Cornwall knew all the inside news. Whoever his and Tanner's boss was must have told him every detail, which made Cornwall even more dangerous than Carly originally assumed. He knew exactly how Tanner and Hank worked, would be able to second-guess them. Suddenly Carly felt the enormous futility of Tanner even attempting to rescue her and Therese.

"Can I please see Therese?"

"I'm afraid not."

"What will you do with us now?"

"I don't know," he answered baldly. "Having

you here has definitely altered my plans."

The phone rang twice. Cornwall considered for a moment, then let it ring a third time before he gestured to Gabriel to answer it.

"*Buenos noches*," Gabriel said. After a brief pause he looked at Cornwall and nodded.

It was Tanner. Cornwall moved to his brother's side and put his ear to the phone. No, it wasn't Tanner, it was Hank; Tanner's Spanish left something to be desired. Cornwall stepped quietly away, allowing his brother to take care of the details. He knew Hank would leave no room for negotiation. He'd simply state the facts and hang up. Too bad it all had to be this way, Cornwall thought, then mentally shrugged. But maybe it was better that it did. Killing Tanner and Hank would leave him free to move on and out of this business. Once this day was over and the book was safely in his hands, he would be through with drug trafficking once and for all. In fact, he could hardly wait to take Therese and . . .

Therese. He swallowed, knowing it would be a long time, if ever, before she forgave him. Maybe having baby sister was a good thing after all. As long as Therese knew there was a threat to Carly, she'd do whatever he wanted. But he would forever have to be on guard. He could never allow either of them to escape.

Cornwall turned to his brother. Gabriel was

cunning and shrewd, and Cornwall could almost kill him for harming Therese. Still, he was perfectly capable of handling this last major shipment—as long as he laid off the nose candy. Gabriel was younger by eight years, pampered by their American mother and his Mexican father. Both he and his brother had been used to money, but it was just like the old man to have spent every cent the family had before he died. If only his stepfather had let him handle the finances when things had gone bad, none of them would have been forced into poverty. But . . .

It had taken them years to build this business, and it would take just a few days to end it. But it was over.

Gabriel hung up the phone.

"Where and what time?" Cornwall asked anxiously.

"Midnight, the brewery."

"Back or front?"

"In the alley."

Cornwall nodded. "It's nine o'clock. Start preparing the men."

CHAPTER TWENTY-TWO

It was impossible to sit still, Carly thought, her mind in a turmoil. Being locked in this bedroom was horrible, especially when she was helpless to do anything but pace back and forth anxiously across the ice blue carpet. At least she hadn't been tied up—but then again, it might have been better if she had. Then her only worry would have been to untie herself so she could find a way to escape. Now, being free in the room, she had to face the truth—the door was locked, the windows were locked, and short of boring a hole through the roof, there was no way out.

Carly hugged herself as she looked out the window. Even if they weren't secured, the two-story drop to the ground would probably kill her. And if it didn't, the guards would.

"Oh, to be home with Ellis," she muttered. She jumped at the sudden knock on the door, then stood stock-still as a key grated in the lock. Was it Cornwall . . . Gabriel . . . *Therese*? As the door swung in, Carly's mouth fell open.

"Jorge!" She rushed forward and pulled him in, closing the door quickly behind him. "You're the last . . ."

He shook his head, pushing her hands away, a formidable expression on his face.

"What is it?" she asked. "Are we being watched?" Scenes from spy movies rushed to mind and Carly quickly scanned the room for hidden cameras.

Jorge pulled her chin around, then shook her head. Once he had her full attention he cupped his hand behind his ear and pointed toward the door.

"They're listening?" she mouthed.

He nodded. She sighed dejectedly and stepped away.

"Why are you here?" she asked in a voice meant to carry.

Jorge merely positioned himself in front of the door, where he stubbornly crossed his beefy arms across his chest.

"Ahhh," she said sarcastically, "my very own guard. How nice."

Jorge rolled his black eyes and smiled, then quietly stepped toward her.

"Is there any way out of here?" she whispered.

He shook his head, then lifted his hand in the age-old gesture of a gun. Her hopes fell.

"Too many guards?" she asked.

He nodded once and folded his arms again.

"What am I going to do?"

Jorge shrugged, and Carly became frustrated —frustrated because he couldn't talk, couldn't communicate; then she was immediately ashamed of her thoughts. But it didn't keep her from pressing him for information.

"Jorge, is my sister still here?" He nodded.

"Is she nearby?" Again he nodded.

"How close?"

He held up three fingers, then touched the door.

"Three doors? She's three doors down?"

A brief smile touched his thick lips.

"And she's all right?"

He blinked.

"Thank you, Jorge."

As if unable to help himself, he ran his hand over her hair, then squeezed her shoulder.

"It's after ten," Hank said, pushing himself away from the barn wall.

"Sure is," Tanner answered but didn't move from his seated position on the hood of the station wagon. He was back in control again, his mind set on the mission ahead.

"We have to send Consuelo and Diego on their way."

Tanner spat out the piece of straw on which he'd been chewing. "Yeah."

"I suppose you want me to go and get her and Huerve at the house?"

"If you don't mind."

"And you'll take care of Diego there?" Hank said, pointing at the man, who was bound and gagged in the corner of the barn.

Tanner smiled. "I'll pick you up at the house."

Hank's brow lifted. "Don't dawdle."

"Won't take but a minute," Tanner said, then watched Hank let himself out the door.

Without hurry, Tanner slid off the car and sauntered toward Diego. Trussed up like a turkey, Diego cringed when Tanner smiled broadly, then wiggled like a maggot in hot ashes as Tanner bent down until they were at eye level.

"Ready to go?" Tanner asked.

Diego shook his head, then dug his heels into the dirt floor and pushed away.

"Come now, amigo, don't tell me you've changed your mind about the good old U.S.A.?" Tanner said as he reached for Diego's collar.

Diego's eyes widened; his head thrashed back and forth.

"I didn't think so." When Tanner twisted his hand around the shirt, Diego whined through the gag.

"What's that? You want me to untie you?" Tanner asked in a low, angry tone; then, with uncontrollable strength, jerked Diego to his feet. "Good. I could never forgive myself if I hit a defenseless man."

As if reconciled to the fact that nothing he could do would stop Tanner, Diego quit moving while Tanner released the ropes and gag.

"Several nights ago Carly Jameson must have felt exactly as you feel now. Except I'll bet she never cried," Tanner said, spinning Diego around.

"Please, señor," Diego said, throwing up his hands.

"Where's all that cocky self-confidence now?"

"I did not hurt . . ."

Tanner's fist crashed into Diego's nose just as the gunshot cracked from across the barn. Half of Diego's head went flying. Warm blood squirted over Tanner's arm and, horrified, he watched the man's body slip from his fingers and fall to the ground. Then he turned and saw Huerve in the doorway, a pistol wobbling in his frail hands.

Hank and Consuelo rushed in, both their pistols aimed at the older man.

"Wait, Hank, Consuelo," Tanner ordered,

then gestured toward Diego's body.

Hank looked from the body to Tanner. "Looks like our plans have changed," he said somberly, relieving Huerve of the pistol.

The night was chill and damp; Tanner smelled rain in the air. Dark clouds had long ago covered the quarter moon, ensuring that his and Hank's position so near the house would go undetected. Both knelt on the ground and watched La Pantera's house, neither speaking as they waited for someone to depart.

Consuelo was probably halfway to Mexico City by now, Tanner thought, knowing she'd see that the book got to Omi. He couldn't help but think of Huerve and the grim look on his wrinkled face. It was amazing that the older man had still agreed to help them, even though his role was a minor one. They'd let him out of the car close to the brewery; then he'd ridden his bicycle the half mile it took and put his old black Bible in place of the book Hank had instructed La Pantera to pick up. Tanner imagined Huerve was home by now. But no one would be waiting for La Pantera, because Tanner knew there was no way he'd bring Carly or Therese out of his home, just as Tanner hoped La Pantera wouldn't suspect that Tanner and Hank would dare enter his home to retrieve the two women.

Thunder rumbled softly in the distance and Tanner sighed silently, then lifted field glasses to his eyes. Guards seemed to cover every approach, but fortunately there didn't seem to be as many patrolling behind the house. He and Hank had left the car about a mile away and walked the rest of the way; Tanner could only hope that four people would make the return trip.

A soft knock sounded on the door and Carly sat up on the bed, alert as Jorge answered the summons. The woman Carly knew as Anita bustled in, a cup and saucer in her hand.

"Señor Cornwall sent you some tea," she said. Carly somberly accepted the cup and Anita turned to leave, but Carly grabbed her arm, halting her.

"Did you take my sister some?"

"Sí."

"Was she all right?"

"Sí, she is fine."

Carly sighed and let the woman go. After Jorge closed the door, Carly sat back against the pillows and sipped the tea, grimacing at the bitter taste. She wished Señor Cornwall had at least thought to send sugar too. Then she looked at Jorge. "It's not the best I've ever had, but you're welcome to some."

He shook his head, and Carly noticed an

almost sad expression flit across his face. "Don't worry, Jorge, everything will work out," she said, wishing she believed her own words. If only there was *something* she could do. Carly sipped the tea again, and as she swallowed, she realized why the tea was so bitter—something had been added to it. The medicinal taste was suddenly very strong.

Her eyes went to Jorge and he looked away. He knew the tea had been drugged. Carly sat the cup on the nightstand without accusing him, hoping, as she settled back down, that she hadn't consumed enough to do her harm.

Hank elbowed Tanner and Tanner lifted his field glasses. The garage door was sliding up and Tanner spotted two cars—a Lamborghini and a dark sedan, the same car that had mowed down the men at the brewery. The sedan backed out and Tanner tensed. They were going after the book. *He* was going after Carly.

A light rain suddenly pelted them, followed by a clap of thunder. "Let's go," he said and began his descent to the house before the car was even out of the garage. He knew all the guards would be watching the car.

With as little noise as possible the two men reached the wall circling La Pantera's house; then they scrambled over the wall and onto the grounds just in time to see red taillights clear the main gates.

The place was well lighted, too well lighted, Tanner thought as he crept along the inside of the wall, Hank hard on his heels. If they could just make it the hundred or so feet to the back of the house, they'd be all right, at least until the time came to leave.

In the distance two men laughed, and Tanner looked over his shoulder. The guards were crowded together, all looking toward the front gates. He turned to Hank and Hank nodded. Both darted across the yard, their feet never making a sound. Tanner hoped that whatever it was that held the men's attention kept them entertained for a few moments more.

He and Hank passed the back door and went to the opposite side of the house where they parted, Tanner staying there while Hank moved on. If one was captured, at least the other would be free to rescue him. Tanner's heart pounded; no lights shone inside this section of the house. He pressed his nose against a window, trying to make out the room, but it was too dark. He tugged on the window but wasn't surprised when it didn't budge.

Still, he had to enter somewhere. He moved to the next window and met with the same resistance; then he stopped, spotting a higher but smaller window to his left. It looked like a bathroom window, which would be the perfect entryway. Raising his hands high, he pushed against the glass and it slid up smoothly. A grin split his face as he gripped the ledge and boosted himself up, but working his large frame through the small opening was a task. He entered one shoulder at a time, then twisted his body until his hips cleared the opening and he was able to pull his legs through. Tanner squinted, then stepped down, right into a sink. He wasn't in a bathroom, he was in the kitchen.

He lowered the window behind him and stepped to the floor, being careful of where he walked. He stopped at the door and peered around. Directly in front of him was another door, probably to the dining room. To his left was a long hall, a light glowing at the end. Avoiding the obvious, he crept toward the light, looking for the stairs. Something told him Carly and Therese were upstairs.

Dark paneling made the hallway seem more narrow than it was, and sweat trickled down his back. He reached the end, where the hall turned to the right, and he stopped, listening, alert for any suspicious noise. The house seemed deathly quiet, and Tanner tensed. It was too damned quiet.

Not knowing why, he suddenly looked over his shoulder. No one was there, yet he had the nagging feeling he was being watched, that someone was toying with him. And if that was so, there was nothing he could do about it. He had to move on. Knotting his hand into a fist, he leaned against the wall, then slowly looked around the corner. Straight ahead, in all its glory, was a brilliantly waxed mahogany staircase, the first step holding a very young and, Tanner surmised, inexperienced guard.

Tanner dug into his pocket and pulled out a coin. Then he leaned his back against the wall and tossed it down the hall. The tinkling of the metal was just loud enough to attract the guard's attention, and Tanner grabbed the boy as he cleared the corner, rendering him unconscious with one quick move.

Then Tanner glanced around the corner again to make sure no one had heard him and was coming to investigate. When he was certain it was safe he hefted the slight body of the guard over his shoulder and quickly raced to the steps, ducking behind them at the last moment. He laid the boy down and quickly divested him of his weapons, then tied his hands and feet with both their belts. Tanner didn't worry that the boy would regain consciousness any too soon; in fact, Tanner knew as he slung the boy's rifle over his shoulder and tugged his cap low, it would be a long time before the young guard awoke. Tanner rose and quietly climbed the stairs.

A loud thump roused Carly momentarily, but she was so groggy she couldn't open her eyes. Yet she knew she had to. She was in danger; she hadn't meant to fall asleep. But she was so tired, had been through so much.

Someone was stroking her hair. It must be Jorge; he liked to touch her hair. She tried to tell him she was all right, just to give her a moment and she'd shake off the drowsiness, but her mouth wasn't cooperating.

He must have understood her though, because he was pulling her up. But her neck seemed made of rubber and she couldn't hold her head up. If she had a drink of water, she thought, licking her dry lips, she knew she could talk. Her mouth was so dry she couldn't even swallow.

"Come on, Carly wake up," someone whispered to her. She smiled. Jorge had lied: he *could* talk.

Suddenly she felt arms going under her arms, hugging her close to a warm body. *Oh, God,* she thought, lifting a heavy hand to push him away. She never dreamed Jorge would try something so underhanded with her.

She strained with all her might, desperately trying to shake the daze she was in, and barely managed to open her heavy lids. Through a misty haze she saw blue eyes.

"Carly." The whisper was harsh.

Why was Tanner here? And he was angry again. She didn't want to fight with him, she just wanted to sleep.

"Carly!" He shook her and somehow her senses became slightly clearer. Again she peeked at him. He was inches away from her nose. Her head rolled to her shoulder and she saw that she was sitting on a bed. But she wasn't in her room. Her bed wasn't blue.

"Go away," she managed to croak. And it worked; he laid her down. But before she knew it he was back, scrubbing her face with a cold, dripping-wet cloth. Her eyes flew open; she struggled, and when she cried out, he stuffed the cloth in her mouth and jerked her upright.

"We have to get out of here now. Do you understand?"

Carly blinked, trying with all her might to absorb the urgency in his tone. Somehow she recognized they were in danger, although she couldn't really remember why, and she tried to cooperate. Swaying on her feet, she tried to nod but fell against him.

He pushed her back, his blue eyes boring into her as he pulled the cloth out of her mouth. "Do you know where Therese is?"

Her throat felt fuzzy. "Thirsty," she muttered. In seconds Tanner was holding a glass of water to her mouth and she guzzled it. Every moment that ticked by seemed to help clear her mind.

"Carly, where's Therese?" Tanner asked in a rough voice.

She held up three fingers. "That many doors."

"She's up here?"

Carly nodded, then swayed again, her gaze landing on the unconscious form on the floor. She swallowed thickly. "You hurt Jorge."

"He's all right," Tanner said, and before Carly knew what was happening he had slung her over his shoulder.

Tanner checked the upstairs hall, then stepped out, squeezing Carly's thigh as he moved to the third door. He was worried; he hadn't seen Hank. If Therese had been drugged too, they were in real trouble. There was no way he could manage them both.

He reached the door and hesitated, wondering whether he should have left Carly in her room, then decided he had to take her with him. If they parted now . . . But he couldn't take the chance of bringing her into Therese's room. If Carly had had a guard, Therese was bound to have two. He quietly stepped back and, spotting a smaller door farther down the hall, hurried toward it. As he opened it he sighed in relief. It was a linen closet. He set Carly on wobbly legs and, seeing that she still wasn't lucid, cupped her chin in his hand and whispered, "You have to stay in here. Do you understand?"

She shook her head as if to clear it, then nodded. Tanner, unable to resist, leaned down and kissed her lingeringly, the thought of losing her tearing at him. Pain filled him, but he turned it into grim determination, refusing to allow his personal feelings to get in the way of what he had to do. He pulled her close and squeezed her tightly, then released her.

"Bend down," he said, "and crawl under that shelf." Her movements were slow, but she managed to do as he said. "Stay here until I come back. And try your damnedest to stay awake."

She clutched his hand and pulled him forward. Her words were garbled and soft, but he could have sworn she said "I love you." He kissed her softly, then made himself stand up and close the door.

Feeling feral, he retraced his steps to where Therese was supposed to be. Quietly he tried the knob. When it didn't turn, Tanner pulled his pistol out and tapped the door with the barrel. Inside, the lock twisted and Tanner leaned his weight into the door. When it opened he flew in, his pistol pointing at the first man he saw, his eyes darting around the room.

"It took you long enough."

Stunned, Tanner closed his eyes; his gut twisted. Then he spun around, his pistol aimed at his target. Three men held guns on him; he recognized the one in the middle.

"Cornwall."

"Drop it, Barnes." A muscle in Cornwall's jaw twitched, then he lifted his chin a notch. "Take his rifle, Manuel."

Tanner relinquished his only other weapon, then stared at the man who'd been almost as close to him as Hank. "Why?"

"Why not?"

Tanner couldn't believe this was happening. Not Cornwall; he never dreamed it was Cornwall.

Cornwall stepped past Tanner and went to the massive bed centered in the room. On it Therese was curled on her side, sound asleep, the side of her face beaten to a pulp. "You son of a bitch!" Tanner said, stepping toward them.

Cornwall's eyes narrowed and he gently touched her battered face. "I probably hate it more than you do."

"I doubt it."

Cornwall shrugged. "You know, I purposely drugged them," he said, changing the subject. When Tanner didn't respond he continued. "I wanted you to know that, although it really isn't going to matter whether you know it or not. Still . . ." He shrugged again, then faced Tanner. "She'll be happy with me. I've always wanted Therese, and Carly won't be any trouble. In fact, the more I've thought about it the better I like the idea. They'll keep each other company."

"What are you talking about?" Tanner asked. A sudden, infinitesimal movement outside the window caught his eye and he glanced away, then reached into his shirt pocket for a cigarette.

Good, Tanner thought. Cornwall was so busy telling his plans he hadn't noticed the movement.

"I'm cutting loose. No more government work, no more dealing. I've accumulated quite a fortune, as you must have seen in the book. But the game's over. I know when to get out. Neither Therese nor Carly will ever want for anything."

"Except their freedom." Tanner avoided looking at the window; he knew without a doubt that Hank was out there.

"Which they'll get one day."

"You're a fool if you think Therese will ever accept a deal like that."

Cornwall glared at Tanner and Tanner smiled. "She'll eventually kill you." He stuck the cigarette between his lips and glanced at the bed. Jesus Christ! Therese's eyes were open. Tanner smiled even wider at Cornwall, then lit his cigarette. Therese wasn't drugged; they were going to get out of this.

"She won't if she knows her sister will be killed."

Tanner raised a brow. "Maybe, maybe not. Have you forgotten the book? It's on its way to Omi right now."

Cornwall smiled. "I'll be long gone before it reaches his hands." He chuckled. "I wish I could see that bastard's face when he finds out I'm the traitor."

"Hmmm—got it all figured out, haven't you. Except . . . what are you going to to about Diego?" Tanner took joy in seeing the smile vanish from Cornwall's face. "He knows all your plans—where you're going."

"We've never met, Barnes. But that was a good try."

"Don't kid yourself; he knows all about you." Did know, Tanner thought, and it went to the grave with him. "You'll be on the run, hunted like a Nazi war criminal the rest of your life. Is that what you really want?"

"Who'll be left to find me? You and Hank are the best. I have you, and my men probably have Hank by now."

"There'll be others."

"They'll never find me."

Tanner had to be cautious. Cornwall knew almost every signal he and Hank had. He also had to lure Cornwall away from the bed and Therese and then put some space between himself and Cornwall. He took a deep drag from the cigarette, taking his time to scope the room. A dresser with a nice, large mirror stood alone on the opposite side of the room. If he could make it over there, not only would he have room to dive to the floor, but he'd be able to signal Hank as well.

He turned his back on Cornwall, hoping Cornwall didn't suddenly decide to play the heavy, and stepped toward his goal.

"Nice house. Is it yours?"

"It belongs to my family."

Tanner reached the dresser and lifted a picture. "Nice-looking man. I can see the resemblence."

Cornwall followed him. "Yes, we do have some traits alike. He's my half-brother."

"La Pantera?"

Cornwall threw his head back and laughed. Tanner reared back and hit him with the picture, frame and all, and dove for the floor.

The window shattered; gunfire erupted. The bedroom door flew open and Tanner gasped. It was Carly, and she was in the direct line of fire. Bullets sprayed through the room, but before Tanner could react a huge body hurled itself on her from behind, knocking her to the ground.

Tanner, desperate to reach her, frantically scuttled on his stomach toward her. A hand gripped him by the ankle, pulling him back. Tanner kicked, saw one of the guards fall, then quickly jabbed with his other foot. Cornwall had him and wasn't about to let go. Tanner's pistol lay right where he'd dropped it, just inches from his fingertips, and with all his might he stretched for it. Another guard knelt on the opposite side of the bed; Tanner saw him from beneath the mattress. Outside, weapons began to go off everywhere; before long Hank would be in trouble. In minutes every guard in the camp would be upon them. Again Tanner kicked, this time connecting with flesh. Cornwall grunted but didn't release him. Tanner's fingertips brushed the pistol; another inch and he'd have it. He glanced hurriedly at Carly. Whoever the man was had completely covered her body with his. With a superhuman surge of strength, Tanner grabbed the gun, rolled unto his side, and fired. Cornwall's grip went slack.

Then Tanner rolled back onto his stomach and fired beneath the bed, hitting the man in the thigh. When the man fell, Tanner fired again, ending any threat he might have posed. Glass shattered again, and Tanner knew it was Hank entering the window.

Tanner aimed the pistol at the only remaining threat in the room—the man on Carly.

"Hank?" he called.

"I'm in, and everything's okay."

Tanner slowly rolled to his feet and waited for the huge man to move. He could hear Carly crying and he felt alive.

"Get off her!" he ordered through clenched teeth.

The man cautiously lifted his weight from Carly's slight form, his hands out in a gesture of surrender. As soon as she was able, Carly lifted her head. "Don't shoot him," she said, her voice breaking.

Tanner ignored her and waved the gun at the huge man, indicating he was to move. Once he was a safe distance away, Tanner rushed to Carly and lifted her to her feet, wrapping her in his arms.

She sobbed, clinging to him with all her strength.

"Up against the wall," he heard Hank order; then Hank was softly but urgently talking to Therese. But none of it mattered—for the moment nothing mattered but the woman in his arms.

CHAPTER TWENTY-THREE

"W've got to go, Tanner," Hank said tensely.

Tanner released Carly, and she ran to Therese. Then he pulled an Uzi from one of the dead men's fingers and grabbed the extra ammo. His eyes went knowingly to Hank. They'd merely passed the first hurdle; it was going to be hell getting out of this alive.

"Therese, grab a weapon," Hank ordered as he, too, gathered extra ammunition.

"Carly, get away from that window!" Tanner shouted, and she quickly ducked away.

"What about him?" Hank asked, nodding toward their only hostage.

Before Carly could speak, Therese stepped forward. "Jorge's going with us," she said and tossed him a pistol. "He's saved my neck quite a few times lately."

"Not to mention mine—twice," Carly added. Then she looked at Tanner, her eyes filling with fear. "I'll need a gun too."

Hating this for her, he stood up and wrapped himself around her one more time. She clung to him, a silent sob shaking her body. Then he let her go and handed her the rifle he'd taken from the boy downstairs.

"Who's left?" he asked, looking at Therese.

She pulled her eyes off Cornwall's body, then said, "Gabriel, Cornwall's brother, has gone after the book. The only ones left are the guards."

"How many?"

"Ten, fifteen. Too many."

"The car's parked about a mile south of here. If we make it off the grounds, we'll separate and meet there. Carly goes with me."

"Mario will be waiting about three miles east of Orizaba with a chopper. If we can get to him, we're home free," Hank added, then asked, "How many guards are in the house?"

"I took care of one earlier," Tanner said.

"There might be one or two left," Therese said. "Cornwall knew you'd come and he left the inside of the house pretty empty. He wanted to deal with you himself."

"Is Gabriel La Pantera?"

"No," Therese said sadly. "All this time I

thought . . ."

Tanner tugged his cap low on his head. "None of us could have known." His gaze touched Cornwall's lifeless body and a raw ache filled him. His mind flashed back to all the years before. Cornwall by his side, Cornwall covering his back, both of them moving beneath an enemy's nose and Cornwall grinning all the while. And then Tanner recalled Carly's words about Cornwall searching Hank's unconscious body that night she'd met him at the Diamond Lounge. He'd thought she'd just been panicky; how could he have overlooked such an obvious hint?

Tanner walked to the bed and pulled off a blanket. With sorrow in his heart he draped it over the body.

"Is everyone ready?" he asked, turning around. "We can't keep Mario waiting."

"First we have to get out of this house," Therese said. "And that isn't going to be easy."

"The floor's open for suggestions," Tanner said, pulling Carly close to his side. She leaned heavily against him, still fighting the effects of the drug.

"There's another car in the garage," Therese said.

"We saw it."

"If we separate now," Therese continued,

"Hank and I can make a break for it with the car, and you three can hotfoot it out of here while we're creating the diversion."

"What are we waiting for?" Hank said, moving to the door.

"No," Carly protested.

"Carly'll never make it on foot," Tanner said, stopping everyone.

"I'm fine as long as I don't stand still," she argued.

"We'll take the car." He ignored her protest. "Let's go!"

He grabbed Carly's hand and followed Hank, Therese, and Jorge out into the hall. Gunfire sounded in the distance and Tanner knew Cornwall's men were running amok, shooting at anything that moved, probably even at each other. It was going to take some kind of miracle to make it through the gate in one piece, he thought as they reached the top of the stairs. Hank halted and gestured to them to step back. Then he lifted the Uzi and leveled it against his shoulder, whipping around the corner and firing twice. Then he sighed and waved them forward. All five of them quickly descended the steps and followed Therese as she led them through the house into a game room.

"Tanner, I know this is pretty farfetched," Therese said, "but if you pulled out of the garage the way you've done a million times, maybe the guards will think you're Cornwall. After all it's dark and you're hair and build are about the same. . . ."

Hank's eyes went to Tanner. "It's worth a try."

"I can't leave you, Therese," Carly spoke up. "Why can't we all go together?"

"The car's a Lamborghini."

Carly closed her eyes, and Tanner felt her anguish. "What if you and Tanner take the car?" she asked Therese.

He sucked in his breath and pulled her around. "I'm not leaving you!"

"We haven't got time to argue," Hank said urgently. "Gabriel will be back soon." He looked at Tanner. "Take Carly and go. We'll give you three minutes, then we'll make our move." He turned to Therese. "We'll have to leave through the back."

Therese nodded, her eyes going to Carly. Carly stepped forward and put her arms around Therese. Tanner saw her body tremble, knew what it took for her to hold back the tears. Therese closed her eyes tightly as she kissed Carly's cheek.

"I'll see you at the chopper," she said softly to Carly.

Carly nodded briskly, then hugged Therese one more time. "I love you," she said as she stepped back.

Tanner took her by the arm, then looked at Therese. "Is there a remote for the garage door?"

"Yes, in the glove compartment."

Tanner planted a solid kiss on her cheek. "Watch out for my partner."

"Will do."

Carly moved to his side and blew a kiss to Jorge.

Tanner thumped Hank on the shoulder. "I'll see you at the chopper."

"You bet."

With one last look at his friends, Tanner led Carly out of the house and into the garage. Without turning on a light, he opened the car door for her, then went to the driver's side.

"Don't lift the gun unless someone fires at us. We may be able to pull this off," he told her as he slipped into his seat and closed the door.

"Fasten your seat belt," she said, and in the darkness she turned to him, her eyes gleaming like stars.

Tanner kissed her and moved his hand up to cup her breast. "I have a lot to explain to you, Carly, but please believe me when I say I love you."

"I hope it's as much as I love you." Her voice broke and her arms went around his neck. They kissed violently, hurriedly; then Tanner pushed her away.

494

"You ready?"

She nodded.

"Reach into the glove box and press the remote." He started the engine.

Gripped by fear, Carly shook like a leaf. She didn't think she could stand it if something happened to Tanner or Therese. The garage door slid open; her heart sank to her stomach and she prayed as she had never prayed before.

The car rolled out of the garage and stopped. No sound was heard. Tanner revved the engine, then shoved it into gear as casually as if they were out on a joyride. He even winked at her. Could it really be this easy? she thought, clutching her hands together. Just at that moment, a guard stepped from the side of the house directly in front of the car. Tanner flashed the lights on, blinding him. The guard threw his arms up and covered his eyes, then shouted and leaped out of the way. But the damage was done—the others were alerted.

"Damn!" Tanner punched the accelerator. The rear end of the car swerved as tires grabbed the concrete and thrust them ahead. Carly gripped the dashboard, her eyes locked on the drive ahead. The gate looked miles away; the car didn't seem to move fast enough.

The first shots came from the man behind them. The back window shattered and a bullet zinged by her head.

"Duck down!" Tanner barked, flooring the pedal as they passed the front of the house. But Carly didn't move. Headlights flashed before them; a car was coming through the gates.

"Oh my God! That must be Grabriel."

Tanner shifted into a higher gear. "If we make it past him, he'll have a hell of a time catching us in this machine."

But what if we don't make it? Carly wanted to ask, hanging on as the car raced ahead.

"Tanner, they're closing the gates!" she shouted, lifting the pistol out of her lap. Two armed men positioned themselves on either side of the wall. White fire sparked from their guns. Glass shattered before her eyes, flying all through the cab as the windshield burst. They lost a headlight.

"Get down, Carly!" Tanner ordered again. But Carly refused to listen. She rolled down her window, aimed at the closest man, and fired twice. She missed, but he jumped back.

The car raced directly at them and Carly screamed. Tanner clutched the wheel; they were going head-to-head, a suicide ride. Just before the point of impact, Tanner jerked the wheel to the right and whipped around the other car. But they still weren't out of trouble. The gates were narrowing by the second. If Tanner didn't hurry they were going to crash through.

Behind them, the other car had spun around on the lawn and was closing in fast. Carly's eyes went from it to the gate. She mentally willed Tanner on, clenching her fist as they neared. She shot randomly, knowing she wasn't hitting a thing, but it made the danger easier to accept. Her mouth flew open; she closed her eyes. They weren't going to clear the gate!

Again Tanner shifted into a higher gear. The Lamborghini seemed to leap with power, then sailed through the closing gates, the screech of metal as they raked each side of the car setting her teeth on edge.

Tanner whooped with joy, not bothering to slow down as they sped away; Carly turned in her seat just in time to see the other car crash through the gates, then lose control as the gates ripped its rear end away. The wrecked car spun into the darkness.

"We made it," Carly said, awe in her voice.

"Of course we did," Tanner said, squeezing her thigh. "I think I'm going to buy one of these cars myself as soon as I get home."

Home. Carly suddenly thought of Therese and Hank and Jorge, and her elation died.

"Do you think they got away?" she asked.

The smile left Tanner's face. He didn't answer.

A yellow light on the tail of the chopper blinked rapidly. As soon as the pilot saw Tanner's face, the blade began to turn. Tanner helped Carly out of the car, and they ran for the open door.

Once inside, he pushed Carly toward a rear seat, leaving three more empty in the back and one next to the pilot. Just enough room, Carly thought, for all of them.

Tanner shouted something at the pilot, then positioned himself at the door. Carly had never seen him so tense, so alert. His hand opened and closed, then gripped the door.

"Get us out of here!" he suddenly shouted, sliding the door closed.

Carly leapt to her feet. "You can't do this, Tanner! You have to wait." The chopper lifted and she lost her footing as it rose.

"Sit down, Carly!" he ordered. But Carly refused to listen and grabbed his arm. "We can't leave them!"

"We have to. There are three cars coming."

Tanner raced to the front and Carly followed hot on his heels. The chopper soared upward, the noise almost unbearable. Tanner shoved her into the copilot's seat, then thrust a set of headphones at her. He reached for another set in the seat behind her, but he didn't sit; he stood, barking orders at Mario.

"Pass over them. I don't think any of them is Hank."

"Who could they be?"

"Gabriel must have sent them. He isn't going to make it easy for us to get away."

Carly craned her neck to look down. But she didn't know what kind of car Hank was driving.

"Hank's not down there," Tanner said with certainty. "Follow the road back to town." The chopper slanted to the left, throwing Tanner against Carly. He caught himself on the back of her seat and, once he was stable, squeezed her shoulder.

"Can you hear me?" he asked, and she nodded. "We'll get them, I promise."

She reached up and squeezed his hand in return. Then he pointed down. "There they are. Hit them with the light."

Mario hit a switch and a spotlight shone down on a car. "Are you sure it's them?" Carly said. Her heart thumped so hard she could feel it pulsing in her ears.

"Yeah, I'm sure. See, they're stopping. Bring her down, Mario."

Tanner moved to the door as Mario brought the chopper down in the middle of the road. The minute it landed, Carly jumped to her feet and rounded the seat. Tanner slid the door open and Carly thrust her head out, her knees going weak with relief when she saw three people leaving the car. She grasped Tanner's arm. "I can't believe we've all made it."

He wrapped his arm around her shoulders. "I can't either," he said, smiling down at her.

She heard Therese and Hank laughing and turned to greet them. Tanner stepped down and clasped Hank, Carly followed him and grabbed her sister. "Are you all right?" she asked.

"It went so smoothly it was almost scary," Therese said, grinning. "You're some kind of sister, you know that?"

Feeling giddy with relief, Carly answered, "I know."

"Come on guys, we haven't got time to chat," Tanner said, his voice laced with tension. In the distance car lights shone. "Looks as if we're about to have some company."

Hank stepped on board. "Uninvited, at that."

Therese smiled. "How rude."

Carly glanced hurriedly around. "Where's Jorge?" Carly asked, panicked.

"He's not coming," Therese said.

Carly glanced at the car and, when she saw his

forlorn little wave, tore out of Therese's embrace. "Wait!" she yelled, racing toward him.

"Carly!" Tanner shouted, racing after her.

"We can't leave him," she screamed. Just before she reached the car, Tanner grabbed her and spun her around. "Let me go!"

"He doesn't want to come."

"They'll kill him if he stays."

"Look," he ordered, spinning her back. Jorge had left the car and was hovering on the edge of a group of trees. He waved her away, shaking his head negatively at her.

Then he disappeared into the trees.

"No!" she cried.

"They'll never catch him, Carly. They'll think he's left with us."

The chopper engine suddenly whined loudly. Tanner lifted Carly bodily and ran as the headlights of the approaching car focused on them.

"Hurry!" Hank shouted, and Carly saw him waving them on. Tanner leaped into the chopper and it left the ground, slinging them all against the wall as it ascended.

Hank was the first to regain his feet, and he quickly closed the door. Therese followed and took the seat near the pilot. Tanner stood, hands on hips, then bent down and jerked Carly up.

She'd never seen him so angry. "Of all the stupid . . ."

"Don't you talk to me that way!"

"You could have gotten us both killed!"

"Lighten up, Tanner," Therese shouted over her shoulder.

He turned and glared at her; she laughed and so did Carly, the anger leaving her immediately.

Tanner looked back at her. "I can see I'm going to have a hell of a time living with you."

"Who said anything about living together?" she asked, her brows rising.

He pulled her close, butting his nose against hers. "Whoever heard of a married couple living apart?"

"What did you say?" she asked, laughing.

"You heard me."

"I love you," she said, kissing him softly.

"I adore you," he said, pulling her back into his embrace. Over his shoulder she saw Therese smile, then her eyes went to Hank and he held up his thumb.

She looked into Tanner's deep blue eyes and saw his love for her shining there. Taking his hand, she pulled him into one of the rear seats while she took the other.

"Now," she said, arching a brow, "I want to

hear all those explanations you promised."

"What?" he said, laughing.

"Beginning with Consuelo . . ."

EPILOGUE

"I love Galveston," Carly said, leaning her back against her new husband's chest. "I love your yacht. . . ."

"I love you," Tanner said, planting a kiss on top her head. A light Gulf breeze caressed them both.

She turned in his arms. "Do tell?"

"I'd rather show."

She grinned. "Kiss me."

And he did, long and lingeringly.

"I'm suddenly very tired," she whispered against his lips.

"Me too." His voice was raspy, his eyes filled with desire. Hand in hand they went below deck and into the captain's quarters. His hands went to her throat where he slowly unbuttoned her blouse, kissing her as he released each one. When the blouse was completely open, he slid it off her shoulders, smiling when he realized she was bra-less.

Carly reached for the hem of his shirt and pulled it up over his head, then carelessly dropped it to the floor. She stepped against him, rubbing gently against his chest, her hands releasing the snap on his jeans.

In moments they were completely undressed and entwined on the bed. Carly trembled, his touch setting her on fire. She reached for him, stroking and touching until he, too, was filled with desire. Then they came together, passionately, heatedly.

Long moments later, Tanner eased his weight off her and Carly snuggled against his side.

"Two days is not long enough for a honeymoon," Tanner said softly.

"We have to be back in Beaumont to greet your parents at the airport," Carly said, twisting a clump of short, curly hair on his chest.

"We could let Therese entertain them for a few days."

Carly laughed. "I'd rather make a good first impression on your mother."

"She'll love you, and so will Dad, although Dad will probably love getting his fingers into the accounts at Jameson Steel even more."

"I hope he and Ellis don't butt heads."

"So what if they do? It'll do them both good."

"I know Ellis's return to work full time has done him all the good in the world. I still don't see why Tina King . . ."

"Don't worry about her. She's been put on desk duty." Tanner lifted himself up and smiled. "I just remembered something," he said, reaching for a drawer in the nightstand. He pulled out a gold chain and dropped it across her breasts.

"Where did you get this?" she asked, laughing.

"Tiny gave it to me that night he brought us home from the hospital. I was supposed to have given it to you then, but . . ."

"We'll have to get him to give us a ride around the island."

"No, no," Tanner said. "I'm not letting you off this . . ."

A loud crackle, followed by static, reached their ears.

"What in the world is that?" Carly asked, her nose wrinkling.

"The radio."

"Oh, no."

"Come on," he said rising and pulling her out of the bed. "That can be one only person."

"This is Anna. Come in Crockett."

Tanner lifted the mike and smiled. "This had better be good, Armand." The mike whined and Tanner adjusted the frequency.

"Would I interrupt my best friend's honeymoon for anything less?"

"Where are you?"

"Miami. We just confiscated Gabriel's shipment. He's been apprehended and all his men gathered up. It's over."

Carly grabbed the mike. "That's wonderful," she said, then frowned when Tanner laughed.

"You have to push the button to talk, sweetheart." She thrust it back at him and blushed.

"Then you tell him."

Tanner shook his head. "Crockett over and out . . ."

"Tanner, that's rude."

He grinned devilishly at her and swung her up in his arms.

"Crockett. Crockett, you there?"

"Yeah," he said, whispering in Carly's ear. "I'm here." Hank's voice grew fainter as Tanner carried her back to his cabin.

They could barely hear the *"Enjoy"* that laughingly came across the wires.